BHAGAVAD-GĪTĀ

A Comprehensive Guide for Young Readers

BHAGAVAD-GĪTĀ

A Comprehensive Guide for Young Readers

PART 1

Chapters 1 to 6

COMPILED BY
Aruddhā Devī Dāsī

Krishna Homeschool

Library of Congress Cataloging-in-Publication Data
Bhagavad-gītā : a comprehensive guide for young readers. Part 1 /
compiled by Aruddhā Devī Dāsī. — First edition.
Utah, USA : Rekha Gupta, 2025.
194 pages
ISBN 978-1-7369610-6-3

Bhagavadgītā—Juvenile literature. 2. Vedic philosophy. 3. Spiritual life—Juvenile literature. 4. Hinduism—Juvenile literature.
I. Devī Dāsī, Aruddhā.

Cover and book design:
Eight Eyes
www.eighteyes.com

Cover illustration by Prithvi Kumar

For more information, contact:

Krishna Homeschool

aruddha108@yahoo.com

Contents

Acknowledgments *vii*

Introduction *ix*

Synopsis of Śrīla Prabhupāda's Introduction to *Bhagavad-gītā As It Is* *xiii*

Elements for Your Study *xvii*

Chapters 1 to 6 Flow Map 1

CHAPTER 1
Observing the Armies on the Battlefield of Kurukṣetra 3

CHAPTER 2
Contents of the Gītā Summarized 23

CHAPTER 3
Karma-yoga 59

CHAPTER 4
Transcendental Knowledge 92

CHAPTER 5
Karma-yoga – Action in Kṛṣṇa Consciousness 124

CHAPTER 6
Dhyāna-yoga 151

This book is lovingly dedicated to the spiritual master of the whole world, His Divine Grace A. C. Bhaktivedanta Swami Prabhupāda, who gave us the priceless gift of *Bhagavad-gītā As It Is.* Through his faithful translation and profound purports, the sacred "love song" of Lord Kṛṣṇa – delivered without compromise – continues to enlighten and transform countless souls across the world.

May this guide serve as a humble tribute to his work, helping young readers and students dive deeper into the divine message of the *Bhagavad-gītā* and experience the life-changing power of its pure and timeless wisdom.

Acknowledgments

My humble obeisances and gratitude to my spiritual master, His Holiness Gopal Krishna Goswami, a dear and dedicated disciple of Śrīla Prabhupāda, who was tireless in his efforts to preach Kṛṣṇa consciousness throughout the world. He always encouraged me to share my experiences of Kṛṣṇa-conscious parenting with devotees.

My gratitude to my husband, Anantarūpa Prabhu, my sons, Rādhikā Ramaṇa and Gopāla Hari, and my daughters-in-law, Amṛta Keli and Devī Mūrti, who greatly supported my efforts in completing this series of books.

My profound thanks to all the contributors of this book, who spent many hours studying the topics in the *Bhagavad-gītā* and creating suitable resources for children. They come from countries around the world. I offer my heartfelt gratitude to the following contributors for their dedicated and excellent efforts in specific areas:

India

Prithvi Kumar for the front cover artwork and beautiful book illustrations.

Pūrṇeśvarī Rādhā Devī Dāsī for critical-thinking, analogy, theatrical, language, and science activities.

Gokula Vallabhī Devī Dāsī for action, introspective, writing, and language activities.

Śyāmalī Devī Dāsī for action, introspective, writing, and language activities.

Portugal

Nikuñja Vilāsinī Devī Dāsī for chapter summaries, themes, solo questions, multiple-choice questions, general activities, and art suggestions.

South Africa

Indulekhā Sakhī Devī Dāsī for theatrical, writing, and language activities.

United States

Amala Nāma Dāsa for adding diacritics and reviewing the text.

Amṛta Sundarī Devī Dāsī for writing and language activities and one art activity.

Madhavi Pasagadi for artistic activities.

My profuse thanks to Nikuñja Vilāsinī Devī Dāsī (Nirvana Kasopersad) for her excellent editorial work. Her expertise in checking content, correcting grammar, and proofreading, with constant attention to quality and detail, proved to be a great blessing as we put this valuable work together.

Many thanks to Raghu and Govinda of Eight Eyes for their excellent design, layout, and cover design, which makes the book polished, attractive, and friendly to children.

I am also grateful to Amala Nāma Dāsa (Amol Bakshi) for reviewing the content with care and attention, for his valuable feedback, and for spotting minute errors with an eye for detail.

This book is the product of many hands, and it would not have existed without the dedication of all these devotees. I am deeply indebted to them for taking time out of their busy schedules to create a valuable resource for children everywhere.

Introduction

The *Bhagavad-gītā* is one of the most important spiritual texts for anyone seeking self-realization and God consciousness. It presents timeless wisdom that guides us in understanding the nature of the self, our relationship with the Supreme, and how to live a life of purpose and devotion. Śrīla Prabhupāda repeatedly emphasized the regular and serious study of the *Bhagavad-gītā*, encouraging everyone to approach it with sincerity and humility. When young people begin studying the *Gītā* from an early age, they establish a strong spiritual foundation that supports lifelong devotional service and steady spiritual growth.

Purpose of This Study Guide

During my travels and seminars on homeschooling and parenting with Śrīla Prabhupāda's books – especially *Śrīmad-Bhāgavatam* – I often received requests from parents, teachers, and youth leaders for a *Bhagavad-gītā* study guide specifically designed for young readers. This book was created in response to those heartfelt requests. Many devotees expressed the need for a comprehensive resource that would make the *Gītā* both accessible and engaging for children and teens while remaining faithful to the original text and purports.

This study guide is designed to help young readers engage deeply with the *Gītā* in a way that is age-appropriate yet rooted in serious scriptural standards. It is structured to meet *Bhakti-śāstri* course requirements, allowing teenagers to use this guide as part of their formal *śāstra* study. With proper guidance, young readers (ages 12–18) can use this book to prepare for and eventually receive their *Bhakti-śāstri* certification.

Target Audience

This guide is intended primarily for young readers between the ages of 12 and 18. It is ideal for Sunday schools, youth groups, homeschoolers, *gurukulas*, or individual students eager to explore the *Bhagavad-gītā* systematically. Parents, teachers, and facilitators can use this book to create a rich and meaningful learning experience for students in various settings.

Goals and Objectives

The main aim of this study guide is to help young devotees understand the philosophical and devotional teachings of *Bhagavad-gītā As It Is* in a way that is clear, engaging, and transformative. It is also meant to help children develop a natural attraction for reading Śrīla Prabhupāda's books and cultivate this habit that will nourish their faith throughout their lives.

The activities and discussions are designed to make scriptural study interactive and relatable, accommodating different learning styles. In doing so, the guide helps students develop *śāstra-cakṣu* – a scriptural vision – through which they can see and understand the world around them. Another important objective is to make the teachings of the *Gītā* relevant to daily life, helping students apply its wisdom in practical ways and preparing them for deeper engagement with scripture in later stages of their spiritual lives.

Structure of the Study Guide

Each chapter of this study guide is organized according to major themes that follow the chronological order of verses within that chapter. These themes simplify complex ideas, making them accessible and relatable for young minds. Activities are built around these themes and follow the sequence of the verses, ensuring a contextual and cohesive learning experience.

Chapter summaries and activities are based on the verses and Śrīla Prabhupāda's purports, with the goal of presenting the teachings in a child-friendly manner while maintaining their depth and integrity.

Types of Activities (Categorized for Varied Learning Styles)

To accommodate diverse learning preferences, the guide offers a variety of activity types:

- **Action activities** – puzzles, games, and hands-on learning.
- **Artistic activities** – drawing, designing, crafting, and creating visual representations of key ideas.
- **Critical-thinking activities** – encouraging logic, analysis, and application of *Gītā* principles.
- **Introspective activities** – personal reflection and journaling to help students internalize the teachings.
- **Science activities** – linking *Gītā* concepts with scientific understanding.
- **Theatrical activities** – skits, role-plays, and dialogues that bring verses to life.
- **Writing and Language activities** – Focused on assessing students' comprehension and ability to clearly express what they have understood rather than grammar and linguistics. These include reflections, essays, and other writing tasks. They also include comic strips – visual storytelling to capture themes in a fun and memorable way.

Special Features

To further support understanding, each chapter includes an **Analogy Anthology** section that highlights and explains significant analogies from the *Gītā* to clarify complex ideas. A **Verse Memorization List** is also provided, featuring selected key verses for students to learn by heart. Additionally, **Sample Answers** are included to help parents, teachers, and learners guide discussions and check comprehension effectively.

Guidelines for Using This Book

This guide can be used in both group and independent study contexts. The activities are flexible and can be selected according to the student's age, ability, and learning style. Parents and teachers are encouraged to actively discuss themes and guide students through reflective and philosophical exercises.

Students should be encouraged to read the verses and purports directly from *Bhagavad-gītā As It Is* alongside this guide. Memorization of selected verses, understanding key analogies, and grasping fundamental philosophical concepts are strongly recommended, especially for those preparing for *Bhakti-śāstri* certification. For this purpose, going through all or most of the activities are recommended.

To receive official *Bhakti-śāstri* certification, students will need to study under a certified *Bhakti-śāstri* teacher or program and fulfill the board's specific requirements, which this guide is designed to support.

This book is Part 1, covering Chapters 1–6 of the *Bhagavad-gītā As It Is*. Two more volumes will follow, each covering six chapters, forming a three-module course that spans all 18 chapters of this sacred text.

It is my sincere prayer that, by Śrīla Prabhupāda's grace, young readers from all over the world and from all walks of life will benefit from studying the *Bhagavad-gītā* and applying its timeless teachings to their daily lives. May this guide inspire them to grow in knowledge, devotion, and spiritual strength.

— Aruddhā Devī Dāsī, October 2025

Synopsis of Śrīla Prabhupāda's Introduction to Bhagavad-gītā As It Is

What Is the Bhagavad-gītā?

The *Bhagavad-gītā*, literally meaning "The Song of God," refers to the conversation between Lord Kṛṣṇa and Arjuna on the Battlefield of Kurukṣetra. The *Bhagavad-gītā* opens on the battlefield where Arjuna, a warrior of unmatched skill, suddenly becomes paralyzed with grief and compassion at the thought of fighting his relatives, teachers, and friends. He sets down his bow, unwilling to fight. In that moment, he turns to his charioteer, Lord Kṛṣṇa, the Supreme Personality of Godhead, and accepts Him as his spiritual master. It is then that the *Gītā* is spoken – Kṛṣṇa's timeless message, relevant for all souls in all ages.

Why Study the Gītā?

1. ***Bhagavad-gītā* was spoken by the Supreme Personality of Godhead.**

"Bhagavān" refers to the Supreme Lord – the one who possesses all six opulences in full: wealth, strength, fame, beauty, knowledge, and renunciation. "Bhagavad" is the possessive form, meaning "of Bhagavān" or "of the Lord." Śrīla Vyāsadeva establishes from the very beginning that Śrī Kṛṣṇa is the Supreme Personality of Godhead. Therefore, the *Bhagavad-gītā* is understood to be the direct words of God.

2. ***Bhagavad-gītā* is the science of the spirit, not a sectarian religious text.**

The knowledge given in the *Gītā* is spiritual science, offering universal truths that can be realized by practice. It is not limited to any religious group or belief system but offers practical guidance for all humanity across all times.

3. ***Bhagavad-gītā* was spoken to all of us, not just to Arjuna.**

Although the *Bhagavad-gītā* was seemingly spoken to Arjuna to convince him to fight, it is a message for humanity at large. Arjuna understood his position as an eternal servant of Kṛṣṇa and therefore surrendered to His will. By his personal example, Arjuna taught us to surrender to Kṛṣṇa in all situations.

4. ***Bhagavad-gītā* encourages us to understand our real position as the loving servant of God.**

Bhagavad-gītā propounds spiritual knowledge and teaches us that Kṛṣṇa is the Supreme Personality of Godhead and we are His eternal loving servants. It encourages us to revive this eternal relationship and become happy.

5. ***Bhagavad-gītā* sets out the real goal of life.**

The real goal is to attain the highest status – becoming a faithful servant of God. This goal is higher than any material success we may wish to achieve in our lives.

6. ***Bhagavad-gītā* teaches us to accept God's word as it is, without any interpretation.**

Writers and scholars sometimes tend to interpret the *Gītā* as an allegory, a moral or religious text, or a political or management course. The *Gītā* should be understood as it is – as the message of the Supreme Lord to all living entities meant to awaken their love for Him – and should not be interpreted in any other way.

How to Study the Bhagavad-gītā?

The *Bhagavad-gītā* is not a text that we can independently read and understand without proper guidance. It is knowledge passed down through the process of *śabda,* spiritual sound (which you will learn about in detail later).
It should be properly received from a line of teachers who carry the message of the Lord as He spoke it originally. This line of teachers is called a disciplic succession or *paramparā*. Any bona fide *paramparā* begins with Lord Kṛṣṇa Himself as the first teacher and is followed by a line of masters who carry and transmit the same message without distortion.

There are four main Vaiṣṇava *paramparās* that are considered bona fide, and Śrīla Prabhupāda, the author of the *Bhagavad-gītā As It Is*, comes in the Brahma-Madhva-Gauḍīya *paramparā*, or *sampradāya*. The *ācāryas* (spiritual teachers) in this lineage are as follows:
1. Kṛṣṇa 2. Brahmā 3. Nārada 4. Vyāsa
5. Madhva 6. Padmanābha 7. Nṛhari 8. Mādhava
9. Akṣobhya 10. Jaya Tīrtha 11. Jñānasindhu
12. Dayānidhi 13. Vidyānidhi 14. Rājendra
15. Jayadharma 16. Puruṣottama 17. Brahmaṇya Tīrtha 18. Vyāsa Tīrtha 19. Lakṣmīpati
20. Mādhavendra Purī 21. Īśvara Purī, (Nityānanda, Advaita) 22. Lord Caitanya
23. Rūpa, (Svarūpa, Sanātana) 24. Raghunātha, Jīva 25. Kṛṣṇadāsa 26. Narottama 27. Viśvanātha
28. (Baladeva), Jagannātha 29. Bhaktivinoda
30. Gaurakiśora 31. Bhaktisiddhānta Sarasvatī
32. A. C. Bhaktivedanta Swami Prabhupāda

When we receive the knowledge through disciplic succession, we can be sure that we are hearing Lord Kṛṣṇa's message as He spoke it to Arjuna, without change.

The Five Truths of the Gītā

The *Gītā* centers on five eternal truths:

- **Īśvara (the Supreme Lord):** Kṛṣṇa, the supreme controller, the all-knowing and all-powerful, yet also the most intimate friend of every living being.
- **Jīva (the living entities):** We, the spirit souls – who are not the material body – are eternally connected to the Supreme Lord in loving service. By nature we are eternal, conscious, and blissful, but we are bound in material existence and can realize our true identity through the process of *yoga.*
- **Prakṛti (material nature):** The Lord's inferior energy made up of the physical and subtle elements, which serves as the field of action for the souls. Material nature also manifests the three modes – goodness, passion, and ignorance – which bind the soul in the material world and cause forgetfulness of

the Lord. We must rise above these modes to realize our true position.

- **Kāla (time):** The eternal force that brings destruction to all material things, working under Kṛṣṇa's will.
- **Karma (action):** The law of cause and effect, binding the soul to repeated birth and death according to its deeds.

Understanding these five truths is essential for liberation.

The Process for the Present Age

In this age of quarrel and hypocrisy (Kali-yuga), traditional sacrifices and austerities are impractical. But the simple and powerful process available to everyone is the chanting of the holy names of God:

Hare Kṛṣṇa, Hare Kṛṣṇa, Kṛṣṇa Kṛṣṇa, Hare Hare
Hare Rāma, Hare Rāma, Rāma Rāma, Hare Hare

This chanting of the *mahā-mantra* cleanses the heart, awakens devotion, and delivers the soul to Kṛṣṇa.

Reflection: Prepare to Study the Gītā

As you approach the *Bhagavad-gītā*, cultivate the proper mood to receive and imbibe its teachings:

- Accept Kṛṣṇa as the Supreme Personality of Godhead.
- Inquire submissively, with a desire to understand rather than challenge.
- Practice humility and surrender.
- Be willing to accept the teachings in full.
- Maintain faith in the conclusions of the *ācāryas*.

Elements for Your Study

Musical Representation

Bhagavad-gītā literally means "the song of God." Generally, songs serve to enamor us by their melodies or help us examine the world around us through their lyrics. They enrich a part of our brain that thirsts for musical and creative expression. So, imagine what "the song of Kṛṣṇa" can do! Kṛṣṇa is the supreme musician and artist, and His wise words can uplift our minds and purify our existence through His love song, the *Bhagavad-gītā*.

Why is it a love song? Kṛṣṇa did not "sing" this divine song just to Arjuna, but to all of us who face dilemmas and struggles in life. Kṛṣṇa's "song" is filled with valuable instructions on how to live life fully, overcome our dilemmas and difficulties, and ultimately surrender our hearts to Him. Unlike mundane songs that do not serve the real self-interest of the hearer, Kṛṣṇa's words are laden with love. And when we immerse ourselves in His beautiful lyrical words, we learn how to reciprocate with His love. This is the essence of *bhakti*, the conclusion of Kṛṣṇa's message.

To remind us that Kṛṣṇa is the orchestrator of the symphony of our lives and the life of Arjuna and His devotees against the backdrop of the *Bhagavad-gītā*, we've used terms related to music and composition for the main categories of each chapter of this book. Read the "Chapter Beats" to get an overview of the chapter; answer the "Solo Questions" for your self-study; review the "Learning Harmonies" to quiz your memory; study and discuss the "Theme Tracks" to see the main themes and key messages of each chapter; memorize important verses under "Sacred Rhythms," and learn and have fun with the activities in "Medley Acts."

Enjoy the tunes of Kṛṣṇa's love song as you study the *Bhagavad-gītā*.

Bhagavad-gītā Study Group:

You are not alone in your studies. As you go through this book, you will meet our *Bhakti-śāstrī Bhagavad-gītā* study group, characters who may be like you and will sometimes guide your study journey. Take note of them, their individual quirks and personalities, and what they have to teach you.

Balu (short for Balarāma)

Madhu (short for Madhusūdana)

Priya

Tara

Tamal

PART 1
Karma-yoga

CHAPTERS 1 TO 6 FLOW MAP

CHAPTER 1. Observing the Armies on the Battlefield of Kurukṣetra: Arjuna observes the armies on both sides of the battlefield and is overwhelmed with sorrow. He fears the destruction of families, sinful reactions, and finds no joy in victory. So, he refuses to fight.

Dhṛtarāṣṭra hopes his sons will win, but Sañjaya explains how Kṛṣṇa is about to guide Arjuna back to action.

CHAPTER 2. Summary of the the Gita: Arjuna surrenders to Kṛṣṇa as his guru. Kṛṣṇa explains *jñāna* – the difference between the body and the soul; *sakāma-karma* – doing duty for rewards; *buddhi-yoga* – working with intelligence; *niṣkāma-karma-yoga* – selfless action with knowledge; and the qualities of a *sthita-prajña* – a steady, self-realized person.

In 2.49, Kṛṣṇa urges Arjuna to reject bad actions through *buddhi-yoga*, so Arjuna asks in 3.1: Which is better – renunciation or action?

CHAPTER 3. Karma-yoga: Kṛṣṇa emphasizes *niṣkāma-karma-yoga* over giving up work. Even a realized person should act to set the right example. He warns that lust is the enemy on the spiritual path – and must be defeated with spiritual intelligence.

Kṛṣṇa now reveals transcendental knowledge that helps overcome the bondage of desire.

CHAPTER 4. Transcendental Knowledge: Real knowledge comes from Kṛṣṇa through *paramparā* (disciplic succession). Knowing the divine nature of Kṛṣṇa's birth and actions brings liberation. Karma is better understood through *jñāna*, which is gained by *yajña* (sacrifice) and approaching a bona fide *guru*.

In 4.39, Kṛṣṇa says peace comes through *jñāna*, but in 4.42, He urges Arjuna to act. Arjuna again asks about *sannyāsa* (renunciation) and *karma-yoga* (action) in 5.1.

CHAPTER 5. Action in Kṛṣṇa Consciousness: Kṛṣṇa says *karma-yoga* and *sannyāsa* both lead to liberation, but *karma-yoga* is easier. Selfless work in Kṛṣṇa consciousness brings freedom. One can attain liberation by focusing on the Supreme. Even *aṣṭāṅga-yoga* leads to success when practiced with *bhakti*.

After mentioning *aṣṭāṅga-yoga*, Kṛṣṇa now explains it in detail.

CHAPTER 6. Dhyāna-yoga – The Yoga of Meditation: *Aṣṭāṅga-yoga* has two stages: *yogarurukṣu* (the beginner) and *yogarūḍha* (the advanced yogi). Controlling the mind with practice and detachment is essential. The goal of meditation is to realize the Supersoul (Paramātmā) within the heart. Even if one fails, a *yogi* gets another chance in the next life. But the *bhakti-yogī* is the highest of all.

In 6.47, Kṛṣṇa declares *bhakti-yoga* as the topmost path. In Chapter 7, He begins to explain it deeply.

CHAPTER 1

Observing the Armies on the Battlefield of Kurukṣetra

CHAPTER BEATS

An overview

King Dhṛtarāṣṭra could not bear the suspense any longer. His sons were on the Battlefield of Kurukṣetra, in the greatest war that would ever be fought. He needed to know what was happening. Worrying thoughts plagued him. Would his sons, the one hundred Kauravas, and their army win the battle against the honorable Pāṇḍavas, his own nephews? Would his sons offer a compromise after facing the powerful Pāṇḍava brothers and their army, with Kṛṣṇa, the Supreme Personality of Godhead, on their side? Would the sacred land of Kurukṣetra, also known as Dharma-kṣetra, influence the result of the war and thus bring about ruin for his impious sons? If King Dhṛtarāṣṭra had any life in his eyes, you would have seen fear in them. But the frown on his face was enough to reveal his distress.

To remove his doubts, the old, blind king asked Sañjaya, his charioteer and advisor, who had just come from the battlefield, about what had happened. You see, Sañjaya had the power to see the battlefield in his mind by the mercy of his spiritual master, Vyāsadeva.

Dhṛtarāṣṭra asked, "O Sañjaya, after my sons and the sons of Pāṇḍu faced each other on the battlefield, what did they do?"

Sañjaya bowed his head and then closed his eyes and spoke as if every word had great connotations: "O King, your son Duryodhana looked at the military formation arranged by the sons of Pāṇḍu. He went to the commander-in-chief and his teacher, Droṇācārya, and spoke: 'O teacher, behold this great army expertly arranged by your disciple, the son of Drupada. It has many great fighters, *mahā-rathas*, like Bhīma and Arjuna.' "

Duryodhana's diplomatic words only revealed his fear and nervousness. He wanted to incite hatred and anger in Droṇācārya so that he wouldn't be lenient in his fight against the Pāṇḍavas. You see, Droṇa once had a feud with King Drupada, whose son, Dhṛṣṭadyumna, was prophesized to kill him. Now Duryodhana wanted to remind his teacher of this feud by mentioning King Drupada and his son. The open-hearted Droṇa, however, had accepted Dhṛṣṭadyumna as a student and had trained him in warfare. Duryodhana's words were to warn Droṇa that he shouldn't have similar mercy on his students, the Pāṇḍavas, who now stood as enemies before him.

Duryodhana then stood up tall, his face lighting up with courage. He pointed to his army, raised his voice, and told Droṇa: "The captains in my army are personalities like you, Bhīṣma, Karṇa, Kṛpa, Aśvatthāmā, Vikarṇa, and Bhūriśravā who are always victorious in battle. I can count on you all and the other experienced heroes who are prepared to lay down their lives for me. Our army, which is protected by general Bhīṣma, is immeasurable, whereas the Pāṇḍava army, which is protected by the less-experienced Bhīma is limited. Still, you all must protect Bhīṣma from all sides."

Bhīṣmadeva blew his conchshell. The sound resounded through the battlefield like a roaring lion, as if in answer to Duryodhana's words – did they really stand a chance against the illustrious Pāṇḍavas and their heroic warriors? Victory could not possibly be theirs with Kṛṣṇa on the side of the Pāṇḍavas. He was not only on their side but had taken on the humble position of Arjuna's chariot driver.

Then the tumultuous sound of bugles, horns, drums, and trumpets filled the battlefield. Amid the haze and dust on the opposite side, one hero stood out, whom Duryodhana had failed to mention. On a golden chariot yoked to six white lustrous horses, was Kṛṣṇa, holding on to the horses'

reins, His golden helmet gleaming in the sun and His long black hair blowing in the wind. Hanumān's insignia on the chariot's flag also blew in the wind. Arjuna stood at the back of Kṛṣṇa, ready to blow his conchshell in answer to Bhīṣmadeva's. Then together, Arjuna and Hṛṣīkeśa Kṛṣṇa pressed their transcendental conchshells to their lips. The divine sound mixed with the sound of the conchshells of the other Pāṇḍava brothers – Yudhiṣṭhira, Bhīma, Nakula, and Sahadeva – followed by the conchshells of other war heroes on their side. The uproarious sound of conchshells vibrated in the sky and earth and shattered the hearts of the Kuru army. Yet, the Pāṇḍava army did not shudder in the least from the sound of the Kurus' conchshells. Their confidence came from Kṛṣṇa.

Arjuna took up his Gandiva bow and eyed the sons of Dhṛtarāṣṭra, who had deceived the Pāṇḍavas, encouraged by their blind father. The battle was about to begin. Arjuna requested Kṛṣṇa to draw the chariot in between the two armies so he could get a better view of his opponents. Out of love for His devotee, Kṛṣṇa immediately did as He was told. Understanding the mind of Arjuna, He said, "O Pārtha, just behold all the Kurus assembled here."

Arjuna looked at his teachers, his childhood mentors, his fathers and grandfathers, his maternal uncles, brothers, sons, grandsons, father-in-law Drupada, and well-wishers and friends. His throat became parched, and his body began to tremble. In a faltering voice, he addressed Kṛṣṇa: "My dear Kṛṣṇa, seeing my friends and relatives ready to fight with me, my limbs are quivering, my mouth is drying up, my whole body is trembling, my hairs are standing on end, and my Gāṇḍīva bow is slipping from my hand. I'm not able to tolerate this any longer. I'm forgetting myself and my mind is reeling. I see only misfortune for everyone, O Kṛṣṇa, killer of the Keśī demon."

Kṛṣṇa smiled. He knew the reason for Arjuna's plight. His dear devotee was so softhearted and compassionate that he couldn't bear the thought of his opponents' imminent death on the battlefield. By the Lord's will, Arjuna had become illusioned.

"O Kṛṣṇa," continued Arjuna, not able to look at Kṛṣṇa directly, "even if I win, I'll be the cause of so much lamentation. So what's the use of winning? What good can come from killing my own kinsmen? I cannot desire any victory, kingdom, or happiness at the expense of killing my own family.

"O Govinda, what is the use of a kingdom or happiness when those for whom we desire these things are ready to give up their life in battle? Why should I wish to kill them even if they want to kill me? O Madhusūdana, I can't fight with them even in exchange for the three worlds, let alone this earth. O Janārdana, what enjoyment will I get from killing the sons of Dhṛtarāṣṭra?"

Kṛṣṇa's expression turned serious. His gentle eyes were fixed on Arjuna. Arjuna was only His instrument, for His devotees' aggressors were already destined to die before entering the battlefield. If there was anything He couldn't tolerate, it was any wrong done to His devotees.

"O Mādhava," continued Arjuna, "if we slay such aggressors we will be overcome with sin. So what can we gain and how can we be happy by killing our own people? These greedy men see no fault in killing family or quarreling with friends, but, O Janārdana, why should we engage in such sin?"

Now looking directly into the Lord's compassionate eyes, Arjuna said, "Imagine what would happen if we destroy our family. When these senior members of society die, family traditions may stop and irreligion increase. Women will thus become unprotected and exploited. And then there will be unwanted population in the form of illegitimate children. The souls of forefathers will fall down because there will be no qualified persons to offer oblations on their behalf. Welfare activities and community projects will wither away and die. O Kṛṣṇa, maintainer of the people, those whose family traditions are destroyed will live in hell.

"Alas, how strange it is that we are ready to commit such sinful acts. Desiring to enjoy royal happiness, we are intent on killing our own relatives. Better if the sons of Dhṛtarāṣṭra kill me unarmed and unresisting on the battlefield."

Sañjaya leaned in closer to King Dhṛtarāṣṭra and said, "Arjuna was anguished. He cast aside his bow and arrows and sat down on the chariot, unable to speak."

THEME TRACKS

Themes and key messages
to contemplate and discuss

THEME TRACKS	REFERENCES	KEY MESSAGES
Theme Track 1 Bigger is not always better.	1.1–11	Having everything material doesn't necessarily mean that you will be successful. Dhṛtarāṣṭra's sons had the biggest army and most powerful warriors, but the King was nervous that his sons would lose the battle, because the Supreme Lord Kṛṣṇa was on the side of the Pāṇḍavas. He also feared that because Kurukṣetra was a holy place, it would influence the outcome of the battle, and since the Pāṇḍavas were virtuous, it would influence them favorably. Similarly, Duryodhana recognized the power of the Pāṇḍava army, even though his army was bigger and, in some ways, better. Therefore, he tried to use diplomacy to influence Droṇācārya, his *guru*, to stay focused in his mission to destroy the Pāṇḍavas.
Theme Track 2 Whoever takes shelter of Kṛṣṇa has nothing to fear even in the greatest calamity.	1.12–19	As Bhīṣmadeva, who was on the side of the Kauravas, blew his conch, the sound indicated that they had no chance of victory because Kṛṣṇa was on the other side. As Kṛṣṇa, Arjuna, and the rest of the Pāṇḍavas blew their conchshells, a transcendental sound filled the battlefield, which shattered the hearts of the Kurus. However, when the Pāṇḍavas heard the opposing army's conchshells, they were not afraid because they were confident that Kṛṣṇa was their shelter and protector.
Theme Track 3 Kṛṣṇa is *bhakta-vatsala*. He is always affectionate to His devotees and takes pleasure in serving them.	1.20–27	Arjuna requested Kṛṣṇa to drive the chariot in between the two armies so he could observe them. Kṛṣṇa took the role of the chariot driver out of love for His devotee. He was also conquered by the love and qualities of His devotee. Arjuna was pure and compassionate and therefore didn't want to fight. Kṛṣṇa was happy to serve him and therefore Arjuna called Him *acyuta*, one who is infallible but one who is also infallible (never fails) in His love for His devotee.
Theme Track 4 Doubts arise when one is not sure about one's duty in service to Kṛṣṇa.	1.28–46	Arjuna was doubtful whether to fight or not. His doubts arose from his softheartedness and compassionate nature. He presented to Kṛṣṇa four reasons why he shouldn't fight: to show compassion to friends and relatives; to understand that there's no enjoyment without family even if they were victorious; to be fearful of sinful reactions; and to see the harmful effects of destroying the family. Arjuna would need to realize that his duty in service to Kṛṣṇa was greater than his reasons not to fight. When one understands how to please Kṛṣṇa, according to His desires, one no longer has doubts.

SOLO QUESTIONS

To enhance your self-study

(Find the answers in the verse and purport references provided in brackets.)

1. What is the significance of Dhṛtarāṣṭra's saying *māmakāḥ* in relation to his sons? (1.1)
2. Why was Dhṛtarāṣṭra fearful? How did he think that the battlefield of Kurukṣetra would influence the battle? (1.1)
3. How was Sañjaya able to see the Battlefield of Kurukṣetra? (1.1)
4. What is the significance of Duryodhana's saying *dhīmatā, tava śiṣyeṇa* to Droṇa, which referred to Droṇa's disciple on the opposing side? (1.3)
5. List the vows Bhīma made after the gambling match. (1.4)
6. Why was Duryodhana confident of Bhīṣmadeva's and Droṇa's full support? (1.11)
7. List four signs of victory for the Pāṇḍavas. (1.14–20)
8. What is the significance of Hanumān on Arjuna's flag? (1.20)
9. List the progressive steps leading toward the destruction of a dynasty. (1.39–42)

LEARNING HARMONIES

Multiple-choice questions
to quiz your memory

(Choose the most complete answer.)

1. What was Dhṛtarāṣṭra's real blindness due to?
   a. Being born blind.
   b. Being attached to his sons.
   c. Being cursed in his previous life.
   d. Being an unrighteous king.

2. Why was Dhṛtarāṣṭra nervous and afraid to hear what was happening on the battlefield?
   a. He thought that the holy place of Kurukṣetra would influence the result of the fight.
   b. He knew that Kṛṣṇa's presence and position could mean victory for the Pāṇḍavas.
   c. He thought that his sons were offering a compromise because they recognized that they would lose to the powerful Pāṇḍavas.
   d. All of the above.

3. Why do you think Duryodhana didn't mention Kṛṣṇa as one of the heroes on the opposite side?
   a. Kṛṣṇa was not a combatant in the army.
   b. He felt Kṛṣṇa was not a threat to him.

   c. He did not recognize Kṛṣṇa's superiority and position.
   d. He assessed things materially, relying only on material strength rather than Kṛṣṇa's supreme presence.

4. Who was Dhṛṣṭadyumna?
   a. The son of Drupada, prophesized to kill Droṇācārya.
   b. The son of Droṇācārya, who was Droṇa's student.
   c. The son of Dhṛtarāṣṭra, who was prophesized to kill Arjuna.
   d. The son of Drupada, who was on the side of the Kauravas.

5. Why did Duryodhana mention Dhṛṣṭadyumna to his teacher Droṇācārya?
   a. To remind Droṇa that Dhṛṣṭadyumna was his enemy, not his student.
   b. To incite hatred in Droṇa against their opponents.
   c. To remind Droṇa that Dhṛṣṭadyumna would kill him so he shouldn't be lenient to the opposing army.
   d. All of the above.

6. Why is Arjuna called *guḍākeśa*?
   a. Because he conquered sleep.
   b. Because he conquered his enemies.
   c. Because he conquered sleep and ignorance.
   d. Because he conquered ego.

7. The six types of aggressors don't include one of the following:
   a. Criticizes and belittles others.
   b. Gives poison and sets fire to someone's house.
   c. Attacks with weapons and steals someone's riches.
   d. Occupies someone's land and kidnaps someone's wife.

8. Kṛṣṇa is called *bhakta-vatsala* because:
   a. He is sometimes stern with His devotees.
   b. He is affectionate to His devotees and conquered by their love.
   c. He is partial to His devotees.
   d. He imparts knowledge to His devotees.

9. Arjuna's four reasons for not fighting were the following:
   a. Shame for his family; guilty of sin; going to hell; fear of Kauravas.
   b. Fear of Duryodhana; attachment to relatives; fear of failure; not confident.
   c. His compassion; fear of sinful reactions; no enjoyment after destroying his family; future destruction of family dynasty.
   d. His soft-heartedness and weakness; his not believing in Kṛṣṇa; his emotions; his physical frailty.

10. According to the last purport of this chapter, which qualities of Arjuna make him fit to receive the knowledge of *Bhagavad-gītā*?
   a. Lamentation and grief.
   b. Thirst for knowledge.
   c. Kindness and soft-heartedness.
   d. Determination and fearlessness.

MEDLEY ACTS

A variety of fun activities
to learn from

THEME TRACK 1 ACTIVITIES

LANGUAGE ACTIVITIES

Kurukṣetra as Dharma-kṣetra

Śrīla Prabhupāda writes in verse 1 purport that "because the battle was arranged to be fought at Kurukṣetra, which is mentioned elsewhere in the *Vedas* as a place of worship—even for the denizens of heaven—Dhṛtarāṣṭra became very fearful about the influence of the holy place on the outcome of the battle."

First let's learn how Kurukṣetra became a holy place. Tamal and his sister, Tara, are doing some research for their *Bhakti-śāstrī* assignment:

Tamal: I came across some very interesting information on how Kurukṣetra became a *dharma-kṣetra*, a holy place.

Kurukṣetra was formerly known as Brahmakṣetra, Bhṛgukṣetra, Āryāvarta, and Samanta-pañcaka.

According to the *Mahābhārata*, King Kuru, a great monarch and ancestor of the Pāṇḍavas, performed great austerities at Kurukṣetra. Lord Viṣṇu, being pleased, granted him two benedictions: 1) Kurukṣetra would be named after King Kuru and become famous as a holy place; 2) Anyone who dies there would go to heaven, or become liberated, while fighting or performing penance. So Kurukṣetra became both a battlefield and a land of performing penance. Many sages and saints, who came to know about Kurukṣetra, also went there to perform penance and austerities, which added to the sacredness of the land.

Tara: Wow! Imagine that! Let's try finding Kurukṣetra on Google Maps.

It is believed that Kurukṣetra was situated on the banks of the Sarasvatī river, which dried up about three thousand years ago.

Directions:
Locate Kurukṣetra on Google Maps. Find (a) Brahma Sarovara and (b) Jyotisar. Research their significance from credible sources.

Now answer the following questions:

1. Why was Kurukṣetra chosen as the battlefield for the *Mahābhārata* war?

2. Dhṛtarāṣṭra thought that the holy land of Kurukṣetra would have a negative effect on the outcome of the war for his sons. Why did he think so?

3. What is the significance of Kṛṣṇa's pastimes with the *gopīs* at Kurukṣetra? Briefly relate the story.

4. Why do people go to Kurukṣetra on pilgrimage today?

Significance of Pilgrimage Places

Balu: These places of pilgrimage look interesting. I love traveling and would like to take a dip in all those rivers! There must be some reason why people in the old days used to make hazardous journeys to these pilgrim places.

Today it's easy to locate a place, book tickets, and go and see it. But it will be boring to go alone.

What could be the deeper significance of visiting these places, other than visiting temples and bathing in rivers?

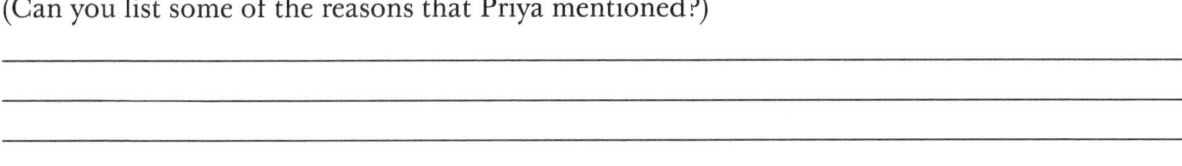

Priya: That's easy. We go to holy places . . .

(Can you list some of the reasons that Priya mentioned?)

____

____

____

____

We should always remember not to treat a place of pilgrimage like a tourist center. As *Śrīmad-Bhāgavatam* (4.28.24, purport) explains:

"A human being who identifies this body made of three elements with his self, who considers the by-products of the body to be his kinsmen, who considers the land of birth worshipable, and who goes to a place of pilgrimage simply to take a bath rather than meet men of transcendental knowledge there, is to be considered like an ass or a cow [i.e. isn't making proper use of the human form of life]."

Removing Weeds from the Paddy Field

Now that you've learned the significance of Kurukṣetra in relation to *dharma-kṣetra,* analyze the analogy from verse 1 purport, which illustrates how the Lord removed unwanted "plants" from the religious field of Kurukṣetra. Refer to the Analogy Anthology section at the end of this chapter and write a short paragraph on the influence the Battlefield of Kurukṣetra had on the outcome of the war. How did it favor righteousness and uproot unrighteousness?

ACTION ACTIVITY

Complex Characters

This chapter introduces some main characters and their complex personalities. We learn of the liberal nature of Droṇa, the diplomacy of Duryodhana, and the partiality of Dhṛtarāṣṭra. We learn of the soft-heartedness of Arjuna and the affection of Kṛṣṇa for His devotees. To understand the *Bhagavad-gītā* it is necessary to understand all these characters. Have fun with the following activities to learn more about them.

1. **Dhṛtarāṣṭra:**
   a. Call out the name of Dhṛtarāṣṭra (learn the correct pronunciation from your teacher) and ask the participants in your study group to call out his traits in response. Get one of the participants to list them down.

   Some of the traits you may collect are
   - Spiritually blind vision
   - "Us" and "Them" mentality
   - Averse to goodness

   b. Then discuss why these traits were attributed to Dhṛtarāṣṭra through incidents from the *Mahābhārata*.

   (Examples: Righteous Pāṇḍu and his sons versus deceptive Dhṛtarāṣṭra and his sons; Dhṛtarāṣṭra's discrimination against his nephews; his lack of spiritual vision; his support for the wayward ways of his evil sons, etc.)

   Read out the list of traits about Dhṛtarāṣṭra. Why do you think these qualities are not favorable and should be avoided? Where do they lead to? Have an open discussion in your class.

2. **Droṇācārya:**

Droṇācārya was a *brāhmaṇa*, and "the *brāhmaṇa's* liberal heart is compared to the sun, which does not withhold its light from the courtyard of anyone, even a thief." [*Surrender Unto Me*; Bhurijana Dasa]

Bring out how this statement is related to Droṇa by enacting or discussing the story of Droṇa and Drupada from the *Mahābhārata*.

3. **Bhīṣma versus Duryodhana:**

One can rarely find a character like Bhīṣma. Discuss the following:

   a. Who was he loyal to externally and who was he devoted to internally? Why did he externally support the Kauravas? Explore what Bhīṣma's stand was and why.
   b. On the other hand, Duryodhana was vindictive and envious of the Pāṇḍavas. He was also a diplomatic politician. He used ploys and techniques like flattering, taunting, and hinting at mistakes for inspiring his army to fight for him. What were they in this chapter?

c. What techniques does a true leader employ to inspire his team to work most productively?

Bhīṣma had no words to respond to Duryodhana's diplomatic words, so he blew his powerful conchshell. If Bhīṣma were to answer Duryodhana in words, what would he have said?

4. **Arjuna:**
   a. Fill in the blanks:

      Arjuna did not fear his enemies because
      - The Pāṇḍavas had ________________ on their side.
      - The emblem of ________________ was present on the ___________ of Arjuna. ________________ had also helped ________________ gain victory in His war against ________________.

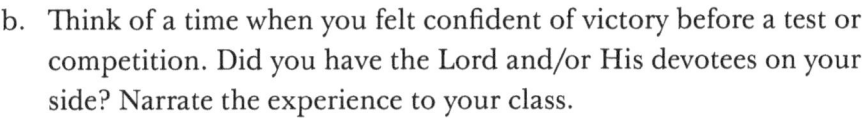

   b. Think of a time when you felt confident of victory before a test or competition. Did you have the Lord and/or His devotees on your side? Narrate the experience to your class.
   c. Arjuna was Kṛṣṇa's pure devotee. What quality of a pure devotee does Arjuna exhibit initially on the battlefield? (Hint: It was only due to the obstinacy of Duryodhana that Arjuna had to fight with his cousins and relatives.)
   d. Then Arjuna became reluctant to fight although he was a *kṣatriya*. Like Arjuna we may sometimes be plagued by doubts when we are asked to do something we are supposed to do. Discuss your experiences in such situations and what you can learn from Arjuna to overcome them.

INTROSPECTIVE ACTIVITY

Bigger Is Not Always Better

There were various signs of victory for the Pāṇḍavas. The first was Kṛṣṇa's presence. When the Supreme Personality of Godhead is on your side, there is always victory. Śrīla Prabhupāda writes in his purport to verse 20: "The emblem of Hanumān on the flag of Arjuna is another sign of victory because Hanumān cooperated with Lord Rāma in the battle between Rāma and Rāvaṇa, and Lord Rāma emerged victorious. . . . Lord Kṛṣṇa is Rāma Himself, and wherever Lord Rāma is, His eternal servitor Hanumān and His eternal consort Sītā, the goddess of fortune, are present. Therefore, Arjuna had no cause to fear his enemies whatsoever."

The Pāṇḍavas chose Kṛṣṇa rather than material strength and opulence to fight the war. Lord Kṛṣṇa briefly tells the story:

Once the war became inevitable, the Kauravas and the Pāṇḍavas sought support from friends and allies. Duryodhana, being the diplomat he was, approached Me for help. Arjuna knows only Me, so he arrived in Dvārakā just as the guards were ushering Duryodhana in. They both entered My chamber. As I was sleeping, Duryodhana sat waiting at the head of My bed, whereas Arjuna remained at My feet with folded palms and affectionate eyes.

When I awoke, I naturally saw Arjuna first. When I learned what they had come for, I offered them each a choice: either My powerful Nārāyaṇī senā (army) or Me alone. Getting nervous, Duryodhana demanded that I give him the first choice since he had arrived first. But I gave Arjuna the first choice since I had seen him first: "O Kaunteya, what do you choose?" I asked him. "My army or Me? If you choose Me, I will not fight or carry any weapon during the battle."

Without hesitation, Arjuna chose Me. Duryodhana was overjoyed that he was given the army, but pretending to be disappointed, he left.

Reflect on the following questions, and then answer in your notebook or discuss with a partner:

An *akṣauhiṇī* is comprised of 21,870 chariots, 21,870 elephants 65,610 horses (cavalry), and an infantry of 109,350 soldiers.

1. Why was Arjuna happy by choosing Kṛṣṇa and why was Duryodhana happy by getting Kṛṣṇa's army?
2. Why do you think we choose *māyā* over Kṛṣṇa?
3. Even though Duryodhana had Kṛṣṇa's army, and an army of eleven *akṣauhiṇīs* compared to the Pandavas' seven, why didn't he win the war?
4. Why then do you think that having more material wealth and possessions is not necessarily better?
5. How can we view material opulence and position like Arjuna did?
6. Why is Kṛṣṇa the best choice?

THEME TRACK 2 ACTIVITIES

ARTISTIC ACTIVITY

Still-Life Drawing: Transcendental Conchshell

In verses 12 to 19, the Pāṇḍavas blew their conchshells, and Kṛṣṇa blew his transcendental conchshell, Pāñcajanya, which is another sign of victory for the Pāṇḍavas. The *Vedas* consider conchshells to be pure. The blowing of the conch is auspicious and it is therefore blown before and after the *ārati* of the Deities and in receiving saintly personalities. In this chapter we learn of the names of the conchshells used by Lord Hṛṣīkeśa, the Pāṇḍavas, and other great personalities, like Bhīṣmadeva, and their effect on the warriors.

In this art activity you will create still-life drawings of a conchshell. It involves looking at the shell from different perspectives and rendering a quick drawing. You can also meditate on the following references while drawing:

1. Kṛṣṇa blows His transcendental conchshell, Pāñcajanya, on the battlefield of Kurukṣetra.
2. Lord Viṣṇu carries a conch and a lotus for the devotees' protection.
3. The Lord touches Dhruva with a conch to empower him with transcendental knowledge.
4. When the residents of Dvārakā hear the sound of Kṛṣṇa's conch, they give up their dejection and run to meet Him.
5. The conch becomes reddish by the touch of Kṛṣṇa's red lips, which reminds us of swanlike devotees at the reddish lotus feet of the Lord.
6. The ocean gifts Pṛthu Mahārāja the conch at his coronation.

Materials needed: Plain sheets of paper, charcoal stick/charcoal pencil, a medium-sized conch, pencil

Steps:

1. Sit comfortably on a chair or on the floor. Place the conch at a suitable height.
2. See the conch from different angles and perceive the change in perspective (see Images 1 to 3).
3. Pick one view of the conch and draw a quick outline with a pencil within a minute (Image 4: view from bottom).
4. When you get comfortable, use charcoal to add depth and value (Image 5).
5. Similarly, sketch the conch from other angles of vision: from the top, sideways, front view, etc. (Example: Image 6)

6. *Variation – Study of harmony and pleasing design:* The concept of golden ratio/sacred geometry states that many things in nature, like flowers, plants, tornadoes, body parts, galaxies, etc., are mathematically proportioned. The ratio of the upper arm to the lower arm with fingers stretched is 1:1.6. The ratio of the hand to the forearm is again 1:1.6. The ratio of fingers to the palm is the same 1:1.6, and even the knuckles are placed in that proportion.
7. The underlying spiral structure, like that of the conch, is easily seen in nature and designed by artists. Using Resource 1, study the golden ratio. Can you see the five rectangles being divided into a square and a smaller rectangle in the ratio of 1:1.6? (Answer shown in Resource 2)
8. Reflect on the underlying harmony in nature and the harmony of Arjuna's will to Kṛṣṇa's will, leading to his victory and Kṛṣṇa's pleasure.

Image 1

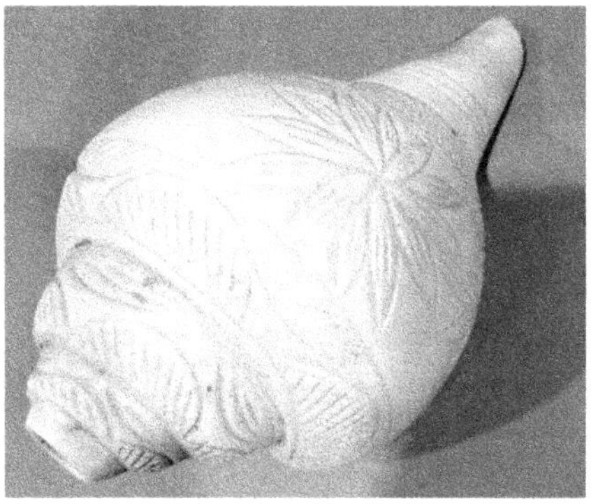

Image 2

Image 3

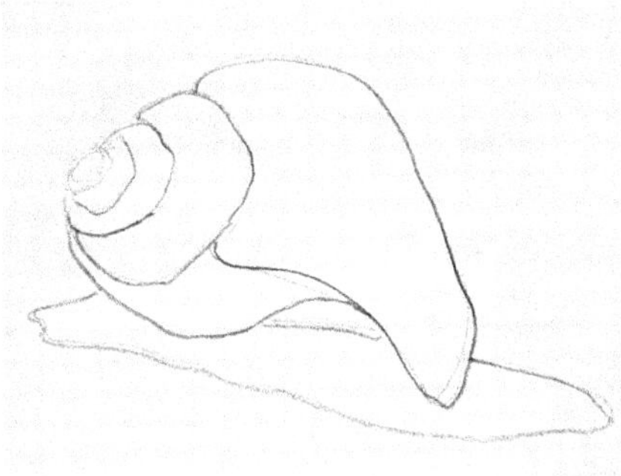

Image 4

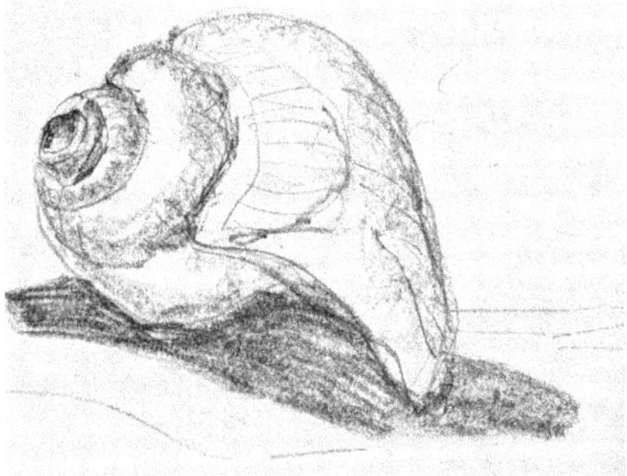

Image 5

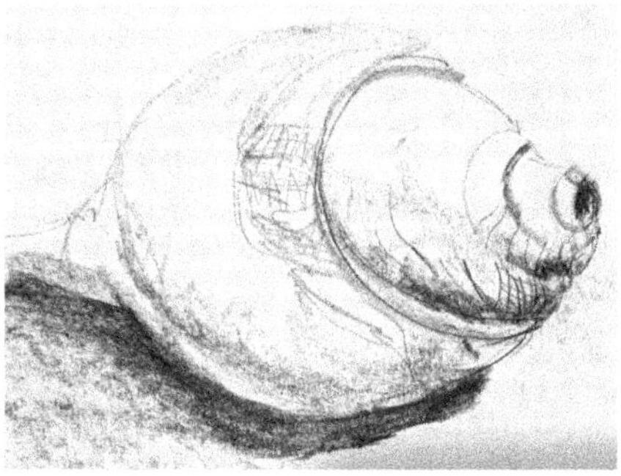

Image 6

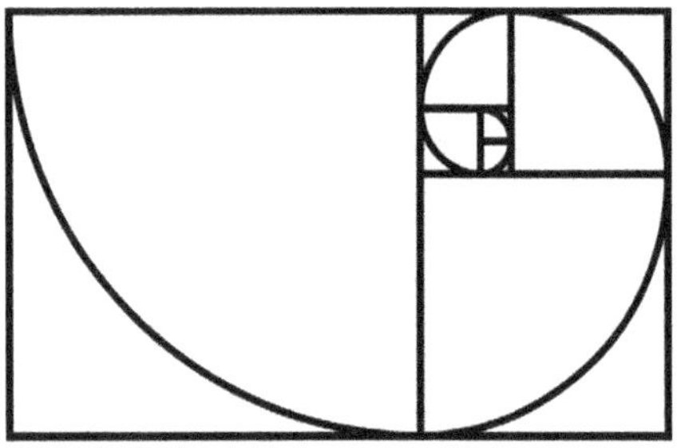

Resource 1

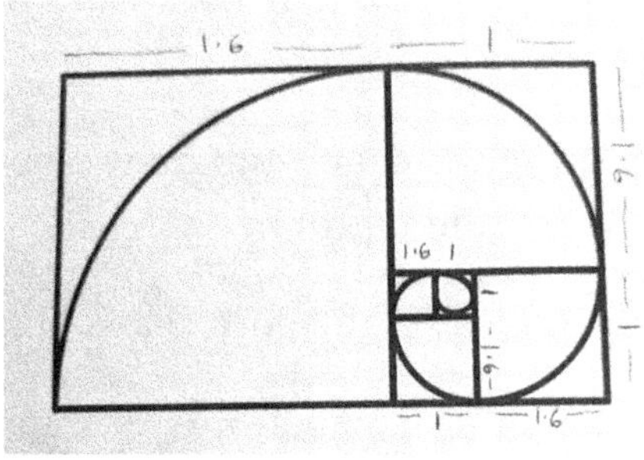

Resource 2

Alternative exercise: Draw a flag of Hanumān, which is on Arjuna's chariot. This is another sign of victory for the Pāṇḍavas, referred to in verse 20. Can you say why?

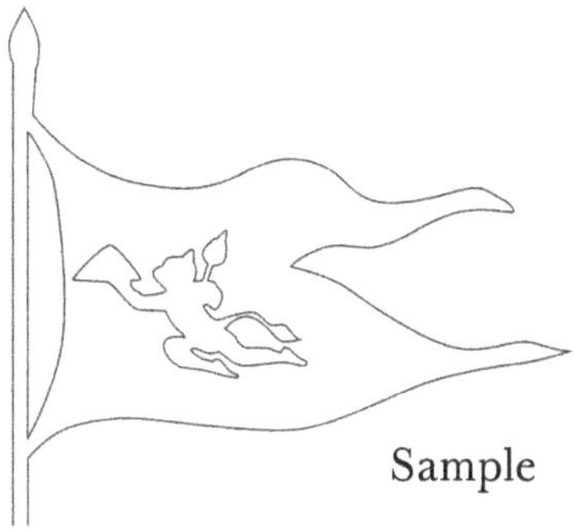

Sample

THEME TRACK 3 ACTIVITIES

LANGUAGE ACTIVITY

Kṛṣṇa as Bhakta-Vatsala

In verses 21 and 22, Kṛṣṇa is called *acyuta*, infallible one, or one who never fails. Śrīla Prabhupāda explains in the purport that "infallible" here means that Kṛṣṇa "never fails in His affection for His devotees," and therefore He became Arjuna's chariot driver. Prabhupāda explains that "out of His causeless mercy He was engaged in the service of His friend."

Our study group members are discussing about Kṛṣṇa as *bhakta-vatsala*, His affectionate dealings with His devotees. Let's see what they conclude.

Priya: Isn't it amazing that Kṛṣṇa, who is the Lord of the three worlds, can humble Himself so much that He becomes Ajuna's charioteer? Imagine that! He doesn't care about His reputation. Let alone that, He steals butter from the *gopīs* and is called *Mākhana-cora*. He runs away from the battlefield and is called *Raṇacora*. He becomes a messenger for the Pāṇḍavas and is insulted by Duryodhana. Why does He put Himself through this?

Madhu: Hmmm...good question, Priya. It seems like Kṛṣṇa will do anything for His devotees and bring out their love for Him more. Remember how He took up the chariot wheel and went after Bhīṣmadeva when Bhīṣma had showered Arjuna with arrows. How strong He must be! And what love He must have for His devotee that He would think of breaking His promise of not fighting. That's Kṛṣṇa for you.

Balu: Yes, I remember reading in Kṛṣṇa book how He killed all those powerful demons to protect His devotees, and He even subdued Kālīya, who had made His devotees' lives miserable. I mean, imagine not to be affected by Kālīya's terrible poison! I wonder if we can get some insights into this and create a new antidote for snake poison!

Tara: Yeah, very funny, Balu! (rolling her eyes) But He's like this to all His pure devotees. What about us? Will He go to such an extent to reciprocate with our small service or offerings of love.

Tamal: Sure. That's what makes Him *Bhagavān*! I think He is there for you whether you are a famous warrior and close friend like Arjuna or a silly schoolgirl. (laughs) Kṛṣṇa is *bhakta-*

vatsala for everyone. Remember that day when you fell and sprained your ankle? I think Kṛṣṇa saved you from something worse. Or another time when you had that fantastic idea to make a GoFundMe campaign for our temple. Who do you think inspired that? *ye yathā māṁ prapadyante tāṁs tathaiva bhajāmy aham* [*BG* 4.11]. If you approach Kṛṣṇa, He reciprocates regardless of who you are.

Priya: Wow! Seems like you've been reading *Bhagavad-gītā* ahead of us. Is there anything more about this?

Tamal: Yes! Kṛṣṇa says in *Bhagavad-gītā* (7.16) that He reciprocates with four types of devotees who surrender to Him: the distressed, the seekers of knowledge, the seekers of worldly possessions, and those who are situated in knowledge. So all of us who come to Kṛṣṇa fall into one of these four categories, and He relates to each one of us in a way that helps us progress in our spiritual lives.

Madhu: I told you! That's Kṛṣṇa for you. (grinning)

Reflection: Think of a time when Kṛṣṇa was *bhakta-vatsala* in relation to you. Write a paragraph in your notebook about your realizations.

Another quality of Lord Kṛṣṇa as *bhakta-vatsala* is that He loves to be named in relation to His devotees.

Here are some names of Kṛṣṇa associated with His devotees. Match the name with the meaning. Can you tell one pastime associated with each name?

NAME	PASTIME/EXPLANATION
Nanda-nandana	One loved by mother Yaśodā
Yaśodā-vatsala	Beloved son of all the Vrajavāsīs
Gopījana-vallabha	One who blessed Mucukunda
Vrajajana-nandana	Loved by the *gopīs*
Mucukunda-prasādaka	Nanda Mahāraja's son

THEME TRACK 4 ACTIVITIES

CRITICAL-THINKING ACTIVITY

To Fight or Not to Fight?

In verses 28 to 46 of this chapter and verse 6 of the next, Arjuna presents five reasons to Kṛṣṇa why he shouldn't fight. Arjuna was one of the bravest and best warriors present on the Battlefield of Kurukṣetra at that time. He came well prepared to face the Kaurava army. Why then did he want to leave just by looking at the opposing army?

Our *Bhagavad-gītā* study group has been given the task to analyze and discuss Arjuna's reasons for not fighting based on the following diagrams and information:

Look at what happened to Arjuna when he saw the two armies:

Arjuna visualized (saw) five "Ds" just by looking at those two armies, and he fell into another "D": Distress. These five Ds were the five reasons Arjuna became unwilling to fight and wanted to give up.

On the next page is a mind map that indicates what was happening in Arjuna's mind.

There were different reasons why Arjuna felt all these strong emotions and thoughts:

1. Being a devotee, he naturally had good qualities and good culture and felt strongly about the consequences of war.

2. Being a family member, he was attached to his family, who sadly were his opponents. He didn't want to lose them.

The first reason reflects his spiritual standing, while the second reflects the immediate material illusion he had been put into because of the will of the Lord. Due to this conflict between material and spiritual thoughts, Arjuna fell into a dilemma about fighting.

Dread

3

1. Killing is sinful. I'd have to face reactions for that.
2. I'd rather forgive the wrong that happened to me than face reactions by punishing wrong-doers.

4 **Decline**

When the men die, so many things will go wrong in the kingdom, especially culturally:

1. Offerings to forefathers will stop.
2. Family traditions stop.
3. Women may become polluted with no one to protect them.
4. Unwanted population increases.
5. Community welfare projects stop.

Disinterest

2

1. Not just soldiers, my relatives will also die. I'd be too distressed by the loss of my relatives to enjoy the kingdom I won.
2. Who shall I enjoy it with, anyway, if they all die?

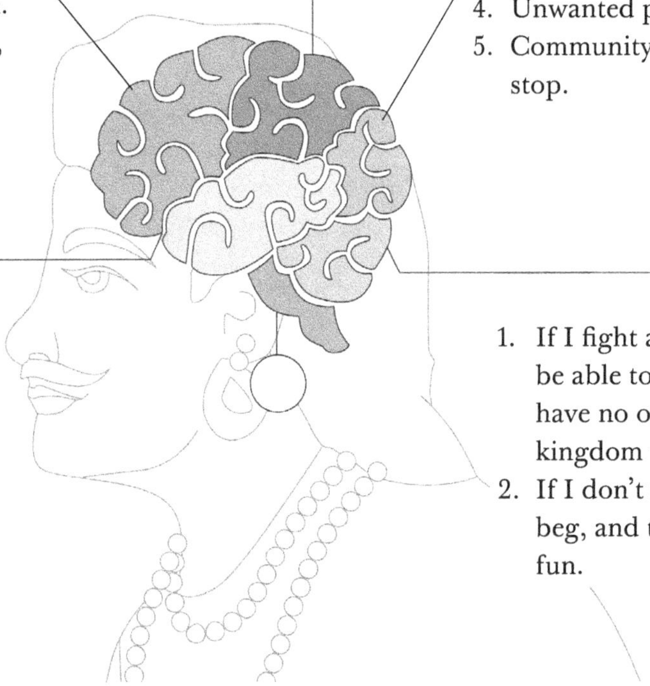

1 **Death**

1. Most people on both sides will be killed.
2. Thousands will perish just to give us the kingdom; why should they?
3. Is it worth gaining a kingdom by taking so many lives?

Dilemma 5

1. If I fight and win, I still won't be able to enjoy because I'll have no one left to enjoy the kingdom with.
2. If I don't fight, I'll have to beg, and that still won't be fun.

Look at the reflections of our *Bhakti-śāstrī* group on Arjuna's distress:

Priya: I'd probably feel the same way in his situation. After all, Arjuna is a devotee—he's too compassionate to hurt anyone – he certainly would find it tough to kill thousands of people! I'd have left the battlefield!

Balu: But he is a *kṣatriya*! He'd not dare – he should just fight! Think about all the things he's saying would happen to society if he doesn't.

Madhu: Maybe he should fight. Maybe he shouldn't. I don't know. Life's always throwing these dilemmas at us, you know. It's one thing when your enemies are strangers, but when it's your own friends and family – even if they're in the wrong – that's the hardest battle of all.

Tamal: Guys, Balu's the only one on track. Arjuna is a *kṣatriya*; it is his job to punish aggressors like the Kauravas – he'd not incur sin for that. And all his compassion – it's based on the bodily concept; it's misplaced!

Tara: That's enough, Tamal! What we all seem to be missing is that Arjuna is a devotee – he has some duty as a *kṣatriya*; he is also soft hearted, but he's got to follow Kṛṣṇa. His primary duty is to do as Kṛṣṇa desires. That's the ultimate criteria. So you should be thinking – what does Kṛṣṇa want him to do?

Now take the reflections from your own study group and say if Arjuna's distress is well founded or not. We will see how Kṛṣṇa begins to remove his distress in the next chapter.

Note: Reflections should be in line with those provided and should capture the essence of Arjuna's distress.

ANALOGY ANTHOLOGY

A collection of analogies
for easier understanding

Analogy: The Lord's Mission

As in the paddy field the unnecessary plants are taken out, so it is expected from the very beginning of these topics that in the religious field of Kurukṣetra, where the father of religion, Śrī Kṛṣṇa, was present, the unwanted plants like Dhṛtarāṣṭra's son Duryodhana and others would be wiped out and the thoroughly religious persons, headed by Yudhiṣṭhira, would be established by the Lord. This is the significance of the words *dharma-kṣetre* and *kuru-kṣetre,* apart from their historical and Vedic importance. – *BG* 1.1, purport

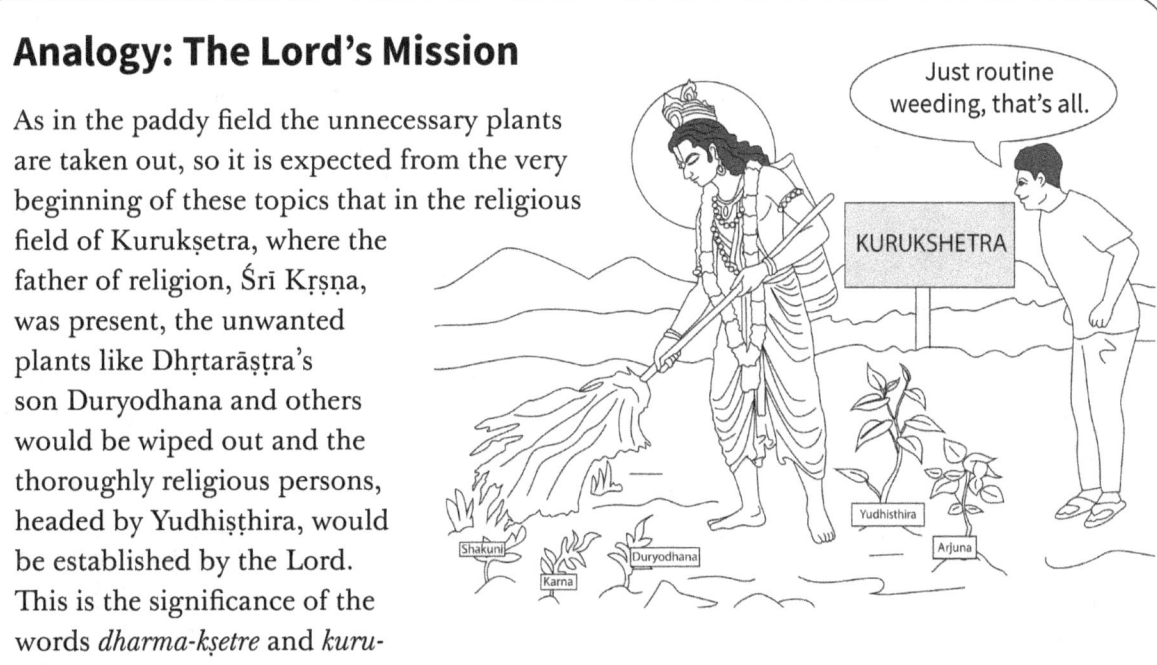

Lord Kṛṣṇa gathered the warriors on the battlefield so that He could wipe out the impious people and establish the rule of Yudhiṣṭhira, the most pious and devoted king.

ANSWERS

Learning Harmonies

1. b; 2. d; 3. d; 4. a; 5. d; 6. c; 7. a; 8. b; 9. c; 10. c

Kurukṣetra as Dharma-kṣetra

1. It was a *dharma-kṣetra*. Only people who follow *dharma* could win here, and all soldiers who died in this battle would receive liberation.
2. Because Dhṛtarāṣṭra knew that his sons were impious and that Kurukṣetra was a holy place, he understood that Kurukṣetra would negatively influence those who were unrighteous and positively influence those who were righteous. Therefore, he felt that his sons, the Kauravas, would lose the war.
3. After a long absence, Kṛṣṇa was feeling great separation from the Vrajavāsīs, especially the *gopīs*, so he invited them to Kurukṣetra on the pretext of observing the solar eclipse. The meeting of Kṛṣṇa and the Vrajavāsīs at Kurkṣetra was most joyous and they enjoyed each other's company. The Vrajavāsīs were astonished to see Kṛṣṇa dressed as a king instead of the simple cowherd boy they had known, so they pleaded with him to come back to Vṛndāvana. Kṛṣṇa promised them that he would after he had conquered all the demonic kings, and by His words and presence He tried to pacify them. These sweet, intimate pastimes that took place here makes Kurukṣetra even more holy and special.
4. Kurukṣetra is the place where the *Mahābhārata* war occurred and where Kṛṣṇa spoke the *Bhagavad-gītā* to Arjuna. Kṛṣṇa's presence had made it sacred. Therefore, pilgrims visit to pay their respects to this sacred land and hear and remember Kṛṣṇa's teachings from the *Bhagavad-gītā*. They also remember the meeting of Kṛṣṇa with the *gopīs* and the other Vrajavāsīs during a solar eclipse.

Significance of Pilgrimage Places (*Potential Answer*)

Pilgrims go to holy places to remember the Lord and His pastimes. By bathing in the holy rivers, visiting the temples, and hearing about the Lord's pastimes in those places, one remembers the Lord and becomes purified. The goal is to hear about and chant the glories of the Lord.

Bigger Is Not Always Better

1. Arjuna was fully aware of Kṛṣṇa's supreme position, and out of love wanted Kṛṣṇa's presence on his side, which would invoke all auspiciousness. Duryodhana, on the other hand, was convinced that material strength would help him win the war, not Kṛṣṇa's presence and personal support. He did not have faith in or affection for Kṛṣṇa.
2. Like Duryodhana, we put our faith in material things and think that this will make us happy and successful. We forget that Kṛṣṇa is the source of all material and spiritual potencies and that putting our faith in Kṛṣṇa and serving Him would naturally make us successful and happy.
3. Duryodhana had a greater army of eleven *akṣauhiṇīs* and the Pāṇḍavas had only seven. But without the approval and favor of Kṛṣṇa, the Kauravas lost the war.
4. Material wealth and possessions may give some temporary material enjoyment and facility, but ultimately can lead to material attachment, greed, hankering, dissatisfaction, and lamentation. Real wealth is our loving relationship with Kṛṣṇa, which makes the soul truly happy. *Māyā's* promises of success and happiness are false.
5. Arjuna was not attached to his kingdom or position for his self-interest. He was attached only in carrying out the desire of Kṛṣṇa and pleasing Him. Similarly, we should see Kṛṣṇa as the source of everything and use material opulence for Kṛṣṇa's pleasure.
6. Choosing Kṛṣṇa means following His instructions as in the *Bhagavad-gītā*. He urges us to think of Him and serve Him in devotion. Each day brings many possibilities of engaging in the service of either Kṛṣṇa or *māyā*. With the right mood, even our small facilities and efforts please Kṛṣṇa, and with misguided intelligence, the greatest of achievements cannot please Him and eventually become sources of misery.

Kṛṣṇa as Bhakta-vatsala

1. E; 2. A; 3. D; 4. B; 5. C

CHAPTER 2

Contents of the Gītā Summarized

CHAPTER BEATS

An overview

Madhusūdana, Kṛṣṇa, observed Arjuna's depressed face and tear-filled eyes. Kṛṣṇa and the Pāṇḍavas had just blown their conches in response to the Kaurava army, showing them that they had indeed come to fight, to win back what was rightfully theirs, to restore *dharma*.

Yet, Arjuna, now overcome with compassion, could not face his cousins, who had usurped him and his brothers of their rightful inheritance, who had tried to plunder and kill them using deceptive plots and cunning ploys.

Kṛṣṇa's reddish lotuslike eyes became stern. As much as he appreciated Arjuna's soft heart and saintliness, Kṛṣṇa rebuked him: "My dear Arjuna, what are you saying? What are you doing? This behavior is not befitting a *kṣatriya* like you, a person who knows the value of life! This won't lead you to the higher planets but to infamy."

Raising His voice, Kṛṣṇa commanded, "O son of Pṛtha, do not succumb to such powerlessness. Give up this petty weakness of heart and arise, O chastiser of the enemy!"

Arjuna did not budge. His lips trembled as he answered Kṛṣṇa: "O Madhusūdana, how can I counter-attack my superiors, like Bhīṣma and Droṇa, who are worthy of my worship? It would be better to lose everything and live by begging than live at the cost of great souls who are my teachers. Even though they want material comforts and success, they are still my superiors. If I kill them, everything we enjoy will be tainted with blood. So I don't know what would be better – to conquer them or be conquered by them."

Arjuna looked up again at his friend, his relative, his master. He could not stop the tears that streamed down his face. "Govinda, I shall not fight. I can't find any way to drive away this grief," he finally said. "I am confused about my duty. Please, Kṛṣṇa, tell me what's best for me. Now I am Your disciple and a soul surrendered to You. Please instruct me."

Kṛṣṇa smiled because His friend had chosen to become His disciple. This was the only way that He could transmit sublime knowledge. Amidst the both armies, Kṛṣṇa spoke for the benefit of everyone present: "You are speaking learned words, O Arjuna, but you are mourning for that which is not worthy of grief. The wise lament neither for the living nor for the dead.

"You see, My dear Arjuna, I've always been existing, and so have you and all these kings, and in the future also each of us will continue to exist. This is because we are the spirit soul within the body. The soul continuously passes in the present body from boyhood to youth to old age. And then at the time of death it similarly passes into another body. A sober person is not confused by this.

"As a person puts on new garments and gives up old ones, the soul accepts new material bodies, giving up old and useless ones.

"Knowing this, you have to tolerate happiness and distress while carrying out your duties. Happiness and distress are temporary just like winter and summer months, so try to tolerate them without being disturbed. Such a tolerant person is worthy of liberation.

"Those who seek the truth know that the material body is temporary and changes and that the soul is eternal and doesn't change. They've concluded this because they've studied the nature of both. The soul is indestructible. No one can destroy the imperishable soul. Therefore, fight, O descendant of Bharata!"

Arjuna stopped trembling and gazed at Kṛṣṇa through his tears. Each word seemed to penetrate his soul, the soul that Kṛṣṇa was describing.

"The soul is never born," Kṛṣṇa continued, His eyes fixed on Arjuna, "which means he doesn't come into being nor will come into being. And the soul never dies. He is eternal, which means he exists forever. He is not slain when the body is slain.

"If you know that the soul is indestructible, eternal, and unborn, how could you kill anyone or cause anyone to kill?

"The soul can't be cut into pieces, nor burned by fire, nor moistened by water, nor withered by the wind. The soul is unbreakable and insoluble. It is invisible, unchangeable and immovable, present everywhere, and is always the same.

"But even if you think that the soul will always be born and will die forever, you still don't need to lament, O mighty-armed Arjuna."

Arjuna began to understand the logic behind Kṛṣṇa's arguments. If the body is just a combination of chemicals and is never born again, then there would be no reason to fear sinful reactions.

"However, O Arjuna, one who is born is sure to die, and after one dies, one is sure to take birth again. Therefore, to discharge your duty, do not lament. All beings are unmanifest in the beginning, then become manifest, and unmanifest again when vanquished. So what need is there for lamentation."

Arjuna began to see this clearer now. Even if he believed that there was no soul and we are a combination of atoms, he should not lament because these material elements would always appear in their manifest form and then become unmanifest as atomic particles. And if he believed Kṛṣṇa that we are indeed the eternal soul, then he should always remember that the body is like a dress; so why should we lament for the changing of a dress?

"Some see the soul as amazing," continued Kṛṣṇa, "some describe the soul as amazing, some hear of the soul as amazing, while others cannot understand the soul at all. I assure you, O descendant of Bharata, that the soul which dwells in the body can never be slain, so you don't need to grieve for any living being."

Did this mean that Kṛṣṇa was encouraging violence on the basis that the soul is immortal? Kṛṣṇa explained next what He actually meant and that violence can only be justified by the sanction of the Lord.

"You should consider your specific duty as a *kṣatriya*. There's no better engagement for you

than fighting on religious principles. So don't hesitate to fight.

"O Pārtha, *kṣatriyas* are happy to fight on the battlefield to maintain justice. For *kṣatriyas* to become nonviolent is unheard of. Your duty is to protect the citizens. When *kṣatriyas* perform their religious duty like this, the doors of the heavenly planets are open for them. If, however, you do not perform your duty of fighting, you will certainly incur sins for neglecting your duties and thus lose your reputation as a fighter. People will think you've left the battlefield only out of fear. For a respectable person, this kind of dishonor is worse than death.

"O son of Kunti, either you will be killed on the battlefield and attain the heavenly planets or you will conquer and enjoy the earthly kingdom. Therefore, get up and fight!"

Arjuna stood up slowly, trying to heed Kṛṣṇa's instructions.

"Just fight for the sake of fighting," Kṛṣṇa reassured him. "Don't consider happiness and distress, loss or gain, victory of defeat – in this way you will never incur sin."

Arjuna let out a sigh of relief. All of a sudden, he felt lighter.

"I've so far described *sāṅkhya*, knowledge through analytical study," Kṛṣṇa continued. "Now listen as I describe working without the desire for fruitive gain. O son of Pṛtha, when you act in such knowledge, *buddhi-yoga*, you can free yourself from all reactions of work. What's more, nothing is lost or diminished when you act in *buddhi-yoga*; even a little advancement on this path can protect you from the greatest fear, the repetition of birth and death."

Arjuna nodded. He understood that even if someone does one percent of spiritual activity in one life, it has permanent results, and the person would start from two percent in his next life. Nothing is lost, unlike material activities that are temporary and give temporary results. He wanted to hear more about *buddhi-yoga*.

"Those who are on this path of *buddhi-yoga* are focused on their purpose. Their aim is one; their faith is not shaken, because they are not interested in the results of their activities. Their resolute determination is based on knowledge, whereas those who are irresolute, their intelligence is swayed by material enjoyment. These men of small intelligence are attached to the flowery words of the *Vedas*, which recommend various fruitive activities to gain material benefits and sense enjoyment. They think there's nothing more than this.

"O Arjuna, rise above the three modes of material nature, which is mainly the subject matter of the *Vedas*, and be free from all dualities and anxieties by being situated in the self. Perform your prescribed duty but don't be attached to the fruits of your action. Never think that you are the cause of the results, and never become detached from doing your duty. Do your duty with an equipoised mind, not being attached to success or failure. Such equanimity is called *yoga*.

"O Dhananjaya, those who want to enjoy the fruits of their work are called misers. Give up this consciousness and surrender to the Lord. Devotional service to the Lord frees one from all good and bad reactions and eventually the cycle of birth and death. Therefore, strive for *yoga*, the art of all work. When your mind is fixed in self-realization you have attained divine consciousness."

Arjuna's face lit up, as Kṛṣṇa's words began to remove the darkness that had been consuming him. "How does such a *sthita-prajña*, a person immersed in divine consciousness, speak, sit, and walk? What are his symptoms?" Arjuna asked.

The Supreme Personality of Godhead answered, "One who gives up all kinds of material desires that come from the mind, O Partha, and is satisfied in the self, as a servant of the Supreme, is said to be a *sthita-prajña*.

"How does he respond to dualities with his

speech? He's undisturbed amidst threefold miseries; he doesn't become elated in happiness; he is free from attachment, fear, and anger; he is undisturbed by any good or evil he may obtain, so he neither praises it nor despises it. Such a person is like a sage of steady mind, fixed in knowledge.

"How does he sit? In other words, how does he control his senses? He's able to withdraw his senses like a tortoise draws its limbs into its shell. One can practice restricting the senses from enjoyment in this way, but one can only be successful by experiencing a higher taste in devotional service. This is the secret of sense control. Even the wise are distracted by the senses. The senses are so strong and impetuous that they carry away the mind by force. Therefore, sense control is only possible by devotion to Me, when one fixes his consciousness upon Me. Such a person has steady intelligence."

"O Lord," Arjuna asked, a smile now making its way to his lips, "What happens when one is unable to control the senses?"

"While contemplating sense objects, one becomes attached to them. From attachment, lust develops; from lust, anger arises; from anger, one becomes deluded and one loses his memory; then one loses his intelligence and falls down in the material ocean."

"And walking? How does one engage his senses?" Arjuna reminded Kṛṣṇa.

"By attaining the Lord's mercy, all one's distresses are destroyed. One who is not connected to the Supreme cannot have a steady mind or intelligence. And how can there be peace without a steady mind? And without peace, how can there be any happiness?"

Arjuna nodded. Kṛṣṇa's words made sense to him.

"What is night for all beings is day for the self-controlled, and what is day for the conditioned souls is night for the introspective sage." Kṛṣṇa continued.

Kṛṣṇa was implying that the wise and self-controlled seek inner truth while others chase worldly pleasures. What seems real and important to most feels meaningless to the enlightened, just as night and day appear opposite to different people. He also explained that the *sthita-prajña* remains peaceful and undisturbed by the flow of desires, but one who strives to fulfill those desires is not. A devotee is therefore happy in the service of the Lord. He gives up false ego, all sense enjoyment and material desires, and at death attains *brahma-nirvāṇam*, entrance into the kingdom of God.

THEME TRACKS

Themes and key messages
to contemplate and discuss

THEME TRACKS	REFERENCES	KEY MESSAGES
Theme Track 1 When one is confused about one's duty in life, one should approach a bona fide spiritual master for guidance and surrender to his instructions.	2.1–10	Arjuna presented more of his doubts to Lord Kṛṣṇa for not fighting. Kṛṣṇa chastised him for having "petty weakness of heart" and did not approve of his compassion for his kinsmen in this situation. Therefore, confused Arjuna surrendered to Kṛṣṇa and accepted Him as his spiritual master so that Kṛṣṇa could remove all his doubts. He was ready to hear from Kṛṣṇa, and Kṛṣṇa smiled because His friend was ready to become His disciple. The talk between master and disciple took place in between both armies so that everyone, friends and enemies, would benefit from hearing Kṛṣṇa's instructions.
Theme Track 2 Knowledge of the differences between body and soul, matter and spirit, is essential and greater than other kinds of knowledge.	2.11–30	Kṛṣṇa explained to Arjuna the nature of the soul and the body so that Arjuna would see no reason to unnecessarily lament. Kṛṣṇa explained that the spirit soul is eternal (never dies) whereas the body is perishable, and in this way He encouraged Arjuna to fight. He also explained that the change of body is natural, the soul is indestructible and therefore cannot be killed, birth and death is inevitable, and one should tolerate all temporary dualities because of this. The Māyāvāda theory of oneness is refuted. Arjuna was not aware that *jñāna-śāstra,* knowledge of matter, the soul, and the supreme controller of both, is greater than *dharma-śāstra* (religious principles) or *artha-śāstra* (politics or sociology).
Theme Track 3 Performing one's prescribed duties gives enjoyment and is a result of *sakāma-karma-yoga.*	2.31–37	Arjuna reasoned earlier that there would be no enjoyment even if he is victorious in the battle. Kṛṣṇa replied that there would be enjoyment in victory or loss, either by gaining a kingdom or going to heaven respectively. He also discussed the problems that would arise from not fighting. If Arjuna neglected his duty of fighting (*sva-dharma*), he would incur sinful reactions, lose his reputation, and be criticized. This process of attaining material enjoyment is called *sa-kāma karma* or *karma-kāṇḍa*, performing rituals and activities for fruitive gain.

THEME TRACKS	REFERENCES	KEY MESSAGES
Theme Track 4 It's better to work with knowledge (*buddhi-yoga*) and detachment (*niṣkāma-karma-yoga*), which does not give any sinful reactions.	2.38–53	Arjuna wanted to avoid war because he was afraid of getting sinful reactions, but Kṛṣṇa warned him that he would incur sin by not fighting. Then Kṛṣṇa explained that one can avoid all reactions by doing one's duty, being detached from the results. He told Arjuna to rise above *sakāma-karma* activities and work with knowledge and detachment, as an offering to Him. In this way, there is no loss or decrease; even a little advancement on this path can save one from the greatest fear (death). Such people have resolute intelligence and are not enamored by material desires. He therefore encouraged Arjuna to fight out of duty, being equal in happiness and distress, gain or loss, victory or defeat. Such equanimity is called *yoga*. Acting in *buddhi-yoga*, work done for the satisfaction of Kṛṣṇa, gets rid of all good and bad reactions and the cycle of birth and death.
Theme Track 5 One can control the senses and mind by devotion to Kṛṣṇa.	2.54–72	A self-realized soul, one who is in divine consciousness, is called a *sthita-prajña*. Kṛṣṇa encouraged Arjuna to develop such consciousness by experiencing the higher taste of devotional service. In this way, sense control becomes easier. A *sthita-prajña* can withdraw his senses like a tortoise withdraws its limbs into its shell. Even the wise are distracted by the senses, but a *sthita-prajña* is of steady intelligence. If one is not able to control the mind and instead contemplates sense objects, attachment develops, then lust, anger, delusion, bewilderment of memory, and loss of intelligence follow, and one falls down into material consciousness. Without a steady mind, there is no peace, and therefore no happiness. Agitated senses carry away the intelligence, and steady intelligence can be achieved by fixing the mind on Kṛṣṇa. A *sthita-prajña* is not agitated by desires and remains peaceful and satisfied. One can achieve this state in the service of the Lord and eventually attain *brahma-nirvāṇam* (liberation from material existence).

SOLO QUESTIONS

To enhance your self-study

(Find the answers in the verse and purport references provided in brackets.)

1. List Arjuna's arguments for not fighting. (1.27–2.7)
2. List six symptoms of Bhagavān in English or Sanskrit (2.2)
3. Arjuna's qualities of kindness and compassion show that he was a great devotee and fit for liberation (2.6), but why did Kṛṣṇa call his softheartedness "petty weakness of heart": *kṣudraṁ hṛdaya-daurbalyaṁ*? (2.3) Why didn't Lord Kṛṣṇa approve of the so-called compassion of Arjuna for his kinsmen? (2.2–2.3)
4. According to scriptural codes, when is a teacher fit to be abandoned? How is Arjuna's abandoning of his teachers justified? (2.5)
5. Arjuna was confused in his duty (*dharma-sammūḍha-cetāḥ*). What process is recommended to dissolve all perplexities? (2.7)
6. How does Kṛṣṇa's statements in verses 12 and 13 support individualism and refute *māyāvāda*, or impersonalism? (2.12–13)
7. Kṛṣṇa's statements about the indestructible nature of the soul are meant to encourage Arjuna to kill. Does this mean that we can kill anyone or commit violence to anyone based on this idea that the soul is eternal? Discuss appropriate and inappropriate application of Śrīla Prabhupāda's statement "violence also has its utility" in relation to the battle of Kurukṣetra and current issues of religious violence. (2.19; 2.21; 2.27; 2.30)
8. List the six kinds of transformations the body is subject to. (2.20)
9. What is meant by *sva-dharma* and what are the two types of *sva-dharma*? Why was it important for Arjuna to perform his *sva-dharma*? (2.31–36)
10. Why is it that the killing of animals in sacrifice, which is not recommended in this age, not considered an act of violence? (2.31)
11. How is Lord Kṛṣṇa's Sāṅkhya philosophy of the body and soul in this chapter and Lord Kapila's Sāṅkhya in *Śrīmad-Bhāgavatam* the same as *buddhi/bhakti-yoga*? (2.39)
12. List the eight stages of spiritual falldown in English or Sanskrit. (2.62–63)

LEARNING HARMONIES

Multiple-choice questions to quiz your memory

(Choose the most complete answer.)

1. What is the primary concern of Arjuna at the beginning of Chapter 2?
   a. His duty as a warrior.
   b. The consequences of war.
   c. The death of his family members.
   d. The loss of his kingdom.

2. What does Kṛṣṇa say about the soul in verse 2.13?
   a. The soul is eternal and cannot die.
   b. The soul is temporary and perishable.
   c. The soul is tied to the body.
   d. The soul is non-existent.

3. In verse 2.19, Kṛṣṇa explains that the soul cannot be killed. What reason does He provide?
   a. The soul is not physical.
   b. The soul is reborn.
   c. The soul is part of God.
   d. The soul is an illusion.

4. What does Kṛṣṇa advise Arjuna to perform in verse 2.47?
   a. To withdraw from battle.
   b. To focus only on the results of actions.
   c. To perform his duty without attachment to the results.
   d. To abandon all duties.

5. What does Kṛṣṇa say about the nature of the mind in verse 2.48?
   a. The mind is the source of all troubles.
   b. The mind must be controlled to achieve peace.
   c. The mind is irrelevant to spiritual practice.
   d. The mind is superior to the soul.

6. According to Kṛṣṇa in verse 2.50, what is the nature of a true *yogī*?
   a. Someone who avoids all actions.
   b. Someone who is indifferent to success or failure.
   c. Someone who only meditates.
   d. Someone who only seeks pleasure.

7. In verse 2.55, what qualities does Kṛṣṇa attribute to a person who is truly detached?
   a. They are indifferent to friends and enemies.
   b. They are free from all desires for sense enjoyment.
   c. They are always joyful.
   d. They do not care for worldly matters.

8. What metaphor does Kṛṣṇa use to describe the person who is steady in their intellect in verse 2.66?
   a. A boat in a storm.
   b. A candle in the wind.
   c. A steady flame.
   d. A tree in the wind.

9. In verse 2.70, what does Kṛṣṇa say about a person who is unaffected by desires?
   a. They are considered wealthy.
   b. They are seen as a fool.
   c. They are happy.
   d. They can achieve liberation.

10. What is the key message of Chapter 2 regarding action and detachment?
    a. One should act without any thought.
    b. One should abandon all actions.
    c. One should act according to duty while remaining unattached.
    d. One should seek only personal gain in actions.

MEDLEY ACTS

A variety of fun activities to learn from

THEME TRACK 1 ACTIVITIES

ARTISTIC ACTIVITY

Create a Sun Catcher

In verse 2 purport, Śrīla Prabhupāda explains the three different aspects of understanding the Absolute Truth: Brahman, Paramātmā, and Bhagavān. He compares this to the three aspects of the sun respectively: the sunshine, the sun's surface, and the sun planet.

Directions:

- Read this part of the purport and refer to Analogy 1 at the end of this chapter to understand why Kṛṣṇa is called Bhagavān throughout the *Gītā*. Discuss with your teacher and class and write a short summary of your understanding in relation to the analogy.
- Meditate on Kṛṣṇa as Bhagavān, the source of everything, and His reflections everywhere in the creation, just as the sun is the source of beautiful spectrums.
- Let us now design a beautiful "sun catcher" to observe the interplay of light and color, reminding us of Kṛṣṇa as the sun.

Materials needed: Any two shiny metal bangles (at least 4 inches in diameter); 5-meter 24-gauge wire (stiff enough to easily bend); small colored crystal beads (plastic or glass) to reflect sunlight; a colorful glass prism or crystal with a hole (optional).

Steps:

1. Slip one bangle inside the other to look like a cross from the top. Using two small pieces of gauge wire, secure the bangles tight at the center. Tie a thread at the same loop to hang it to a ceiling (Image 1).
2. Take enough wire to wrap multiple times along the bangle. Start with one end of the wire wrapped at the center, then two or three times at the beginning of the semi-circle before inserting the beads (Image 2).
3. Insert the crystal beads one by one till the end of the semi-circle, while wrapping the wire twice each time before inserting the next bead (Image 3).
4. Make your own symmetrical pattern with colorful beads all along the four semi-circles (Image 4).

5. Insert some wire or thread into the prism/crystal and suspend it to the bottom center of the suncatcher (Image 5).
6. Hang it to a glass window or in your parent's car where sun rays can pass through the prism and beads. See how your suncatcher displays beautiful reflections as it rotates (Image 6).

Image 1

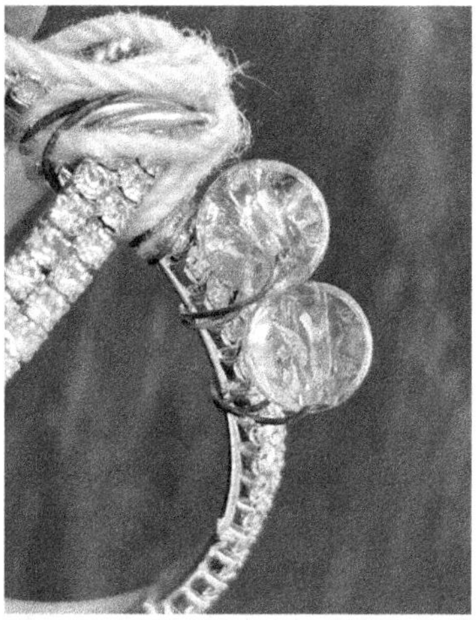
Image 2

Image 3

Image 4

Image 5

Image 6

Optional: Explore other patterns online. Enhance your patterns by hanging some prisms symmetrically all around the suncatcher.

Reflect on the following to unlock the suncatcher mystery:

- Are the suncatchers mere decorative pieces or is there any spiritual significance to them beyond their aesthetic appeal?
- Is there any history to the suncatchers often seen as conduits for positive energy?
- Is the interplay of light and color merely a visual spectacle or does it have any effect on the mind, body, and soul?

CRITICAL-THINKING ACTIVITY

You Have to Fight!

In this activity you will see how Arjuna takes on the role of a disciple by presenting his doubts to Kṛṣṇa and how Kṛṣṇa takes on the role of his spiritual guide.

In the previous chapter, Arjuna presented five reasons why he didn't want to fight. In this chapter, Kṛṣṇa counters those reasons and tries to convince Arjuna to fight. Let us study Kṛṣṇa's counterarguments to Arjuna's arguments.

Divide your class into groups of two. Each of you should have a copy of the *Bhagavad-gītā As It Is* to complete this activity. Your group will be given a set of verse cards from the Resource page at the end of this chapter. These cards contain only verse numbers.

Section 1: Identify Kṛṣṇa's Counterarguments

1. First sort these cards into two groups: Arjuna's arguments and Kṛṣṇa's counterarguments. This part should be reasonably easy – open your *Bhagavad-gītā* and simply check who spoke each verse. (Also remember, Kṛṣṇa didn't do much of the speaking in Chapter 1.)
2. After you have sorted the cards into two piles, complete Arjuna's side of the table on the next page, referring to the critical-thinking activity in the previous chapter and the verses from the text. You should be able to fill out Arjuna's five arguments and the verse numbers.
3. Next, look at the remaining cards. Obviously, these are Kṛṣṇa's counterarguments to Arjuna's arguments. Read each verse translation and understand it. Then try to find out which of Arjuna's arguments Kṛṣṇa is trying to counter in that verse.
4. Fill out the verse numbers and write down a phrase or two to summarize the counterargument on Kṛṣṇa's side of the table.
5. Finally, discuss the answers with your teacher. Did you match all the counterarguments properly?

	VERSE NO.	ARJUNA'S ARGUMENT	VERSE NO.	KṚṢṆA'S COUNTERARGUMENT
1				
2				
3				
4				
5				

Section 2: Dive deeper

Now that you have identified the arguments and the corresponding counterarguments, it is time to understand Kṛṣṇa's points more deeply.

1. Stay in pairs. You will now perform a role-play.
2. Each pair in the class picks one argument.
3. Study the verses both Kṛṣṇa and Arjuna speak for the argument you have chosen. Read the translation and the purport and understand the essence.
4. Write a short, one-minute role-play based on your understanding of the verses. You should accurately capture the essence of both the argument and the counterargument.
5. Present your role-play to the class.

INTROSPECTIVE ACTIVITY

Have you ever been in a dilemma like Arjuna? Reflect on what it was. Did you address your dilemma like Arjuna did and resolve it? If you didn't do anything, how would you now address future dilemmas, learning from Arjuna's example of seeking clarity from Kṛṣṇa and surrendering to Him? Refer to verses 7 to 10 and their purports to get further insights and write a short paragraph of your experience and realizations.

THEME TRACK 2 ACTIVITIES

WRITING ACTIVITY

Essay: Spiritual Knowledge Is More Important Than Religion

In verse 2 purport, Śrīla Prabhupāda explains the three different aspects of understanding the Absolute Truth: Brahman, Paramātmā, and Bhagavān. He compares this to the three aspects of the sun respectively: the sunshine, the sun's surface, and the sun planet.

In a one-page essay, discuss the significance of Śrīla Prabhupāda's statement: "Knowledge of matter, soul and the Supreme is even more important than religious formularies." (*BG* 2.11, purport)

Guidelines (refer to verse 11 purport):

- Why did Kṛṣṇa chastise Arjuna and call him a fool?
- Who is truly learned according to Kṛṣṇa?
- What is real knowledge?
- How is this knowledge more important than following mundane religion?
- If one is learned, what is one free from?
- Relate an incident from *śāstra* or your own life to illustrate this theme?
- Conclude by giving the essence of knowledge and why it is superior.

LANGUAGE ACTIVITY

Refuting the Māyāvāda Theory

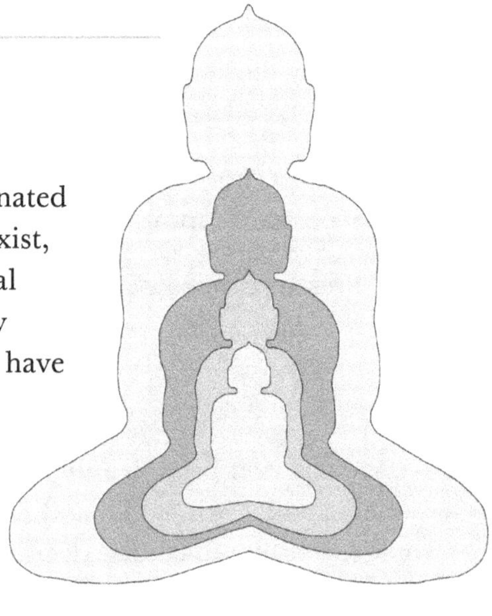

Balu is excited after reading verse 12 of this chapter. He is fascinated that his existence is eternal, there was never a time he did not exist, and there will never be a time he shall cease to exist. In his usual dreamy way, he chats to Tamal about the various bodies he may have had in previous lifetimes and the unusual habitats he may have experienced.

Tamal brings to his attention that this verse is more important than that – it establishes the differences between the temporary body and individual soul, the difference between the *jīvas* and the Supreme soul, and the spiritual eternality of all souls. Tamal reminds Balu that in this verse Lord Kṛṣṇa was not only able to counter Arjuna's argument about having compassion for his relatives but He also refutes the Māyāvādī theory.

The Māyāvādī theory states that the individual soul is separated or broken from original consciousness by the covering of *māyā*, or illusion. According to Māyāvādīs, individuality exists only in the conditioned state. Under the influence of *māyā*, one experiences individual consciousness. After liberation, the soul merges into the impersonal Brahman and loses its individual existence.

Balu was initially disappointed with the scholarly interpretation of the verse but eventually became eager to learn how to contest the Māyāvādī theory of oneness. After reading verses 12, 13, 23, and 24 and their purports, help Balu by matching the Māyāvādī arguments and their respective refutation below:

MĀYĀVĀDĪ ARGUMENTS	REFUTATION
1. Kṛṣṇa and the *jīvas* are one.	a. The soul is unbreakable, insoluble, and can be neither burned nor dried. It is unchangeable and eternally the same. (*BG* 2.23–24)
2. There is homogenous merging of all individuals after liberation.	b. Kṛṣṇa has maintained spiritual individuality all along; if He is accepted as an ordinary conditioned soul in individual consciousness, then His *Bhagavad-gītā* has no value as authoritative scripture. *Māyā* is His inferior energy, so Kṛṣṇa cannot be overcome by it. (*BG* Introduction; *BG* 2.12, purport)
3. The individual soul is separated from original consciousness by illusion.	c. Kṛṣṇa identifies Arjuna and all the assembled kings as eternal individuals in the future. (*BG* 2.12) "The individual soul is eternally the atomic particle of the spirit whole, and he remains the same atom eternally, without change." (*BG* 2.24, purport)
4. Individuality exists only in a conditioned state.	d. Kṛṣṇa and the living entities have individuality in the past, present, and future. (*BG* 2.12)
5. Kṛṣṇa's individuality is material and not spiritual.	e. The bodily conception was already condemned in verse 11 by Lord Kṛṣṇa. Why would He propose this based on the body again?
6. The plural "us" mentioned in verse 12 refers to the material bodies, not to the individual souls.	f. The Lord is eternally the maintainer of the individual living entities both in their conditioned and in their liberated situations. (*Kaṭha Upaniṣad* "*nityo nityānāṁ*") The *jīvas* cannot be cut; they are eternally separated parts of the Supreme Soul. (*BG* 2.23)

ACTION ACTIVITIES

Analyzing the Soul

In this chapter Kṛṣṇa uses *sāṅkhya* to analyze the soul, showing us that life is not made up of material elements. What features of the soul shows us that life comes from life and not something material? First let's understand some of these features, explained in verse 17 and purport, through the following simple activities.

Activity 1: Experience the Soul
Often we think, " I have a soul" and "I am this body." But actually the reverse is true:

"I am soul" and "I have this body."

How to understand this? Here is a small experiment.

Imagine you have a pencil in your hand and your teacher has called upon you to question you as follows. What would you answer?

- Is this your pen?
- Is the pen different from you?
- Where is the pen?
- Just as the pen is different from you, can you say that the hand is different from you?
- How are you standing?
- In the same way, are the legs different from you?
- How do you eat?
- Is the mouth different from you?
- How do you see?
- Are your eyes different from you?
- Now can you say that you are different from your body?
- Who are you?

What can you conclude by this experiment?

Activity 2: Size of the Soul

The approximate size of the tip of a hair is 120 μ (atomic mass unit).

So if we divide this into a hundred then again into a hundred, the size is like that of a bacterium, which can be seen under a microscope.

Then why can't we see it? (Also refer to the science activity in this section.)

The size of the soul is 1/10,000th part of the tip of a hair.

"If we divide the tip of a hair into a hundred parts, and then divide each part into further hundred parts, we will get the size of the soul. These souls are innumerable in number." (*Śvetāśvatara Upaniṣad*)

Activity 3: Consciousness: A Symptom of the Soul

Your mentor calls two students in front of the class and asks them to stand facing each other. She asks student 1 to gently pinch student 2. She then asks them the following questions:

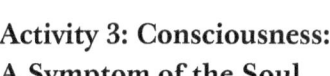

To student 2: Did you feel the pain?

To student 1: Did you feel the pain?

Mentor to student 1: Why did you not feel the pain?

Student 1: Because that is not my body.

Mentor: So we understand that we are conscious of our body only. We are not conscious of another body. Why?

Student 1: The soul in my body is different from the soul in another body.

Mentor: Now, let us consider a dead body. If we pinch a dead body, will it feel the pain? Why?

Student: No. Because there is no consciousness in the body.

Mentor: That is because there is no soul. So what do we conclude from this?

Transmigration of the Soul

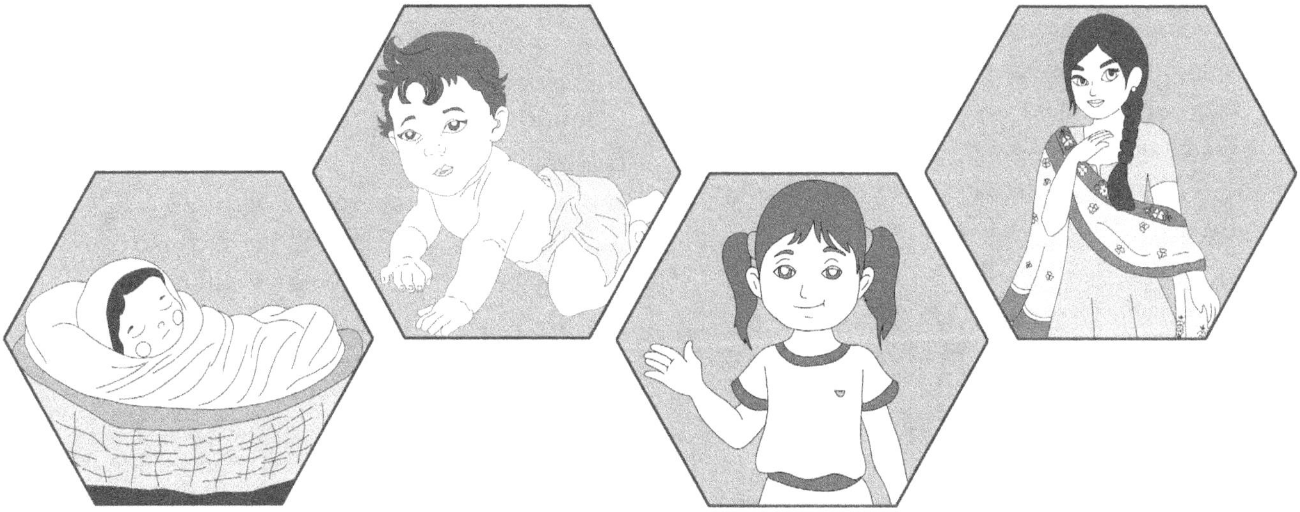

From verses 13 and 22, we learn that while the body changes, the soul does not. Research shows that the human body is in constant flux. About 330 billion cells of our body (that is about 1 per cent of our body cells) are replaced every day.

Let's see practically how this has happened in your body so far.

Directions:

- Collect some photos of yourself at different stages of your life, from young childhood to recent milestones. They could be pictures of the day you were born, your first word, your first meal, your first day at school, your 13th birthday, etc. You can photocopy them.
- Then collate the pictures according to age in a small album or chart and label each picture.
- Look at these pictures and try to recall any incident or situation related to that time in your life. You may narrate some memories in class.

Although your body has changed a lot, you still remember some things. You still feel it is you.

That something that has changed is your body.

That something that has not changed is you, the soul.

Now, how does this relate to verse 13 about changing bodies after death? Explain the process of transmigration of the soul, referring to verses 13 and 22 and their purports, in a short paragraph.

SCIENCE ACTIVITY

Soul Science

Kṛṣṇa introduces the most fundamental concept of spiritual science in this chapter – the existence of the soul. Material science relies on *pratyakṣa* (direct perception) and *anumāna* (inference*) to understand things, but the soul cannot be perceived by the material senses nor understood by material science.

As Śrīla Prabhupāda explains in the purport to verse 17, the soul is an atomic spiritual entity that material scientists cannot measure, leading some to falsely deny its existence.

To understand the soul, we need a different approach: *śabda-pramāṇa*, which means receiving knowledge from a bona fide spiritual authority. The perfect authority is Lord Kṛṣṇa, who explains the nature of the soul in the *Bhagavad-gītā*, and this knowledge is confirmed by realized spiritual teachers like Śrīla Prabhupāda.

While we cannot directly observe the soul with our senses, we can trust the knowledge passed down through these authorities, which forms the foundation of spiritual science.

Śabda-pramāṇa: A Systematic Approach to Spiritual Knowledge

Śabda-pramāṇa is a methodical, reliable way of gaining knowledge, much like how material science relies on tested and verified data. Here's why it's a form of science:

1. **Systematic and Verifiable**: Spiritual knowledge transmitted through *śabda-pramāṇa* is not random; it's part of a structured tradition passed down by realized authorities. Just as scientific knowledge is verified through experimentation, spiritual knowledge can also be verified by faithfully following the recommended rules and regulations for spiritual life and confirming the expected results first hand.

2. **Subtle Knowledge**: Material science deals with the physical world, while *śabda-pramāṇa* reveals knowledge of the soul – something beyond the physical realm. Material science attempts to uncover physical laws through human endeavor, whereas spiritual science transmits, through realized authorities, laws that govern the transcendental soul, *karma*, and the afterlife.

3. **Universal and Objective**: Like scientific truths, the teachings of *śabda-pramāṇa* are non-sectarian and universal. The truths about the soul apply to all living beings, independent of time, place, or culture.

4. **Authority**: In material science, we rely on experts who are conditioned souls with the four defects; in spiritual science, the ultimate authority is Kṛṣṇa, whose teachings are passed

* Drawing conclusions based on evidence or reasoning, without direct observation.

down through His representatives. Their teachings ensure the purity and consistency of the knowledge.

5. **Progressive Understanding**: In both material science and spiritual practice, knowledge deepens over time. As we practice spiritual teachings, our understanding of the soul becomes clearer and more profound.

Activity:

1. Read *BG* 2.17 and Śrīla Prabhupāda's purport. Summarize the key points Prabhupāda makes to show that life is not merely a product of material combinations.
2. Research a modern case study that suggests the existence of the soul (e.g., a near-death experience (NDE), out-of-body experience (OBE), or reincarnation). Present this case to the group and explain how it supports the idea of the soul's existence beyond the body.
3. Reflection: Discuss how these studies and verses from the *Bhagavad-gītā* strengthen your faith in the existence of the spirit soul, even when it cannot be directly perceived. How does understanding the soul as a spiritual reality affect your view of life and death?

By embracing the method of *śabda-pramāṇa*, we can deepen our understanding of the soul and our true spiritual nature, transcending the limitations of material science.

INTROSPECTIVE ACTIVITY

Mirror, Mirror on the Wall

The real identity of the individual, according to the *Bhagavad-gītā*, is the soul within the body. The labels associated with the body – such as name, gender, or occupation – don't reflect who we really are: the soul within the body.

Let us explore our true identity through this story of a 13-year-old girl named Geeta, who is struggling with poor self-image.

"Mirror, mirror on the wall, who is the fairest of them all?" Geeta asks the magic mirror hanging on the wall of her room. Some classmates at school had ridiculed her again today because of her dark skin. In her world, fair skin was often seen as superior, leaving Geeta feeling inferior.

No one knew how she came to possess the magic mirror, but the mirror always spoke the whole truth to her.

"Do you see your real self in me today, O Geeta?" the mirror answers her question with another.

"What is my real self, O Mirror? All I know is that I am sad today. I am just a girl in a blue dress with lacy frills, but I have a dark complexion, so everyone makes fun of me."

"Ah! That layer of covering you still do see.
Try to look deeper, to find your real 'me,'" the mirror encourages.

The mirror guides Geeta to probe deeper and deeper until she cries out in joy:

"Isn't that little spark there the real me?
They call it the soul – no one can see.
Beyond all temporary mistaken identities,
It is eternal, full of knowledge and bliss.

Inconceivable is the soul, let me explain,
More beautiful than the outer skin,
Invisible, insoluble,
Not slain when the body is slain,
Unbreakable, indestructible.

So that's exactly who I am!
Knowing this can make one calm.
All these troubles seem small,
As we transcend this disturbing realm."

Fortunate was little Geeta to see her real self in the mirror each day.

Exercise:
How did Geeta's self-image change when she realized she was a spirit soul and not the dark-skinned girl in the mirror?

- Have you been in a similar situation, or do you judge yourself by your appearance? Do you judge yourself by others' standard of beauty?
- How can you overcome a similar predicament, understanding your true spiritual identity? Does it help you focus on what is real and of ultimate value?
- Discuss in class how to overcome cases like Geeta's in a school situation.
- Recap Kṛṣṇa's instructions on *jñāna* with reference to key *ślokas* and analogies. (*BG* 2.11–30)

THEME TRACK 3 & 4 ACTIVITIES

CRITICAL-THINKING ACTIVITY

Niṣkāma- and Sakāma-Karma-Yogas

In this chapter, Kṛṣṇa attempts to convince Arjuna to fight by first presenting the concept of *sakāma-karma-yoga* (2.31–37), and then *niṣkāma-karma-yoga* (2.38–53).

1. *Sakāma-karma-yoga* refers to performing your duty with a desire to enjoy the results of your activities. For example, in verses 2.31–37, Kṛṣṇa instructs Arjuna on *karma-kāṇḍa* and tells him to fight out of duty as a *kṣatriya*. As a result, Arjuna would either enjoy a kingdom on Earth in victory or enjoy heavenly pleasures in defeat.
2. *Niṣkāma-karma-yoga* refers to performing your duty without a desire to enjoy personal gains. In this case, one performs one's duty to please the Supreme Lord. Later in the chapter, Kṛṣṇa urges Arjuna to work without attachment to victory or defeat, but just to carry out His will.

Arjuna understood these instructions and decided to act in the service of the Lord.

Read verses 31–37 to understand *sakāma-karma-yoga*, and verses 38–53 to understand *niṣkāma-karma-yoga*.

Our *Bhakti-śāstrī* study group also read these verses and was asked to write short reflections on them. Here is what they came up with:

Balu:
Reflection (2.47): "Kṛṣṇa says, 'You have a right to perform your duty, but not to the results.' That's tough! I'm always focused on results; I mean that's logical, isn't it? You work because you want to get something! I now get it that you can work but to please the Lord – that is logical too, because when you water the root, you nourish the tree. Scientific!

Tara:
Reflection (2.48): "*Niṣkāma-karma* is doing everything for Kṛṣṇa without expecting anything in return. That means whatever I do, I should simply do to show my love to Him – I could be dressing the Deity or speaking about Him and similar such things. I don't need to do these things for myself all the time and keep craving for admiration from others in return . . . could be hard for me, but worth a try!

Madhu:
Reflection (2.58): "I struggle with discipline and often give in to my cravings, especially good food. The tortoise analogy especially struck a chord with me: it retreats into its shell to protect itself. So sense control is also a kind of protection from getting carried away, and I am going to try."

Priya:
Reflection (2.53–56): "The idea that inner growth happens when we rise above the activities of the three modes made so much sense. People's natures intrigue me, but their natures are within the three modes! It was also interesting the see how Arjuna analyzes the nature of a *niṣkāma karma-yogī* in the later verses. That is food for thought for me!"

Tamal:
Reflection (2.53): "Sometimes I feel proud that I'm a knowledgeable guy and a hard worker, but Kṛṣṇa shows me it's a meaningless attachment when I forget even the simplest things or when I'm not able to perform well. Just as He gives everything, He can similarly take away everything. He's ultimately in charge of the results. So how can I be proud of my efforts?"

Your study group can now create a similar reflection board after studying these verses.

ACTION ACTIVITIES

Kṣat in Sanskrit means "hurt," and *trāyate* means "to give protection." So a *kṣatriya* is one who gives protection from harm. (*BG* 2.31, purport)

Comparative Study: Karma-Kāṇḍī and Bhakti-Yogī

Kṛṣṇa advises Arjuna to do his prescribed duty as a *kṣatriya*, but greater is to act as a *bhakti-yogī* – to do his duty as a *kṣatriya* according to Kṛṣṇa's desires. Choose one of the following activities to contrast a *karma-kāṇḍī* with a *bhakti-yogī*:

Visual Poster: Create a poster illustrating key differences between a *karma-kāṇḍī* and a *bhakti-yogī*, including relevant verses.

Role-Play: Act out a dialogue between a *karma-kāṇḍī* and a *bhakti-yogī*, showcasing their beliefs and practices.

Digital Presentation: Use slides or a video to present your analysis and conclusions to the class. Include relevant analogies from verses 42 to 46 (refer to Analogy Anthology at the end of this chapter).

Pointers for your activity:

- **Karma-kāṇḍa:**
    - The *karma-kāṇḍa* sections of the *Vedas* focus on sacrifices aimed at pleasing the demigods to obtain temporary benefits, such as sons, health, wealth, longevity, and heavenly pleasures. For a *kṣatriya* the doors of the heavenly planets are wide open (*svarga-dvāram apāvṛtam*). (*BG* 2.31–33)
    - A *karma-kāṇḍī* diligently performs prescribed duties based on their *varṇa* and *āśrama*. Success leads to elevation to heavenly planets, while neglect incurs sins (*BG* 2.34).
- **Contemporary Challenges:**
    - In today's world, performing these sacrifices properly is difficult due to the unavailability of pure ingredients. Additionally, accurately determining one's *varṇa* is often impossible (*BG* 2.35).
    - Without understanding one's *varṇāśrama-dharma*, it's challenging to know one's prescribed duties. Even if a *varṇa* is known, changing occupations per Vedic prescriptions may not be feasible (*BG* 2.36).
- **Kṛṣṇa's Guidance to Arjuna:**
    - Kṛṣṇa instructs Arjuna to fulfill his duties as a *kṣatriya* and fight (*BG* 2.31). He then advises that, rather than adhering strictly to *karma-kāṇḍa* duties, one should embrace the true purpose of the *Vedas*: surrendering to the Supreme through *bhakti-yoga* (*BG* 2.42–46). Even as a *kṣatriya* he could still be a *bhakti-yogī,* using his duty for Kṛṣṇa's pleasure.
- **Transcending Material Dualities:**
    - The *Vedas* mainly deal with the three modes of material nature and associated dualities. The purpose of the *Vedas* is served by knowing the purpose behind them. Kṛṣṇa encourages Arjuna to transcend these modes by tolerating dualities and achieving full Kṛṣṇa consciousness through *bhakti-yoga* or *buddhi-yoga* (*BG* 2.45–48).
    - Engaging in *buddhi-yoga* fulfills the Vedic purpose, making additional *karma-kāṇḍa* rituals unnecessary (*BG* 2.45).

- **Results of Practices:**
    - Performing *varṇāśrama* duties and *karma-kāṇḍa* rituals may lead to elevation to higher planets after death, but one remains trapped in the cycle of birth and death (*BG* 2.30).
    - In contrast, practicing *bhakti-yoga* liberates one from this cycle and fosters a profound understanding of the Supreme Lord and one's eternal relationship with Him, ultimately leading to the supreme goal of love of God (*BG* 2.47).

Work with Detachment

In verse 47, Kṛṣṇa encourages Arjuna to fight, to do his prescribed duty (*karmaṇy evādhikāras te*), without being attached to the results. He explains that one has a right to perform one's duty but one is not entitled to the fruits.

Today our *Bhagavad-gītā* study group is discussing this statement, showing how it can be misinterpreted:

1. **Misunderstanding detachment:**

    Balu: Does this verse mean we can do our work carelessly since we shouldn't worry about the results?

    Priya: No, Balu, quite the contrary. This verse explains that we should focus and put in real effort when we perform our duties.

2. **Using it as an excuse:**

    Madhu: Maybe we don't need to take our responsibilities that seriously because the verse says we aren't entitled to the fruits of our actions.

    Tara: I don't think so. This can lead to laziness or not doing our best work, which goes against this message about being responsible in our actions.

3. **Ignoring accountability or simply wanting results:**

    Tamal: You're right, Tara. This verse doesn't mean we can act without thinking about the consequences. It emphasizes that we must be accountable and do our duties faithfully but not be attached to the results, for we are not the real cause of the results – the Lord is.

The group was asked to explore this more through role-play, and so can you:

1. Divide the class into small groups of four to five students.
2. Each group will read verse 47 and purport and discuss its meaning, focusing on the concept of duty and attachment to results. Explore the following questions:
    - What does it mean to perform one's duties without attachment to results?
    - How can one balance the desire for good outcomes with the principle of duty?
    - Can you think of examples from daily life or history where this principle was applied effectively?

3. Your group will brainstorm examples of inappropriate applications of the phrase in modern contexts, such as:
    - Workplaces where employees neglect their responsibilities.
    - Workplaces where employees are only in the mood of competition.
    - Students who do not put in effort because they believe grades do not matter.
    - Students who work only for the sake of being number one in class.
    - Individuals who use this teaching to justify laziness or lack of ambition.
4. Now your group will create role-play scenarios based on your discussions. Present a short skit that illustrates:
    - A correct application of "*karmaṇy evādhikāras te*."
    - An inappropriate application of the phrase.
    - After each skit, your group will briefly discuss why their portrayal is either a positive or negative example.

WRITING ACTIVITY

Letter: No Loss or Diminution

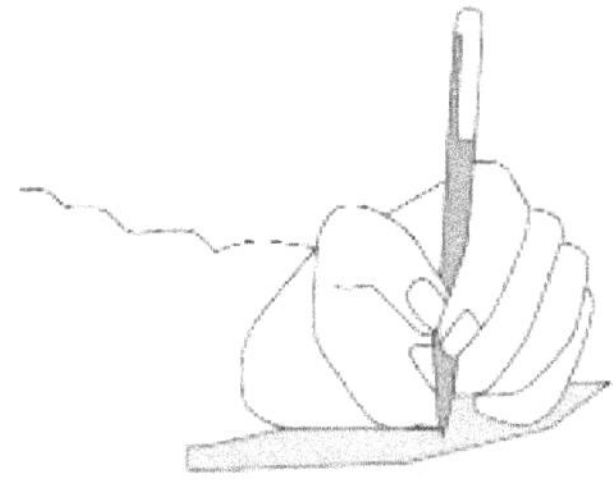

Your devotee friend's brother or sister, or other family member, has strayed away from Krsna consciousness. Your friend is disappointed and worried, so you decide to console him or her from your understanding of verse 40 in this chapter, which states that there is no loss or diminution (*pratyavāyo na vidyate*) whenever one comes in contact with Kṛṣṇa conscious activities.

Write a letter to your friend explaining how *bhakti-yoga* is beyond the three modes and thus any advancement made on this path, however small, is eternal and continues to the next life, unlike material advancement, which is temporary and ends at the time of death.

Prabhupāda elaborated on this concept during a lecture in Paris on August 10, 1973:

"But if you cultivate spiritual consciousness or Kṛṣṇa consciousness, that will go with you. And if you have finished in this life, say, ten percent, then next life you begin eleven percent."

Then discuss with a partner how this knowledge of the soul (*aṇu-ātmā*) and the Supreme Soul (*vibhu-ātmā*) and the process of *bhakti* allows our intelligence to become resolute in purpose. If our mind sways by material temptation or mental disturbances, our intelligence can help us focus on what's important. In this way we can become fixed in Kṛṣṇa consciousness with the help of resolute intelligence (*vyavasāyātmikā buddhiḥ*) as explained in verse 41.

Discuss the significance of resolute intelligence in your life and how it can help you overcome personal challenges.

THEME TRACK 5 ACTIVITIES

LANGUAGE ACTIVITIES

A Sthita-Prajña

Refer to verses 54–72 to understand who a *sthita-prajña* is and complete the following activities:

Prajña literally means "perfect knowledge," and a *sthita-prajña* is one of steady intelligence.

Cross out the qualities that a *sthita-prajña* will not have:

1. No desire for sense gratification arising from petty materialism
2. Elated when there is happiness
3. Gets angry very fast
4. Free from attachment, fear, and anger
5. Disturbed by the three-fold miseries

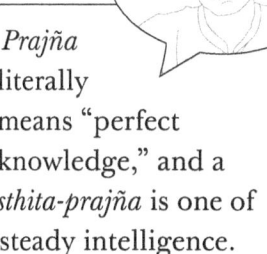

6. Neither praises nor despises good or evil
7. Is always situated in Kṛṣṇa consciousness
8. Like a tortoise that withdraws his senses when required

Give three examples of a *sthita-prajña* that you know from *śāstra*. Explain why you consider them *sthita-prajñas*.

Now that you know the qualities of a *sthita-prajña*, do you think it's necessary to cultivate these qualities before becoming a *sthitha-prajña*? See how you can start practicing some of these quality traits now in the following scenarios:

	SITUATION	RESPONSE
1.	You are selected to be the school head boy/girl.	
2.	You win the school marathon but are disqualified for a flimsy reason.	
3.	Your pet cat dies.	
4.	The billboards in the city are a great distraction. They arouse your senses.	
5.	You are pulled into a fight between two of your friends and one of them blames you.	

Poem: The Sthita-Dhīr Muni

In the quiet depths of his steady soul,
Where storms of life have no control,
The *sthita-dhīr muni* stands serene,
Untouched by joy, unmoved by the sheen
Of sorrow or fleeting bliss,
In the service of the Lord, he finds his abyss.

When the winds of misery howl and roar,
He is still, as a mountain's core.
Not shaken by the trials of fate,
Nor eager for pleasure's fleeting state.
Sense delights may call his name,
But to him, they are all the same.

His mind, a river, flowing still,
Not bound by the world's errant will.
Success or failure, loss or gain,
Cannot disturb his inward reign.
For in the Lord, his mind does stay,
Unshaken by what comes his way.

No anger flares, no joy takes flight,
His heart is bathed in sacred light.
In every breath, his soul is free,
A servant to the Lord, is he.
Beyond the rise and fall of days,
He walks in wisdom's timeless ways.

Referring to verse 56 and purport, discuss the following questions:

1. How does the *sthita-dhīr muni's* approach to happiness and distress help him remain stable in both victory and defeat?

2. In what ways does dedicating one's life to the service of the Lord prevent attachment to sense enjoyment or detachment from worldly affairs for the *sthita-dhīr muni*?

3. How can the mindset of the *sthita-dhīr muni*, who is unaffected by external joys or sorrows, be applied to modern challenges such as career success or failure?

4. Why is it significant that the *sthita-dhīr muni* neither becomes elated with happiness nor discouraged by miseries? How does this neutrality reflect a deeper spiritual truth?

5. In what manner does the *sthita-dhīr muni's* relationship with sense objects differ from mere detachment, and how does this reflect his deeper spiritual understanding?

6. How do the analogies in verses 58 to 72, such as the tortoise withdrawing its limbs (2.58) or the ocean remaining undisturbed by rivers flowing into it (2.70), illustrate the control of the senses through Kṛṣṇa consciousness. (See Analogies 3 and 6 at the end of the chapter.) How can you apply these examples to managing distractions and desires in your own life?

INTROSPECTIVE ACTIVITY

The Higher Taste

Verse 59 elaborates that restricting sense enjoyment externally while we nurture desires for sense gratification internally will never work. Only when we experience a higher taste (*paraṁ dṛṣṭvā*) will we give up our taste for lower desires and enjoyment.

Discuss examples from Śrīla Prabhupāda's preaching to illustrate this. Reflect on things in your own life that you've given up for some more fulfilling activity. Then think of spiritual activities you've replaced for mundane activities, because you've developed a higher taste for those devotional activities.

Here are some examples of developing experiences with higher tastes that you could try out:

1. Experiencing auspiciousness that gives health and happiness; e.g., Waking up refreshed and energetic each morning after a good night's sleep rather than staying awake all night watching TV.

2. Developing good habits; e.g., Going with your friends on *harināma* instead of being locked up in your room doing your own stuff.

3. Cultivating a taste for serving Kṛṣṇa and His devotees; e.g., Giving up standing first in line for *prasādam* in the temple and instead trying to experience the bliss in serving *prasādam*.
4. Practicing *bhakti*; e.g., Giving up reading some mundane book in favor of Kṛṣṇa book, *Mahābhārata*, or any spiritual literature.

- Add more to this list and share more examples of the higher taste you've experienced in spiritual activities that automatically replaced lower habits.
- As you can see, it is easier to control the senses when you have a higher taste for Kṛṣṇa conscious activities. Cite examples from verses 58 to 72 that illustrate control of the senses by the process of Kṛṣṇa consciousness.

ANALOGY ANTHOLOGY

A collection of analogies
for easier understanding

Analogy 1: Aspects of the Absolute Truth

The Absolute Truth is realized in three phases of understanding, namely Brahman, or the impersonal all-pervasive spirit; Paramātmā, or the localized aspect of the Supreme within the heart of all living entities; and Bhagavān, or the Supreme Personality of Godhead, Lord Kṛṣṇa... These three divine aspects can be explained by the example of the sun, which also has three different aspects, namely the sunshine, the sun's surface and the sun planet itself. One who studies the sunshine only is the preliminary student. One who understands the sun's surface is further advanced. And one who can enter into the sun planet is the highest.
– *BG* 2.2, purport

Just like the sun has three aspects – sunshine, sun disc, and sun-god – the Absolute Truth is also realized in three phrases – Brahman, Paramātmā, and Bhagavān.

Analogy 2: The Soul's Proof

This very small spiritual spark is the basic principle of the material body, and the influence of such a spiritual spark is spread all over the body as the influence of the active principle of some medicine spreads throughout the body. This current of the spirit soul is felt all over the body as consciousness, and that is the proof of the presence of the soul.
– *BG* 2.17, purport

Just like medicine's influence spreads throughout the body, the influence of the soul spreads throughout the body and is proof of the soul's presence.

New beginnings, new hopes.

Analogy 3: Changing Bodies

As a person puts on new garments, giving up old ones, the soul similarly accepts new material bodies, giving up the old and useless ones.
– *BG* 2.22

The body changes but the soul is the same.

Analogy 4: The Seasons of Life

This too shall pass.

O son of Kuntī, the nonpermanent appearance of happiness and distress, and their disappearance in due course, are like the appearance and disappearance of winter and summer seasons. They arise from sense perception, O scion of Bharata, and one must learn to tolerate them without being disturbed. – *BG* 2.14, purport

Just like summer and winter are seasons of weather and we tolerate them, we should tolerate happiness and distress, which are seasons of life in the material world.

Analogy 5: Withdrawing the Senses

One who is able to withdraw his senses from sense objects, as the tortoise draws its limbs within the shell, is firmly fixed in perfect consciousness.
– *BG* 2.58

A person firmly fixed in perfect consciousness withdraws his senses from sense objects, just like a tortoise withdraws its limbs within the shell.

"I'm retreating to enjoy the real treat within!"

Analogy 6: One Roaming Sense Can Mislead a Yogī

As a strong wind sweeps away a boat on the water, even one of the roaming senses on which the mind focuses can carry away a man's intelligence.
– *BG* 2.67

Even one of the roaming senses can carry away a man's intelligence, just like one strong wind can sweep a boat away.

SACRED RHYTHMS

Important verses
to memorize

***BG* 2.7**

kārpaṇya-doṣopahata-svabhāvaḥ
pṛcchāmi tvāṁ dharma-sammūḍha-cetāḥ
yac chreyaḥ syān niścitaṁ brūhi tan me
śiṣyas te 'haṁ śādhi māṁ tvāṁ prapannam

Now I am confused about my duty and have lost all composure because of miserly weakness. In this condition I am asking You to tell me for certain what is best for me. Now I am Your disciple, and a soul surrendered unto You. Please instruct me.

***BG* 2.13**

dehino 'smin yathā dehe
kaumāraṁ yauvanaṁ jarā
tathā dehāntara-prāptir
dhīras tatra na muhyati

As the embodied soul continuously passes, in this body, from boyhood to youth to old age, the soul similarly passes into another body at death. A sober person is not bewildered by such a change.

***BG* 2.14**

mātrā-sparśās tu kaunteya
śītoṣṇa-sukha-duḥkha-dāḥ
āgamāpāyino 'nityās
tāṁs titikṣasva bhārata

O son of Kuntī, the nonpermanent appearance of happiness and distress, and their disappearance in due course, are like the appearance and disappearance of winter and summer seasons. They arise from sense perception, O scion of Bharata, and one must learn to tolerate them without being disturbed.

***BG* 2.20**

na jāyate mriyate vā kadācin
nāyaṁ bhūtvā bhavitā vā na bhūyaḥ
ajo nityaḥ śāśvato 'yaṁ purāṇo
na hanyate hanyamāne śarīre

For the soul there is neither birth nor death at any time. He has not come into being, does not come into being, and will not come into being. He is unborn, eternal, ever-existing and primeval. He is not slain when the body is slain.

ANSWERS

Learning Harmonies

1. b; 2. a; 3. a; 4. c; 5. b; 6. b; 7. b; 8. a; 9. d; 10. c

You Have to Fight!

	VERSE NO.	ARJUNA'S ARGUMENT	VERSE NO.	KṚṢṆA'S COUNTERARGUMENT
1	1.28–30	Death (of everyone)	2.11–30	Soul has no death. Body always has death.
2	1.31–35	Disinterest (as he won't be able to enjoy)	2.31–32	If you win, you'll enjoy in this world. If you lose, you will enjoy in heaven.
3	1.36–38	Dread (of sin)	2.33–37	You will not incur sin if you follow *dharma*.
4	1.37–43	Decline (of *dharma*)	2.45–46, 3.24	*Dharma* can be maintained by understanding that the purpose of Vedic rituals is to satisfy Me (Kṛṣṇa).
5	2.6	Dilemma	all (2.18, 2.31, 2.37, 2.48)	Every argument, He says, "Therefore fight!"

Refuting the Māyāvāda Theory

1. f; 2. c; 3. a; 4. d; 5. b; 6. e

Analyzing the Soul

Activity 1: Conclusion – The "my" and "your" is the soul, and is the actual "me" or "you." It is present in our body and yet is aloof from it. It witnesses and experiences everything as a silent spectator.

Activity 2: The soul is not material; it is spiritual. Material things can be measured while spiritual things cannot.

Activity 3: Conclusion – Consciousness is the symptom of the soul. The soul exhibits consciousness. The emotions and feelings of anger, sadness, and happiness are all signs of consciousness. A dead body cannot exhibit this.

Soul Science *(Potential Answers)*

1. The soul is spiritual and not just a result of material combinations; the soul is beyond material instruments and senses; Life and consciousness come from the soul, not from the physical body.

Science can't explain life because the soul is non-material and transcendent.

2. Case Study: Near-Death Experience (NDE) – Example: Pam Reynolds, who was clinically dead during surgery; reported detailed observations of the procedure, including events she couldn't have known; proving consciousness exists independently of the body.

Her experience suggests that the soul or consciousness exists beyond the physical body and brain.

3. Reflection: Modern NDEs and teachings in the *Bhagavad-gītā* reinforce the belief that the soul exists beyond material perception, even when it can't be directly seen or measured.

View on life and death: Understanding the soul's eternal nature shifts the perspective on life and death. We can see death as a transition rather than an end, which gives life a deeper spiritual purpose.

A Stitha-Prajña

Not qualities: 2; 3; 5

Poem: The Stitha-Dhīr Muni

1. The *sthita-dhīr muni* views both happiness and distress as temporary, external events that don't affect his inner peace. Focused on serving the Lord, he remains undisturbed by material outcomes like victory or defeat.
2. His devotion to the Lord frees him from seeking personal pleasure or gain. The *sthita-dhīr muni* engages in worldly duties without attachment because his focus is on blissful devotional service, not on fleeting material experiences.
3. By focusing on duty and not being attached to results, one can remain calm through career successes or failures. Like the *sthita-dhīr muni*, seeing outcomes as temporary helps maintain balance and inner peace. We can also see that Kṛṣṇa does not care about the results but more on our effort to please Him. This helps us to be less attached to the results.
4. His neutrality shows his detachment from material life, understanding that both happiness and sorrow are temporary. This reflects the deeper truth that lasting fulfillment lies in connection with Kṛṣṇa, not in material dualities.
5. The *sthita-dhīr muni* neither clings to nor rejects sense objects; he sees them as temporary and doesn't go after them for himself. But because his objective is service to the Lord, he uses everything in the Lord's service and therefore transcends both attachment and detachment.
6. The tortoise withdrawing its limbs (2.58) symbolizes how one practicing Kṛṣṇa consciousness can withdraw the senses from harmful distractions, just as the tortoise protects itself by retreating. The ocean analogy (2.70) shows how, even when desires flow in, one remains undisturbed if they are fixed in spiritual consciousness. Applying these examples, we can learn to manage our desires and stay focused on higher spiritual goals, without being swayed by external temptations or distractions in everyday life. (Students can discuss their personal desires and distractions and see how to apply this principle.)

RESOURCE FOR "YOU HAVE TO FIGHT"

Photocopy, cut, and distribute these cards in the class before the activity. (Only make half the number of copies as there are students in your class.)

1.28–30	12.33–37	2.11–30	1.36–38
2.6	1.31–35	2.45–46	2.31–32
2.18 2.31 2.37 2.48	1.37–43		

CHAPTER 3

Karma-yoga

CHAPTER BEATS

An overview

After Arjuna heard Kṛṣṇa's words, he furrowed his eyebrows in thought and asked the Lord, "O Janārdana, O Keśava, you explained that I should follow *buddhi-yoga*, the path of knowledge in devotional service. Then why are you telling me to fight in this war if you think that having knowledge is better than fruitive work? Please tell me one thing – what will be most beneficial for me?"

Arjuna now gazed at Kṛṣṇa's stern face. The pearls of sweat on Kṛṣṇa's brow and the dust that settled on His curly locks made Him look more attractive.

Lord Kṛṣṇa replied, "O sinless Arjuna, I've explained that there are two classes of men who try to understand the self: one is the person who tries to understand through *sāṅkhya-* or *jñāna-yoga*, speculative study, and one is the person who understands by *buddhi- or karma-yoga*, by devotional service. Performing *buddhi-yoga* doesn't mean that you should abstain from work, nor does performing *jñāna-yoga* mean that you should renounce everything. Action is natural. You can't refrain from doing something, even for a moment. You can't prematurely renounce your work or your prescribed duties, because your unfulfilled desires can lead to sinful activity. One who doesn't act but inwardly dwells on sense objects is called a pretender. On the other hand, if someone tries

to control the senses by the mind and engages in *karma-yoga*, acting but without being attached to the results of his activities, he is far superior."

Arjuna frowned in thought. He had thought that *buddhi-yoga*, intelligence in spiritual advancement, meant retiring from active life and doing penances and austerities in a secluded place. He was now beginning to understand why he couldn't avoid doing his duty by fighting on the battlefield.

Kṛṣṇa reiterated his instruction regarding work: "So perform your prescribed duty, which is better than not working. You cannot maintain even your physical body without working."

Arjuna sighed and understood the truth in Kṛṣṇa's words.

"Work as a sacrifice for Viṣṇu," Kṛṣṇa affirmed, "otherwise work causes reactions and

then bondage in this material world. Therefore, O son of Kuntī, do your prescribed duties for the satisfaction of Viṣṇu to be free from bondage.

"The demigods are also pleased by sacrifices and will supply everything in nature and all necessities to you. But if you enjoy their gifts without offering them back to the demigods, who in turn offer them to Viṣṇu, you are simply a thief."

Arjuna could understand that our life is dependent on the supplies of the Lord's agents, but if we take the supplies and use them only for our own satisfaction, we become thieves and will be punished by material nature's laws.

"But the devotees of the Lord are released from all sin," continued Kṛṣṇa, "because they eat food which is offered first for sacrifice. Those who prepare food for their own sense enjoyment, eat only sin.

"You see, my dear Arjuna, *yajña*, or sacrifice, produces rains, and rains produce food grains, which are necessary for living beings to live. And from where does *yajña* come? From prescribed duties."

A glimmer of a smile appeared on Arjuna's lips. He knew what Kṛṣṇa would say next.

"Work is prescribed in the *Vedas*, which come directly from the Supreme Lord. So, in acts of sacrifice the Lord is also eternally present. My dear Arjuna, one who doesn't follow the cycle of sacrifice, established by the *Vedas*, leads a life of sin.

"However, one whose goal is self-realization and who works for the Lord's pleasure, being fully satisfied by acts of service, no longer has any duty to perform. He is not obligated by the Vedic injunctions. But he still acts out of duty and without being attached to the results. Working in this detached way, one can attain the Supreme.

"Understand this, My dear Arjuna. A great man wants to set the example for others. He knows that whatever action a great man performs, common men will follow. Even I am engaged in prescribed duties although I am not in want of anything nor need to obtain anything. If I stopped doing My prescribed duties, all men would follow My path."

Arjuna admired Kṛṣṇa, whom he knew didn't have any duty to perform, yet he could see that the Lord Himself was participating in the Battlefield of Kurukṣetra as the leader of the *kṣatriyas*, whose duty was to protect the distressed.

"Can you imagine what would happen if I didn't do My duty as a *kṣatriya*?" Kṛṣṇa continued. "There would be unwanted population, and I would destroy the peace of all living beings. So just as the ignorant perform their duties with attachment to the results of their activities, similarly the learned should act, but without attachment. They should do their duty simply to lead people on the right path.

"In the same way, a learned person shouldn't stop ignorant men from performing their duties. He should not unsettle the ignorant who are fully engaged in material activities, although they are inferior. Rather, he should engage them in devotional activities and gradually uplift their consciousness.

"The spirit soul who is covered by the false ego thinks that he is the doer of activities, but actually they are carried out by the three modes of material nature. Those in knowledge do not work to gratify the senses, because they know the difference between work in devotion and work for fruitive results.

"Therefore, O Arjuna, surrender all your work to Me, with full knowledge of Me. Without desiring profit or claiming that you are the owner of anything, become free from lethargy and fight!"

Arjuna looked at his bow that he'd left aside. Kṛṣṇa's words were beginning to remove the doubts from his mind.

Kṛṣṇa said, "Those who do their duties, following My instructions faithfully and without envy, become free from the bondage of fruitive work. But the envious disregard these teachings. They are bereft of all knowledge and are ruined in their endeavors for perfection.

"Even a person situated in knowledge must act according to his own nature. Everyone is under the influence of the three modes of nature, so no one can repress their nature. It is better to discharge one's own prescribed duty even in a faulty way than do another's duties perfectly. To follow another's path is dangerous. So do your duty and don't imitate others.

"Don't become attached to sense objects nor averse to that which obstructs material enjoyment."

Arjuna pondered about a person's attachment to sense objects. The *jīva* is spiritual and pure and yet when in touch with material nature acts sinfully. He asked, "O descendant of Vṛṣṇi, what impels people to sin, even unwillingly, as if by force?"

Kṛṣṇa smiled for a moment and then said in a grave voice, "It is lust only, Arjuna, which

comes from contact with the mode of passion and which then transforms into anger. Lust is the all-devouring sinful enemy of this world.

"As fire is covered by smoke, as a mirror is covered by dust, or as the embryo is covered by the womb, the living being is similarly covered by different degrees of lust. Thus one's consciousness becomes covered and is never satisfied.

"And where can this lust be found? In the senses, mind, and intelligence. So, dear Arjuna, curb this lust, which destroys knowledge and self-realization, by regulating the senses.

"The senses are superior to matter; the mind is higher than the senses; intelligence is still higher than the mind; and the soul is higher than intelligence. So if you know that you are higher than the material senses, mind, and intelligence, you can steady the mind by using spiritual intelligence. In this way, by spiritual strength, you can conquer this enemy known as lust."

THEME TRACKS

Themes and key messages
to contemplate and discuss

THEME TRACKS	REFERENCES	KEY MESSAGES
Theme Track 1 *Niṣkāma-karma-yoga* is better than *jñāna-yoga* or renouncing work.	3.1–3.9	Kṛṣṇa encourages Arjuna not to renounce his propensity to fight but to act in *buddhi-* or *karma-yoga*, not being attached to the results of his activities. This is called *niṣkāma-karma-yoga*. Inaction is unnatural, and if one prematurely renounces one's work or prescribed duties, one's unfulfilled desires can lead to sinful activity. Such a pretender restrains his senses from action, but his mind dwells on enjoying the senses. By renouncing activities, one cannot attain liberation. Prescribed duties as laid down in the scriptures are meant to purify us from material desires. Still, these actions can produce fruitive results. Therefore, Kṛṣṇa advises to work for Lord Viṣṇu, without personal desire but for His satisfaction. Such work is called *yajña*, or sacrifice, which does not produce *karma*, or fruitive reactions.

THEME TRACKS	REFERENCES	KEY MESSAGES
Theme Track 2 If one cannot perform *karma-yoga*, one can perform *karma-kāṇḍa* activities prescribed in the *śāstra*, which ultimately purify one from material desires.	3.10–3.16	Kṛṣṇa explains that if we have material desires and work with a desire for material gain, we can perform our work in a religious way. This means that we can perform our activities according to the rules and regulations laid down in the *Vedas* (*karma-kāṇḍa*), which will gradually purify us from material desires. Those who want their material desires fulfilled should please the demigods with offerings of sacrifice, of whom Lord Viṣṇu is the chief recipient. Lord Viṣṇu is present in such acts of sacrifice. Therefore, Lord Kṛṣṇa encourages to follow the cycle of sacrifice, which will free one from all sin. If we eat food offered in sacrifice, we will not incur any sin, but if we eat only for personal sense enjoyment, we eat only sin.
Theme Track 3 A devotee performs *niṣkāma-karma-yoga* to set the right example.	3.17–3.29	A self-realized person has no duty or obligations; he doesn't have a taste for material pleasures, but he works without attachment for results to set the example for others. Common men follow a great person, so he has to teach by his own practical behavior. Even great kings and Kṛṣṇa Himself engaged in prescribed duties to set the example for others. Kṛṣṇa therefore advises us to perform our work out of duty without being attached to the fruits. In this way one can attain liberation. However, we should not disturb the ignorant who are engrossed in material activities for sense gratification, nor should we induce them to stop their *karma-kāṇḍa* activities, but we should show them how a learned Kṛṣṇa conscious person acts and behaves and then gradually engage them in devotional activities for their gradual development of Kṛṣṇa consciousness.
Theme Track 4 We should do our duties as an offering to Kṛṣṇa and depend on Him. We should do our prescribed duty and not the duty of others.	3.30–3.35	Kṛṣṇa tells Arjuna to fight as an offering to Him, with full knowledge and dependence on the Lord, and without personal desires and sense of proprietorship (knowing Kṛṣṇa as the supreme proprietor of everything and that everything should be used in His service). Those who execute their duties according to Kṛṣṇa's injunctions, without envy, are not bound by fruitive actions. One should also work according to one's nature. Kṛṣṇa advises that it is better to perform one's own duty in a faulty way than doing another's duty perfectly.
Theme Track 5 We should conquer lust, the greatest enemy.	3.36–3.43	Arjuna asks Kṛṣṇa what causes a person to perform sinful acts, as if by force, because the nature of the soul is spiritual, free from sin. Kṛṣṇa explains that lust is the enemy of spiritual advancement. When the pure soul misuses its independence, one's service attitude is transformed into a desire to enjoy. In other words, love is transformed into lust. Lust can be transformed into love by desiring everything for Kṛṣṇa. In addition, we should try to control lust by following the injunctions of spiritual life, practicing sense and mind control, and cultivating knowledge of the soul.

SOLO QUESTIONS

To enhance your self-study

(Find the answers in the verse and purport references provided in brackets.)

1. Kṛṣṇa consciousness is sometimes misunderstood as inertia, or disinterest in performing activity. What is the correct understanding? (3.1)
2. Who is considered a *mithyācāraḥ*, or a pretender? (3.6)
3. Why is *karma-yoga* in Kṛṣṇa consciousness considered far superior than restraining the senses of action? (3.7)
4. Who is considered a thief? (3.12)
5. Explain the meaning of *vikarma*. (3.15)
6. Why is a fully Kṛṣṇa conscious person not obliged to follow the Vedic injunctions? Why then does he still act? (3.17)
7. What is the meaning of *ācārya* and what is an *ācārya's* responsibility? (3.21)
8. Why did Kṛṣṇa perform prescribed duties? (3.23)
9. Why doesn't a Kṛṣṇa conscious person need to follow the Vedic rituals? (3.26)
10. What are the results of following Kṛṣṇa's teachings and of disregarding His teachings? (3.31–32)
11. Explain Kṛṣṇa's response to Arjuna's fourth reason for not fighting. (3.20-24)
12. Why should one follow one's own path in prescribed duties instead of another's? (3.35)

LEARNING HARMONIES

Multiple-choice questions
to quiz your memory

(Choose the most complete answer.)

1. What is the central theme of Chapter 3?
   a. Knowledge of the Absolute.
   b. The practice of devotional service.
   c. The importance of performing one's duty.
   d. Renunciation of material life.

2. According to Lord Kṛṣṇa, which is most superior?
   a. Renunciation of action.
   b. Performing one's prescribed duties.
   c. Meditation and silence.
   d. Renunciation of wealth.

3. What is Arjuna's main concern that prompts Lord Kṛṣṇa to explain *karma-yoga*?
   a. Arjuna fears incurring sin by killing his relatives.
   b. Arjuna wants to gain more power through knowledge.
   c. Arjuna is seeking to renounce his material possessions.
   d. Arjuna desires to become a king.

4. According to Lord Kṛṣṇa, what is the greatest enemy of the soul?
   a. Greed.
   b. Lust (*kāma*).
   c. Ignorance.
   d. Anger.

5. What does Kṛṣṇa say is the origin of lust, which is the enemy of the soul?
   a. The mind.
   b. The senses.
   c. Contact with the material mode of passion.
   d. The ego.

6. Lord Kṛṣṇa describes *yajña* (sacrifice). Why does He say sacrifices should be performed?
   a. To please the demigods.
   b. For material prosperity.
   c. To maintain universal cooperation between humans, nature, and the demigods, and to satisfy the Supreme Lord.
   d. For attaining *mokṣa* (liberation).

7. What does Lord Kṛṣṇa say about the consequences of working for one's own sense gratification?
   a. It leads to success and satisfaction.
   b. It creates bondage and suffering.
   c. It leads to liberation.
   d. It destroys relationships.

8. Why is it important for leaders or great men to perform their duties?
   a. To secure their wealth and position.
   b. To set an example for others to follow.
   c. To avoid criticism from others.
   d. To accumulate good *karma*.

9. What is the role of the senses in *karma-yoga*?
   a. The senses must be completely suppressed.
   b. The senses should be controlled through detachment and discipline.
   c. The senses should be indulged to experience the material world.
   d. The senses play no role in *karma-yoga*.

10. What is the best way to control the mind and senses?
    a. Through meditation and *yoga*.
    b. By forcibly controlling desires.
    c. Through regulated activities and performing one's duties.
    d. By renouncing all worldly pleasures.

MEDLEY ACTS

A variety of fun activities to learn from

THEME TRACK 1 ACTIVITIES

ACTION ACTIVITY

JAM (Just-a-Message) Game

In the second chapter, Kṛṣṇa extols the path of intelligence, or *jñāna-yoga*, over the path of action, or *karma-yoga*. Yet, Kṛṣṇa instructs Arjuna to follow the path of *karma*, leaving Arjuna confused. He thus questions Kṛṣṇa in this chapter: If *jñāna* (intelligence) is superior to *karma* (fruitive work), why is Kṛṣṇa urging him to engage in work and fight in this war? Arjuna pleads with Kṛṣṇa, asking for guidance on just one clear path, saying, "Please tell me only one thing."

1. Kṛṣṇa clarifies that while *jñāna* is indeed superior to *karma*, he recommends the path of *karma* for Arjuna, given Arjuna's *niṣṭhā* (his spiritual position, faith, or purity of heart).

2. To reach the platform of meditating on Brahman, a person must first purify their heart of the impressions collected over lifetimes. This purification is achieved through *karma- yoga*, or the path of action, by performing one's prescribed duties. Thus, Kṛṣṇa instructs Arjuna to first follow the path of *karma*, purify his heart, and only then, in due time, pursue *jñāna-yoga*, rather than renounce prematurely.

3. Kṛṣṇa wants Arjuna to fulfill his prescribed duties as a *kṣatriya* by participating in the war.

4. *Jñāna-yoga*, or the analytical study of spirit and matter, suits those inclined toward speculation. However, the process of working in Kṛṣṇa consciousness doesn't require one to renounce everything, and at the same time doesn't bind one to the material world.

5. For one who is not purified, adopting the role of a renunciant (*sannyāsī*) creates a disturbance in society because the person is still inclined to sin. Therefore, Kṛṣṇa recommends the path of *karma-yoga* for Arjuna.

Play a fun game to remember this topic:

- The teacher acts as the judge, and each student participates individually.
- The topic for discussion is *"Arjuna says – Please tell me one thing,"* based on the points above.
- Start from one end of the class. The teacher asks the first student: "Please tell me one thing."
- If the student is able to speak without making any theoretical or grammatical mistake, without stuttering, without taking much time, and using their own words, the next participant continues.

If the participant doesn't make any mistakes they stand up. At the end all those standing up are considered the winners.

CRITICAL-THINKING ACTIVITY

Karma-Yoga Vs Karma-Sannyāsa

As we've learned from the game in the previous activity, Kṛṣṇa gave arguments supporting the superiority of *karma-yoga* over *karma-sannyāsa* (renunciation from activities) in verses 4 to 9. He argued that premature renunciation leads to disturbance in society and therefore one should act in one's own position.

Our *Bhagavad-gītā* study group is trying to understand why a disturbance is created, both personally and socially, when a person does something he is not ready for but also cannot go back upon.

The students were asked by their *Bhakti-śāstrī* mentor to come up with real-life examples and then relate them to Kṛṣṇa's teachings to Arjuna. Here is what they came up with:

Balu: Well, I understand it's like doing a *Bhakti-śāstrī* course when you don't have enough knowledge about Kṛṣṇa consciousness or when you are too young. You take it up initially because everyone else is doing it, and then when you cannot keep up, you quit. You look bad, you lose confidence, and you feel stuck.

Tara: To me it's like taking initiation when you are not ready. It sounds exciting initially, but if you haven't chanted in a regulated way before, you may eventually want to give it up because it is too much. You know you have to keep to your vows – after all, you promised your spiritual master, but you can quit if you don't have the discipline.

Madhu: Yes, I relate to that example, Tara. It's the same with taking vows to follow the regulative principles at initiation. If you are not ready, but you jump in, nah, that is not genuine at all. There's no going back once you've promised to follow, but if you aren't ready to stick it out because you lacked self-control in the first place, you're in trouble – and you can create some disturbance for those around you.

Priya: It's like a person starting a personal development plan, say for self-regulation or self-discipline . . . these things take time to become a habit. But if you are not patient, you may follow for a while and quit, thinking you got it all sorted. However, your weaknesses will come to haunt you back later, and you'll feel out of control again. It's better to understand how long it will take for something to give results before prematurely thinking you're done.

Tamal: It is like taking on a service in the temple that's greater than your capacity. You think you'll do a great job, that you'll somehow figure it out and become the big guy, but you mess it up. And that affects the service and how people think about you – they'll find it hard to trust you again, even to make you responsible for something simpler.

Divide your class in groups and discuss the above examples in your group. Then, using the above examples, come up with a list of arguments from all five students as to why it is better for Arjuna to continue fighting, following the Lord's instruction (*karma-yoga*), rather than give up his duty and become a *sannyāsī* (*karma-sannyāsa*). After understanding the arguments clearly, write Arjuna's thoughts in the speech bubble.

THEME TRACK 2 ACTIVITIES

ARTISTIC ACTIVITY

Cycle of Sacrifice

In verses 10 to 13 Kṛṣṇa explains that if we have material desires we can perform our activities according to the Vedic injunctions (*karma-kāṇḍa*), which will gradually purify us. He encourages the cycle of sacrifice, which will free us from all sin.

Verses 14 and 15 describe the cycle of sacrifice. See diagram below.

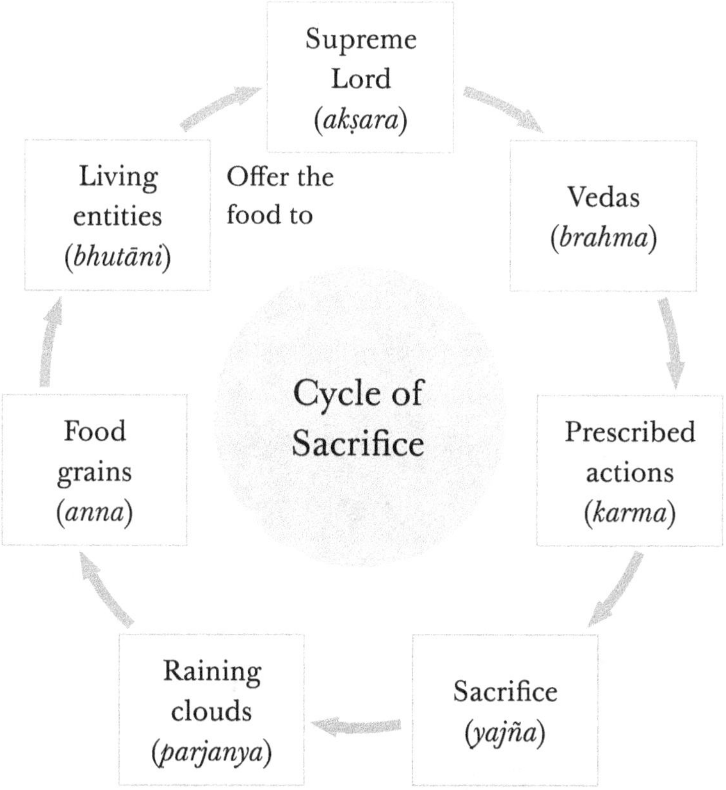

Cycle of Sacrifice

All living entities subsist on food grains, and food grains are obtained when there's rain. Rains are obtained by the performance of sacrifice (*yajña*) and prescribed action that's recommended in the *Vedas*. The *Vedas* is spiritual wisdom given by the Supreme Lord so we can connect to Him through performing *yajña* and our prescribed duties.

The cycle is complete when we offer the grains we receive, in the form of food, to the Lord. Then our food becomes sanctified. By consuming that food as *prasāda,* our existence becomes pure and our memory sanctified. Then we are able to remember Kṛṣṇa and become further purified of material desires. If we eat food offered in sacrifice, we will not incur any sin, but if we eat only for personal sense enjoyment, we incur sinful reactions.

Let us design a diorama to demonstrate the cycle of sacrifice.

Materials needed: A cardboard box; glue gun and glue; popsicle sticks; construction paper; green cardstock paper for grass cotton balls; markers; images of a working farmer, Lord Viṣṇu, a devotee, food grains, fire sacrifice, and demigods from old magazines or the internet; toy animals and persons for living entities; other items from home.

Steps:

1. Cut two adjacent rectangular faces of a cardboard box. Make sure to leave an inch from the edges so that the faces are intact (Image 1).
2. Glue a blue sheet of construction paper on one side for the sky and a piece of green paper on the other side for the grass. A brown patch from the box can be left exposed on this side to show the ground (Image 1).
3. On the blue upper side, glue cotton balls for clouds, using white paper for the raindrops and orange paper for a bright sun. Then, over the clouds, glue the pictures of the demigods. To the right, glue the pictures of Lord Viṣṇu and the devotee offering grains at the feet of the Lord (Image 2).
4. On the bottom ground part, glue the images of the farmer, grains, and *yajña* to a small popsicle stick, and then stick the popsicle sticks with images on the ground, using a hot glue gun to make them stand (Image 3).
5. Place toys or images of different living entities, trees, houses, ponds, hills, etc., of your choice.
6. Connect the components using markers to represent the cycle of sacrifice (Image 4).

Image 1

Image 2

Image 3

Image 4

Further explore the following points:

1. Are the *yajñas* meant only for humans or other living beings also, as they also subsist on food grains? Justify your answer.

2. The demigods reside in the higher planets with much opulence, so they are not nutritionally dependent on the *yajñas*. So are the ghee and other ingredients offered in the fire during *yajña* wasted? What exactly happens when a fire sacrifice is done?

3. Modern scientists describe that rains are due to evaporation, condensation, and precipitation. How do we reconcile the concept of the cycle of sacrifice with this? Are both explanations contradictory or complementary?

SCIENCE ACTIVITY

Balancing the Universal Ecosystem

Ecology is the branch of modern science that studies how living things interact with each other and their environment. Modern ecology, as you learn in your school textbooks, offers a perspective of how living beings interact with their immediate environments based on what can be perceived through the senses (*pratyakṣa*). In verses 10–16, however, Kṛṣṇa offers a more comprehensive understanding of how the universal ecology functions:

1. Demigods, His agents, are in charge of supplying different human necessities, i.e. natural resources.

2. These necessities are supplied when humans perform *yajña*, or sacrifice, and please the demigods.

3. The process of performing *yajña* is mentioned in the *Vedas*, which were created personally by the Lord.

4. Kṛṣṇa Himself is the chief benefactor of all *yajñas*, and one who performs *yajña* to please Him not just lives a life free of sin, but also becomes purified and advances spiritually.

One can achieve universal ecological harmony through practice of *yajña*, that is, by directly pleasing the Lord or by pleasing His agents, the demigods.

Performing a *yajña* is similar to conducting a scientific experiment. Just like we set up a science experiment, a *yajña* needs to be set up using proper ingredients and spatial measurements, *mantras*, and auspicious time. Just like a science textbook describes the procedure for an experiment, the Vedic scriptures describe procedures to conduct different *yajñas*. And just like a science experiment has expected results, a *yajña* also yields specific results for a performer – either some material benefit or spiritual progress.

Verses 10–16 describe how the process of *yajña* harmonizes the universal ecosystem, its results, and the consequences of not performing *yajña*.

Look at the following set of images that help us understand this. As a class, discuss the prompts that follow based on the diagram. Refer to the verses mentioned.

THE UNIVERSAL ECOSYSTEM | **THE PROCESS OF YAJÑA** | **RESULTS AND CONSEQUENCES**

Verses 10–12:

1. How can we call this an ecosystem?
2. Who heads it? Who else has special powers?
3. Why is it important to satisfy these powerful beings to keep ecological balance?

Verses 14:

1. Explain how the system of *yajña* works, using the rain as an example.
2. What spiritual principle does this remind us of?
3. What would happen if *yajña* were not performed?

Verses 11, 12, 13, 16:

1. What benefit does one get by performing *yajña*?
2. Is it fine not to perform *yajña*? Why, or why not?

What conclusion can you draw about the importance of *yajña* from this activity?

WRITING AND THEATRICAL ACTIVITY

The Goal of Yajña: Pleasing Yajña-Puruṣa

Śrīla Prabhupāda writes in his purport to verse 16: "If by performing *yajñas* one does not become Kṛṣṇa conscious, such principles are counted as only moral codes. One should not, therefore, limit his progress only to the point of moral codes, but should transcend them, to attain Kṛṣṇa consciousness."

In the Tenth Canto or in Kṛṣṇa Book, we read of the famous pastime of Kṛṣṇa lifting Govardhana Hill. It all started when the Vrajavāsīs were preparing for an elaborate *yajña* to

King Indra, the demigod in charge of the rain, so they would be assured of sufficient rainfall. Kṛṣṇa convinced His father, Nanda Mahārāja, that the worship of Govardhana Hill was more beneficial. By later manifesting as Govardhana Hill Himself, He showed His devotees that serving Him was greater and more pleasing to Him than their worship of the demigods. He was the source of rain, grains, and everything in creation that was necessary for their survival. Therefore, to worship and honor Him, the *yajña-puruṣa* (the enjoyer of all sacrifices), was higher than trying to please the demigods for getting the natural resources of life.

With a partner, write a short skit of the conversation between Kṛṣṇa and Nanda Mahārāja, in which Kṛṣṇa tries to convince him to abandon the Indra *yajña* and instead perform Govardhana-*pūjā*. Referring to Kṛṣṇa Book for this activity, come to the conclusion that worship of Kṛṣṇa and His pure devotees is the greatest form of worship and means to attain spiritual perfection. Then, with a partner enact the skit in front of your class.

You may begin as follows:

Kṛṣṇa: Bābā, what sacrifice are you getting ready for? Who will receive all these grand offerings? Please tell Me what this sacrifice is for and why you are doing it.

Nanda: O Kṛṣṇa, You're only seven years old – just a little boy. This business of demigod worship is too complicated. I don't think You'd understand.

Kṛṣṇa: Please don't keep secrets from Me, Bābā. I'm not an outsider. I'm your son. Tell Me what you and the other cowherd men are doing.

Nanda: Well, we're getting ready to do *pūjā*. We are going to make a sacrifice to Indradeva, the demigod who sends us the rain. When the sacrifice begins, You can come and sit by me to watch how it's done.

Kṛṣṇa: Father, can you tell Me more about it? Everyone is working hard to gain something, but if they understand their work and why they are working, they achieve success. So I want to know all about this *pūjā* so everything will be successful. Tell Me, is it a Vedic sacrifice or just a popular ceremony?

Nanda: All right, all right. I'm not sure You will understand everything, but there is no harm in telling You. We are not the only ones who worship Lord Indra. Because he is the lord and master of the rain-giving clouds, it is traditional to worship him to thank him for sending rainfall. Without rainfall, we cannot . . .

LANGUAGE ACTIVITY

Saṅkīrtana-Yajña: The Yajña for This Age

In his purport to verse 14, Śrīla Prabhupāda explains, "Yajña, specifically the *saṅkīrtana-yajña* prescribed for this age, must therefore be performed to save us at least from the scarcity of food supply."

Here, Śrīla Prabhupāda expresses the need to perform *yajña* in this age, but specifically *saṅkīrtana-yajña.*

harer nāma harer nāma
harer nāmaiva kevalam
kalau nāsty eva nāsty eva
nāsty eva gatir anyathā

"In this Age of Kali there is no other means, no other means, no other means for self-realization than chanting the holy name, chanting the holy name, chanting the holy name of Lord Hari." (*Bṛhan-nāradīya Purāṇa*)

Why is *saṅkīrtana-yajña* emphasized for this age more than any other type of *yajña*?

Study the similarities and differences of traditional Vedic *yajña* and *saṅkīrtana-yajña* in the table below:

	VEDIC YAJÑA	SAṄKĪRTANA-YAJÑA
1.	Lord Kṛṣṇa is the recipient of all Vedic sacrifices.	Lord Kṛṣṇa is the recipient of performing *saṅkīrtana*, hearing and chanting His holy names.

	VEDIC YAJÑA	SAṄKĪRTANA-YAJÑA
2.	Primary constituents: 1. Qualified *brāhmaṇas* needed. 2. Aim of the doer (*bhavanā*): done by *karma-kāṇḍīs* for material benefit. 3. Learning (*svādhyāya*): Performer focuses on the *karma-kāṇḍa* section of the *Vedas,* the performance of rituals for fruitive gain. 4. Rites involved (*karma*): elaborate fire sacrifices. 5. Offerings (*tyāga*): Expensive ingredients and requirements, such as ghee and an appropriate sacrificial arena. Must be pure and offered following strict rules. 6. Enjoyer of sacrifice (*devatā*): usually the demigods, with Lord Viṣṇu as the chief beneficiary. 7. Results (*phala*): material opulence and prosperity.	Primary constituents: 1. *Brāhmaṇas* not required. 2. Aim of the doer (*bhavanā*): done by devotees to please Kṛṣṇa, without expectation of any result. 3. Learning (*svādhyāya*): Performer has knowledge of the *BG* and *SB*, which emphasizes hearing and chanting the Lord's names and glories. 4. Rites involved (*karma*): Chanting the holy name. 5. Offerings (*tyāga*): Singing and dancing with *kartāla* and *mṛdaṅga*, which is easy to perform. 6. Enjoyer of sacrifice (*devatā*): Lord Kṛṣṇa. 7. Results (*phala*): devotional service to Kṛṣṇa and love of Kṛṣṇa.

1. Can you now conclude why *saṅkīrtana-yajña* is suitable for Kali-*yuga*? Explain your conclusion.

2. Why do you think that the demigods are pleased with the performance of *saṅkīrtana-yajña*? Refer to the watering-the-roots analogy from Chapter 2. Also refer to the analogy of the king and his ministers that Śrīla Prabhupāda often uses.

3. Besides the Govardhana pastime of Kṛṣṇa removing the pride of Indra and showing His supremacy to the demigods and as a result the demigods becoming pleased by His worship, can you think of any other pastime in which the demigods are pleased by the worship of Kṛṣṇa?

ACTION ACTIVITIES

Executing the Saṅkīrtana-Yajña

In essence, *saṅkīrtana* is any activity that promotes the chanting and distribution of the holy name. Therefore, distribution of books, meant to bring people to ultimately chant the holy name is also called *saṅkīrtana*. This activity will give you an experience of participating in the *saṅkīrtana-yajña* for this age.

- Form two or three groups in your class or with siblings or friends.

- Choose a location in your town or city. It could be at a market, the town's square, a residential area, or any place where you can approach the public. With the guidance of your parent or teacher, make sure that you are allowed to do this in these areas. You may also set up a stall if permitted.
- Meet the local people and talk to them about the Hare Kṛṣṇa *mahā-mantra* and the glories of the holy name. Encourage them to take Śrīla Prabhupāda's books. Also distribute *prasādam*, possibly the sweet you prepare in the next activity.
- Note your experiences and summarize them in a short report.

The Power of Prasāda

We've learned that the goal of *yajña* is to please the Supreme Personality of Godhead, and if we offer Him the grains that are supplied as a result of performing *yajña*, He is pleased and sanctifies the food we offer Him. The food then becomes *prasāda*, literally meaning "mercy." If we eat food only for sense enjoyment, we "verily eat only sin." (Verse 13)

Śrīla Prabhupāda further elaborates in his purport to verse 14: "A person in Kṛṣṇa consciousness, who eats food only offered to Kṛṣṇa, can counteract all reactions of past material infections, which are impediments to the progress of self-realization. On the other hand, one who does not do so, continues to increase the volume of sinful action, and this prepares the next body to resemble hogs and dogs, to suffer the resultant reactions of all sins."

He continues: "The material world is full of contaminations, and one who is immunized by accepting *prasādam* of the Lord (food offered to Lord Viṣṇu) is saved from the attack, whereas one who does not do so becomes subject to contamination."

Such is the power of *prasāda*. Let's try to understand and experience the significance of offering food to the Lord and distributing the *prasāda* as outlined in the activity below:

- With your classmates discuss the importance of *prasāda* as discussed in this chapter in relation to *yajña*.
- Discuss the idea of serving others and how *prasāda* distribution also forms part of *yajña*.
- Divide your class into groups and assign each group to prepare a simple vegetarian dish, like "Simply Wonderful" sweets, to be offered as *prasāda*.
- Ensure all ingredients are pure and suitable for offering; emphasize cleanliness and devotion in preparing the sweet.

- Once the sweet is prepared, set up a small altar or designated space to offer it to the Lord with the appropriate prayers and *mantras*.
- Focus on your intentions while offering, understanding that it is meant for Kṛṣṇa's pleasure.
- After the offering, distribute the *prasāda* to fellow students, teachers, or community members. Reflect on how sharing *prasāda* can help spread Kṛṣṇa's mercy and create a better community.
- Conclude with a group discussion on the experience. Discuss how you felt while preparing, offering, and distributing *prasāda*, and what you learned about the importance of selfless service and the impact of *prasāda*.

THEME TRACK 3 ACTIVITIES

LANGUAGE ACTIVITIES

Prescribed Duties

In this chapter Kṛṣṇa emphasizes that we should perform our prescribed duties and not the duties of another. We learn that *yajña* is born from prescribed duties. This means that we can use our prescribed duties as an offering of sacrifice to the Lord.

First let's understand what our prescribed duties are and why it's important to follow them.

Which of the following can be categorized as prescribed duties (PD) or not prescribed duties (NPD)

	ACTIVITY	PD/NPD
1.	Arjuna wanted to leave the battlefield because he was not in favor of killing unnecessarily.	
2.	Kṛṣṇa performed His daily morning rituals without fail.	
3.	A doctor performs the duties of an engineer.	
4.	The hunter Ekalavya wanted to learn the skills of a *kṣatriya.*	
5.	Dronācārya became the *guru* of Dṛṣṭadyumna, who was the son of Drupada, his enemy.	
6.	A cook cooks in the kitchen despite the hot or cold seasons.	

From your daily activities, list those which you can categorize as prescribed duties.

Then think of how you can do them with the consciousness to please Kṛṣṇa.

Dialogue: Misunderstanding Inactivity

The statement in verse 3.17, *tasya kāryaṁ na vidyate*, "for him there is no duty," can be misinterpreted and misused. Read the following dialogue between Bhakta Neil and Brahmacari Vidura Dasa and answer the questions that follow to get the proper understanding:

BG Class Speaker: . . . for him there is no duty.

Bhakta Neil: Wow! What a great class. I know what I'm going to do . . .

Vidura Dāsa: Me too!

Bhakta Neil: Quit university . . . be a sloth.

Vidura Dāsa (at the same time)**:** Do more service.

Wait. Have we been listening to the same class?

Bhakta Neil: Why? Did I miss something? The *Bhagavad-gītā* states that as devotees we have no duty to perform.

Vidura Dāsa: Not exactly . . .

Bhakta Neil: Well, from what I understood I don't have to fulfill my prescribed duties. So no more school for me. I'll just sit under a tree and chant.

Vidura Dāsa: Not exactly . . .

Bhakta Neil: But the verse says I have no purpose in fulfilling prescribed duties or any reason to perform work.

Vidura Dāsa: Not exactly.

Bhakta Neil: Then what exactly did I miss?

Questions:

1. Answer Neil's question. What did he miss in the class?
2. How is Neil misusing the statement "for him there is no duty" in verse 17?
3. Is Kṛṣṇa consciousness inactivity? Explain with examples from this chapter.
4. How will following prescribed duties help Neil in his spiritual life?
5. What do you want to pursue after school? How can you use the knowledge you acquire from work/studies in your services?

The Ācarya Principle

Common men do whatever a great man does. The world follows his exemplary actions. This is the reason I execute My duties perfectly according to the scriptures. I don't have anything to do with this world; I have no prescribed duties, neither am I in want of anything. My objective of coming to this material world is to reciprocate with the love of My devotees and to establish religious principles. But I perform prescribed duties to set the example of an *ācārya*, a perfect teacher who leads by example. Otherwise, without a proper example, people will deviate from their duties. Imagine what chaos there would be in society!

As a householder, I set the example of how to sanctify householder life. Once, when Nārada Muni visited Dvārakā, he was astonished to see Me simultaneously present in the palaces of My 16,108 queens and engaged in My duties. In one place I was doing welfare work for the citizens, establishing wells for drinking water, building houses and gardens for guests, and temples and monasteries for saintly persons. As a *kṣatriya* king I was practicing fighting with a sword and shield. In one palace, I was meditating; in another place I was giving charity to the elders; somewhere else I was making peace with enemies; and in other palaces I was arranging for the marriages of My sons and daughters.

Nārada was grateful that I had revealed My internal potency to him. I expressed to him, "My dear Nārada, O sage among the demigods, you know that I am the supreme instructor and perfect follower of all religious principles, as well as the supreme enforcer of such principles. I am therefore personally executing such religious principles in order to teach the whole world how to act. My dear son, it is My desire that you not be bewildered by such demonstrations of My internal energy."

(Based on *Kṛṣṇa, the Supreme Personality of Godhead*, Chapter 69, The Great Sage Nārada Visits the Different Homes of Lord Kṛṣṇa)

In a short paragraph, describe how you intend to follow the *ācārya* principle as outlined by Lord Kṛṣṇa above. In other words, how do you intend to follow His example of performing your prescribed duties as best as you can? Also include ideal examples, besides Kṛṣṇa, who inspire you.

INTROSPECTIVE ACTIVITY

An Exemplary Leader

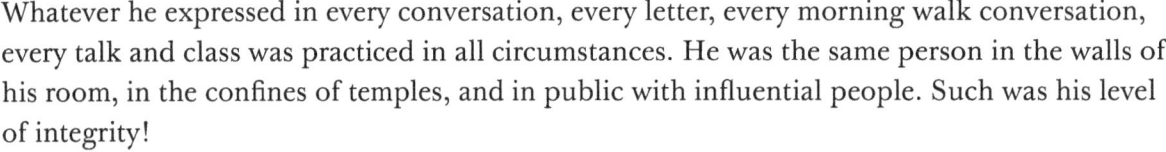

We see all kinds of leaders around us: those who lead the nation, those who lead institutions and organizations, or departments within an organization. Others may be teachers or parents. You may be a leader to your younger siblings or your friends. Whatever the situation, *Bhagavad-gītā* teaches us to be exemplary leaders.

It is easier to learn from the behavior and character of an exemplary leader. Śrīla Prabhupāda was an extraordinary leader, an *ācārya*, not only because he brought the teachings of Lord Caitanya to thousands of people all over the world, but also because of his exemplary integrity in character. He was never duplicitous. He exhibited ideal character and dealings in his personal and public life. Whatever he expressed in every conversation, every letter, every morning walk conversation, every talk and class was practiced in all circumstances. He was the same person in the walls of his room, in the confines of temples, and in public with influential people. Such was his level of integrity!

Although we may not be of such a high standard, we are all leaders within our circle of influence. This means that we can influence others by our actions and behavior.

Keeping in mind Śrīla Prabhupāda as an exemplary leader, look inward to understand how deep you have cultivated this quality of integrity as a leader.

Track your actions and behavior in a journal for a week so you can understand in which areas to improve:

1. Observe yourself during the day. Note down when you find yourself promising more than you can deliver, when you pretend to be someone else, and when you are being just a "people pleaser."

2. Be kind to yourself when you catch yourself being more dishonest and duplicitous than you thought. We may not be at the level of Śrīla Prabhupāda, but being aware of and acknowledging our shortcomings is part of developing integrity as a leader.

3. Bring your journal to class the following week and discuss your realizations with your teacher or class.

Although leaders are mindful of their own behavior and strict with themselves, they are not quick to judge others. They don't criticize and correct others just because they are leaders.

So, every time you need to correct anyone, please ask yourself these four questions:

1. Do I have the right information?
2. Am I the right person to correct him/her?
3. Is my approach to correct him/her proper?
4. Is this the right time to make the correction?

Only if you can answer "yes" to all the above questions, may you go ahead and correct someone, praying intently to Lord Kṛṣṇa to protect you from committing offenses.

After a few weeks of trying to be a good leader in any situation, discuss your experiences with your classmates. See if anyone benefited from your leadership and in what other ways you could improve.

ACTION ACTIVITY

Interview: Preaching Skills

Verses 26 and 29 discuss the followers of *karma-kāṇḍa* principles. The *karma-kāṇḍa* path involves Vedic sacrifices, which result in elevated birth or life in the heavenly planets. Draw up a questionnaire and interview a few senior devotees (maximum five) to discover how to preach to *karma-kāṇḍa* followers.

Begin your interview by sharing with the respondents what you already understand about preaching to *karma-kāṇḍīs* as explained in Chapter 3:

Lord Kṛṣṇa advises us not to approach or disturb those ignorant of Kṛṣṇa consciousness and who engage in fruitive work, because by their fruitive activities they are gradually elevated to Kṛṣṇa consciousness. However, as the devotee is kind, he can show *karma-kāṇḍīs* how to use the results of fruitive work in Kṛṣṇa's service and engage them directly in devotional service.

In your interview, please ensure the following points are covered:

- Ways in which the senior devotees themselves practically applied their knowledge of *karma-kāṇḍa* in preaching to *karma-kāṇḍa* followers.
- Examples of when they failed in their preaching attempts to *karma-kāṇḍa* followers. What did they learn?
- Examples of when they were successful. What did they learn?

You can choose to conduct the interview in person, telephonically, or online. Afterwards, present and discuss your findings in the classroom.

THEME TRACK 4 ACTIVITIES

LANGUAGE ACTIVITY

Varṇāśrama-Dharma and Kṛṣṇa Consciousness

This chapter summarizes the necessity and goal of *varṇāśrama-dharma* and the transcendental position of Kṛṣṇa consciousness.

Study the tables below. Table 1 presents the importance of *varṇāśrama-dharma*, table 2 addresses the *parā-dharma* (highest *dharma*) of Kṛṣṇa consciousness, and table 3 reflects the assimilation of the two. Fill in the tables with your personal understanding of the subject. Also reflect on the corresponding verses from Chapters 2 and 3.

Table 1: *Varṇāśrama-dharma*

WHY FOLLOW VARṆĀŚRAMA-DHARMA?
List the four *varṇas* and *āśramas* and the duties of each.
One needs to perform one's *sva-dharma*, specific duties, according to religious principles to achieve liberation. *Varṇāśrama-dharma* is therefore a gradual purificatory process and "man's stepping stone for spiritual understanding." (*BG* 2.31)
If you neglect your duties, you will incur sins. (*BG* 2.33)
"By working without attachment one attains the Supreme." (*BG* 3.19)
Conclusion:

"Human civilization begins from the stage of *varṇāśrama-dharma,* or specific duties in terms of the specific modes of nature of the body obtained."
BG 2.31, purport

"Without being fully in Kṛṣṇa consciousness, one should not give up his occupational duties. No one should suddenly give up his prescribed duties and become a so-called *yogī* or transcendentalist artificially."
BG 3.33, purport

Table 2: Kṛṣṇa Consciousness (*parā-dharma*)

HOW IS KṚṢṆA CONSCIOUSNESS TRANSCENDENTAL TO VARṆĀŚRAMA-DHARMA?
Note the natural function of the soul (*BG* 3.5) and how all actions are meant for the purpose of pleasing Kṛṣṇa (*BG* 3.26).
Reflect on the fact that Kṛṣṇa consciousness is not restricted to any *varṇa* or *āśrama*. It transcends material duties and is centered on selfless devotion.
Anyone from any *varṇa* or *āśrama* can practice Kṛṣṇa consciousness under the guidance of a bona fide *guru* or in association of devotees.
One should be sincere and not pretend to be advanced or renounced to advance in Kṛṣṇa consciousness.
Conclusion:

"A person who is fully Kṛṣṇa conscious, and is *fully* satisfied by his acts in Kṛṣṇa consciousness, no longer has any duty to perform."
BG 3.17, purport

Table 3: Assimilation of *varṇāśrama-dharma* and Kṛṣṇa Consciousness

UNDERSTANDING AND PRACTICAL APPLICATION
Sva-dharma on the material plane and spiritual plane are both ordained by Kṛṣṇa. When the prescribed duties are performed for the pleasure of Kṛṣṇa, they are no longer material duties.
"O best among the twice-born, it is therefore concluded that the highest perfection one can achieve by discharging the duties prescribed for one's own occupation according to caste divisions and orders of life is to please the Personality of Godhead." (*SB* 1.2.13)
Conclusion:

"Materially, prescribed duties are duties enjoined according to one's psychophysical condition, under the spell of the modes of material nature. Spiritual duties are as ordered by the spiritual master for the transcendental service of Kṛṣṇa."
BG 3.35, purport

After filling out the tables individually, discuss your answers in pairs or small groups. Share your thoughts on how *varṇāśrama-dharma* can be harmonized with Kṛṣṇa consciousness and how one's duties can be transformed into devotional acts. Use examples from your community to illustrate this.

Other resources for your reference:

- Bhīṣmadeva's explanation of *sva-dharma* in *SB* 1.9.26–28.
- Lord Kṛṣṇa's description of the four *varṇas* and worship of the Lord with one's occupational work in *BG* 18.41–46.

THEME TRACK 5 ACTIVITIES

INTROSPECTIVE ACTIVITIES

Transforming Lust into Love

In verses 36 to 43, Kṛṣṇa discusses the nature of lust and its role in our lives. In this activity we will draw general principles from Kṛṣṇa's analysis of lust in verses 36 to 43 and discuss the application of these principles in our own practice of Kṛṣṇa consciousness.

First study the general principles drawn from these verses, along with their applications in our daily life:

Resource 1: General Principles

1. **Nature of Desire**: Kṛṣṇa explains that lust (*kāma*) is a powerful force that drives human actions and can lead to bondage if left unchecked. When the soul comes in contact with the material creation, its eternal love for Kṛṣṇa is transformed into lust. Lust arises from the material mind and senses and is born from the mode of passion. The senses, mind, and intelligence are the sitting places of lust. Lust is the opposite of love: the propensity for sense enjoyment is the opposite of a service attitude.
2. **Controlling the Senses**: Kṛṣṇa emphasizes the need to control the senses and mind to prevent lust from leading one astray. This requires self-discipline, awareness of one's desires, and using spiritual knowledge and intelligence.
3. **Higher Knowledge**: Understanding the temporary nature of material pleasures can help us transcend lust. Knowledge of the self (*ātma*) and the Supreme (Kṛṣṇa) helps in recognizing the futility of pursuing material desires.
4. **Engagement in Devotional Service**: Directing one's energy towards service to Kṛṣṇa purifies the heart and helps diminish lust. Engaging in *bhakti* helps transform *kāma* into pure devotion.
5. **Awareness of the Impact of Lust**: Kṛṣṇa explains that lust is the all-devouring sinful enemy of this world. Lust leads to anger, confusion, and ultimately, the destruction of one's intelligence and spiritual progress. Lust cannot be satisfied and burns like fire.

Resource 2: Application in Kṛṣṇa Consciousness Practice

1. **Self-Reflection**: Regularly assess your desires and motivations. Reflect on how material desires may influence your actions and decision-making. This self-awareness can help you identify areas needing improvement.
2. **Sādhana (Practice)**: Commit to a consistent *sādhana* that includes chanting, reading scriptures, and engaging in devotional activities. This practice helps in focusing the mind and reducing distractions caused by lustful desires.
3. **Mind Control**: Develop techniques to control the mind, but more importantly, engage the mind in focusing on the chanting of the holy names. Recognize when lustful thoughts arise and then engage in spiritual practices.
4. **Service to Others**: Engage in acts of devotional service within your community. Giving Kṛṣṇa consciousness shifts the focus from personal desires to others' well-being, promoting humility and devotion.
5. **Knowledge**: Study the scriptures to gain a deeper understanding of Kṛṣṇa's teachings. This knowledge equips you to differentiate between temporary pleasures and lasting spiritual fulfillment.
6. **Prayers for Purification**: Regularly pray for the strength to overcome lust and for purification of the heart. A sincere prayer can invoke Kṛṣṇa's mercy and help in purifying material desires.

Now do the following activity, which will help you apply these principles in your life and make them habits.

Materials needed: Pen, paper, 3 jars/containers

Steps:

1. Study verses 36 to 43 and note the important principles. Refer to Resource 1.
2. Copy or type the principles on a piece of paper and place it in Jar 1.
3. Every morning read the principles and resolve to act consciously and not give in to lust or anger.
4. During the day recall your vow as much as possible.
5. Before going to bed, reflect on your day. Recollect the times when you were able to remember your relationship with Kṛṣṇa and act with responsibility and affection. Write your reflection and add it to Jar 2.

6. Recollect the moments, if any, when you were carried away by urges of desire to enjoy or acted out of anger. What prompted the action: fear of losing happiness, loss of control, or inconvenience/distress?
7. What would have been the outcome if you had practically applied some of the principles from Resource 2? Note it on a paper and add to Jar 3.
8. Continue this practice for at least two weeks. This will facilitate a new habit of conscious and regulated action and help you conquer lust.

Comic Strip: Transforming Distractions into Devotion

Read the following comic strip featuring Madhu and Priya from our *Bhagavad-gita* study group. Then reflect on your daily distractions and how you can transform them into acts of devotion.

ANALOGY ANTHOLOGY

A collection of analogies
for easier understanding

Analogy 1: Cure for the Material Epidemic

When there is an epidemic disease, an antiseptic vaccine protects a person from the attack of such an epidemic. Similarly, food offered to Lord Viṣṇu and then taken by us makes us sufficiently resistant to material affection, and one who is accustomed to this practice is called a devotee of the Lord.
– *BG* 3.14, purport

Just like a vaccine protects you from getting sick during an epidemic, eating food that's first offered to Lord Viṣṇu protects your mind and heart from being overly attached to material things.

Analogy 2: The Supreme Wealthy Person

The cashier may count millions of dollars for his employer, but he does not claim a cent for himself.

Similarly, one has to realize that nothing in the world belongs to any individual person, but that everything belongs to the Supreme Lord.
– *BG* 3.30, purport

Just as the cashier handles money that isn't his, we may manage or possess things in this world, but they truly belong to the Supreme Lord.

Analogy 3: Avoiding Accidents

One has to follow those rules and regulations, unattached to them, because practice of sense gratification under regulations may also lead one to go astray – as much as there is always the chance of an accident, even on the royal roads.
– *BG* 3.34, purport

Even if you follow rules, there's still a chance to make mistakes – just like accidents can happen even on the safest, well-built roads.

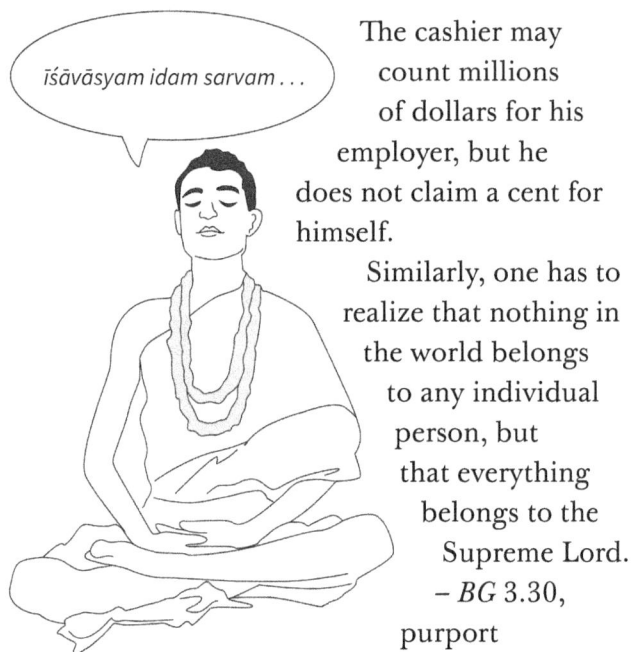

Analogy 4: Unsatisfied Lust

It is said in the *Manu-smṛti* that lust cannot be satisfied by any amount of sense enjoyment, just as fire is never extinguished by a constant supply of fuel.
– *BG* 3.39, purport

No matter how much you try to satisfy lust through enjoyment, it will only grow more, just like adding fuel makes a fire burn bigger, not go out.

SACRED RHYTHMS

Important verses
to memorize

***BG* 3.21**

yad yad ācarati śreṣṭhas
tat tad evetaro janaḥ
sa yat pramāṇaṁ kurute
lokas tad anuvartate

Whatever action a great man performs, common men follow. And whatever standards he sets by exemplary acts, all the world pursues.

***BG* 3.27**

prakṛteḥ kriyamāṇāni
guṇaiḥ karmāṇi sarvaśaḥ
ahaṅkāra-vimūḍhātmā
kartāham iti manyate

The spirit soul bewildered by the influence of false ego thinks himself the doer of activities that are in actuality carried out by the three modes of material nature.

ANSWERS

Learning Harmonies

1. c; 2. b; 3. a; 4. d; 5. c; 6. c; 7. d; 8. b; 9. a; 10. c

Karma-yoga Vs Karma-sannyāsa

List of arguments from the five students' realizations: premature *karma-sannyāsa* can cause more harm than good because a person may think he is ready and take to renunciation immaturely; he may take it up out of a situational need than actual qualification/preparedness; he may feel stuck later and not have a way out; he may develop desires for enjoyment that cannot be fulfilled in that situation; he may lose confidence in his own ability to practice spiritual life; he may break vows that lead to sinful reactions; he may cause social disturbance because people may lose faith seeing his failure; he may lead a pretentious dual life – externally perfect, internally imperfect, etc. It is therefore better for a person to stick to his own duty and capacity when it comes to practicing spiritual life – by performing his duty according to his nature and capacity, he can gradually get purified and eventually take *sannyāsa*.

Arjuna's thoughts (*sample answer*): Kṛṣṇa clarified that *niṣkāma-karma yoga*, or performing my prescribed duty without expectation of result, is better than not working. It is my natural inclination to fight, and I can satisfy Kṛṣṇa by doing that – satisfying Kṛṣṇa, after all, is the highest goal. If I take *sannyāsa*, I won't be able to please Kṛṣṇa like this. I'd still want to fight, for its my nature, so I'd be pretending to myself and everyone else that I am renounced when I'm not – that would not just be pretentious, but also cheating. I'd rather not do that.

The Cycle of Sacrifice

1. Only humans are meant to perform *yajña* as they have the bodies and higher intelligence to do so.
2. *Agni,* or fire, is the means by which the offerings – ghee, grains, etc. – go to all the demigods, the ultimate recipient being Lord Viṣṇu, the *yajña-pati.* The demigods in turn provide all the necessities for the living beings by the sanction of Lord Viṣṇu.
3. They are not opposing; both work together.

Balancing the Universal Ecosystem

Image 1: 1. The verses describe interactions of living beings with each other and the environment, which fits the definition of an ecosystem; 2. Kṛṣṇa heads it; the demigods have specific powers and they are subordinate to the Lord; 3. The demigods, in charge of natural resources, such as light, rain, etc., can supply them in adequate quantity to maintain prosperity on earth. We cannot manufacture these resources, so we have to depend on these higher powers for them. Therefore, the demigods should be properly respected so they continue providing these resources.

Image 2: 1. When the Lord or His deputy Indra is properly honored with a share of sacrifice, he is pleased and sends rain. Rain nourishes plants, which in turn sustain all life; 2. It reminds us that we are dependent on the mercy of the Lord and cannot manufacture the necessities of life on our own; 3. Without rain, environmental balance would be affected, and this would affect normal life.

Image 3: 1. One's necessities/material needs are supplied, and one makes spiritual progress; 2. By not performing *yajña*, one does not acknowledge the ownership of the Lord over everything, and one "steals" the Lord's property without being grateful. One also incurs sin. Conclusion: learner's own conclusions based on above.

Saṅkīrtana-yajña

1. *Saṅkīrtana-yajña* is easier and more practical to perform in this age because there are no hard and fast rules for chanting the holy names, there are no external requirements or ingredients, and one can chant at any time and in any situation.
2. Just as when one waters the root of a tree and the branches and leaves become nourished, by worshiping Kṛṣṇa, the root of existence, the demigods (who are his parts and His devotees) naturally become satisfied. Śrīla Prabhupāda compares the demigods to ministers in the cabinet of a king, and Lord Kṛṣṇa to the king. The ministers are servants of the king and are obliged to do their jobs as directed by the king. So, if we

satisfy the king (Kṛṣṇa), we need not satisfy the ministers (the demigods) separately.

3. In many of Kṛṣṇa's pastimes, when Kṛṣṇa defeats any of the demons and becomes recognized as an extraordinary person, the demigods shower flowers from the heavens, showing their pleasure. Another example: "Out of great affection for the cows of Vraja, Kṛṣṇa became the lifter of Govardhana Hill. At the end of the day, having rounded up all His own cows, He plays a song on His flute, while exalted demigods standing along the path worship His lotus feet and the cowherd boys accompanying Him chant His glories." (*SB* 10.35.22)

Prescribed Duties
1. NPD; 2. PD; 3. NPD; 4. PD; 5. PD; 6. PD

Misunderstanding Inactivity

1. *BG* 3.17 states that a person who is fully Kṛṣṇa conscious and is fully satisfied by his acts in Kṛṣṇa consciousness no longer has any duty to perform. This verse only applies to one who is fully self-realized.
2. Bhakta Neil wants to abandon his prescribed duties by dropping out of university.
3. No. Whatever a Kṛṣṇa conscious person does is enough to fulfill his duties. He does his work but stays detached from the results, acting only for Kṛṣṇa. Kings like Janaka were self-realized, so they had no personal obligation to follow the Vedic duties. Still, they carried them out to set a good example for everyone else.
4. To take care of his body, stay disciplined, purify his heart, and set a good example, Neil needs to follow his duties. Everyone has a natural tendency to seek sense pleasures, and these can cloud the heart. Doing prescribed duties helps purify the heart and frees a person from material attachments.

Varṇāśrama-dharma and Kṛṣṇa Consciousness
(*Potential Answers*)
Table 1 Conclusion: *Varṇāśrama-dharma* is a system that helps people know what their duties are based on their natural qualities and stage of life they are in. By doing these duties, a person can grow spiritually and become closer to God.

Table 2 Conclusion: Kṛṣṇa consciousness is transcendental and can be practiced by anyone, regardless of their *varṇa* or *āśrama*, as long as they sincerely follow the path of *bhakti*.

Table 3 Conclusion: The highest goal of both *varṇāśrama-dharma* and Kṛṣṇa consciousness is to please Kṛṣṇa, with no difference between material and spiritual duties when performed in devotion.

CHAPTER 4

Transcendental Knowledge

CHAPTER BEATS

An overview

Kṛṣṇa had just explained to Arjuna that one should steady the mind, and overcome lust, by one's spiritual intelligence and strength. Now He wanted to give Arjuna divine knowledge that would strengthen his intelligence and help him overcome his unsteady mind.

Kṛṣṇa again observed Arjuna's perturbed eyes scanning the battlefield. The air was thick with tension as the warriors on both sides were preparing to fight, but Arjuna still stood frozen on his chariot.

"Listen, My dear Arjuna," Kṛṣṇa began, "I revealed this everlasting science of *yoga* to the sun-god, Vivasvān, eons ago. He, in turn passed it down to Manu, and Manu then imparted this knowledge to Ikṣvāku. Like this, it was passed down through generations of kings, but over time, it was lost. Now, I'm imparting this wisdom to you because you are My devotee and friend."

Arjuna was surprised. He asked, "How could

You have taught this science to Vivasvān long ago? He is much older than You."

Kṛṣṇa smiled and responded, "Both you and I have had many births, Arjuna. I remember all of them, but you do not. I am unborn and My divine body never deteriorates; I am the Lord of all living beings, yet I still appear in every millennium in My original spiritual form. Whenever righteousness declines and unrighteousness rises, I come to this world to protect the virtuous, annihilate the wicked, and re-establish the principles of *dharma*. One who understands the transcendental nature of My appearance and activities in this world is not born again but reaches My eternal abode."

Arjuna's eyes lit up. He couldn't believe that he was standing in front of the Supreme Lord, who was also his relative and best friend. He bowed his head in reverence.

Kṛṣṇa continued, "Many, many persons in the past who took shelter of Me became purified by knowledge of Me – and they thus grew to love Me. In the manner and mood a person surrenders unto Me I reward them accordingly. All paths that lead to Me directly or indirectly are My paths, because all paths realize different aspects of Me. Men worship the demigods for some material gain and they quickly get fruitive results, but these material gifts are temporary.

"I am the creator of all paths, O Arjuna, and I have created the four *varṇas* (social classes) for people with material desires. Even though I create this system and act within it, I am beyond it. No work contaminates Me, and I do not aspire for the fruits of My activities. Anyone who understands this about Me will not be bound in the reactions of work."

Arjuna smiled. Here was Kṛṣṇa acting as a *kṣatriya,* yet He was not affected by the activities of the material world.

"My dear friend," Kṛṣṇa continued, "You should act in the footsteps of those who've understood My divine nature."

"And how did they act?" asked Arjuna, curious.

"Well, first you have to understand what action is. Even the intelligent are confused by what is action and what is inaction. Action, or *karma*, is acting for some material result. You do your duty only to get some reward. But you should act without being attached to the results, dear Arjuna. Work for Me. This is called inaction, or *akarma*. Such activities do not give good or bad reactions, so you don't enjoy or suffer any of the effects of work. In this way, you are performing inaction although performing action."

Kṛṣṇa explained that such *karma-yogīs* are in full knowledge. The fire of knowledge burns up all their reactions of work. Not caring for the results of their activities, they are ever satisfied. They do their duties to the best of their ability and

leave everything to the Lord. Although engaged in activities, they perform no fruitive action (*karma*). In the perfected stage they are free from material desires, free from false ownership, and work only for the bare necessities of life. As a result, they are not affected by sinful reactions. Such Kṛṣṇa conscious persons are non-envious, steady in both success and failure, tolerant to dualities, and act with full knowledge for the sake of Yajña, Kṛṣṇa, who is the recipient of all sacrifice. So every activity is offered as an act of sacrifice to the Lord.

"There are all kinds of sacrifice," Kṛṣṇa continued to explain. "Demigod worship performed by *karma-yogīs*; Brahman worship by *jñāna-yogīs*; mind control by *brahmacārīs*; restricted sense enjoyment by *gṛhasthas*; self-control by followers of the Patañjali *yoga* system; charity, the sacrifice of one's possessions; austerity; mysticism; scriptural study; and *prāṇāyāma*, controlling the breathing process.

"O best of the Kurus, without sacrifice one can never be happy in this life or the next. All sinful reactions are destroyed by performing such sacrifices, and as such, the eternal spiritual realm (Brahman atmosphere) is attained. Thus, many types of sacrifice are prescribed in the *Vedas*. These sacrifices are through the body, mind, and words of different performers. If you know and practice them, you will be liberated."

Kṛṣṇa smiled and then explained that the sacrifice performed in transcendental knowledge was higher than giving in charity or any other sacrifice. Real knowledge culminates in Kṛṣṇa consciousness. And how to obtain such knowledge? Kṛṣṇa gave the answer:

"Learn the truth by approaching a spiritual master. Inquire from him submissively and serve him. Because these self-realized souls have seen the truth, they can give you this knowledge. When you obtain such knowledge, you will never be in illusion again, because you will see that all living

beings are but a part of Me; in other words, they are Mine.

"Even if you are the greatest sinner, if you are on the boat of transcendental knowledge, you can easily cross over the ocean of miseries. O Arjuna, the fire of knowledge burns to ashes all reactions to material activities, just as a blazing fire turns wood to ashes.

"In this world, there is nothing more sublime and pure as transcendental knowledge. One who subdues the senses can achieve such knowledge and then quickly acquires supreme spiritual peace. However, ignorant people who doubt the scriptures, do not become God conscious; rather, they fall down. They are never happy in this world or the next.

"O Dhanañjaya, conqueror of riches, those who perform devotional service give up the fruit of their actions. Their doubts are dispelled by transcendental knowledge, and thus they are situated in the self. Consequently, they are not bound by the reactions of work."

Kṛṣṇa stared into Arjuna's eyes and said firmly, "Therefore, the doubts that have arisen in your heart should be slashed by the weapon of knowledge. O Bharata, armed with *yoga*, stand and fight!"

Kṛṣṇa's words began to settle in Arjuna's mind. He looked at his bow, the Gāṇḍīva, resting at his side, and the battlefield that stretched out before him. The transcendental knowledge he was receiving from Kṛṣṇa began to remove the fog from his mind. He was beginning to understand his real duty.

THEME TRACKS

Themes and key messages
to contemplate and discuss

THEME TRACKS	REFERENCES	KEY MESSAGES
Theme Track 1 Transcendental knowledge is received in *paramparā,* disciplic succession, starting with Kṛṣṇa Himself, whose appearance in this world is transcendental.	4.1–10	*Rājarṣis,* or saintly kings, had understood the science of spiritual knowledge from the *Bhagavad-gītā* in disciplic succession (from Kṛṣṇa to the sun-god to Manu to Ikṣvāku, etc.), but this chain had been broken. Therefore, Kṛṣṇa found it necessary to speak this knowledge again, this time to Arjuna, for the benefit of the world. Arjuna then inquired that if the sun-god was born before Kṛṣṇa, how did Kṛṣṇa speak this knowledge to him? Kṛṣṇa explained that He remembers all His previous appearances in this world, unlike Arjuna. Kṛṣṇa then revealed the divine nature of His appearance and the reasons for His descent: to deliver the pious, annihilate the miscreants, and reestablish religious principles. By understanding the nature of His appearance one can attain His eternal abode.

THEME TRACKS	REFERENCES	KEY MESSAGES
Theme Track 2 Kṛṣṇa is the creator and the culmination of all spiritual paths.	4.11–15	Kṛṣṇa reciprocates with a worshiper's mood in different spiritual paths according to their different intensities of love for Him. The paths of *bhakti* and *jñāna* give liberation whereas the path of *karma*, including worship of demigods for quick material gratification, leads to bondage. Therefore, Kṛṣṇa created the four *varṇas*, according to their qualities and work, for people with material desires. (The *jīvas* act according to their past desires; Kṛṣṇa is not responsible for their suffering.) However, although Kṛṣṇa acts as a *kṣatriya*, work doesn't affect Him. By understanding this about Kṛṣṇa, liberated souls in previous ages did their work without material desire as an offering to Him. So Kṛṣṇa advises Arjuna to similarly do his duty.
Theme Track 3 A *niṣkāma-karma-yogī* (detached worker) performs *akarma* – inaction in action.	4.16–23	The intricacy of *karma* is difficult to understand; therefore Kṛṣṇa explains *karma* (action), *akarma* (inaction), and *vikarma* (forbidden action). A detached worker (*niṣkāma-karma-yogī*) acts but does not accrue reactions to his work; therefore, his work is considered to be *akarma*, or inaction although performing *karma* (action). The fire of knowledge burns up the reactions of his work. Such a detached worker has many divine qualities.
Theme Track 4 Sacrifice (*jñāna*) done on the platform of knowledge leads to liberation, which is attained by following the instructions of a bona fide *guru*.	4.24–42	There are various types of sacrifices meant for ultimate liberation from material existence. However, sacrifice done in spiritual knowledge (*jñāna-yajña*) is superior and gives liberation. The process for acquiring such knowledge is to serve and inquire from a bona fide spiritual master in disciplic succession. Such knowledge is the purest, gives pure vision, removes illusion, and destroys all sins and reactions to material activities. A person who has faith in the scripture, is dedicated to the instructions and process given in the scripture, and who endeavors to control the senses is eligible to receive this knowledge and thus attains supreme peace.

SOLO QUESTIONS

To enhance your self-study

(Find the answers in the verse and purport references provided in brackets.)

1. How is the knowledge in the *Bhagavad-gītā apauruṣeya*, or superhuman? Why should it be accepted without mundane interpretation? (4.1)

2. Why are misinterpretations of the *Bhagavad-gītā* considered demonic? (4.2–3)

3. Why could Kṛṣṇa remember His conversation with Vivasvān, the sun-god, even though he was older than Kṛṣṇa? Describe Kṛṣṇa's spiritual nature. (4.5–6)

4. What are the six kinds of *avatāras*? (4.8)

5. List the eight stages of devotional life, from *śraddhā* to *prema*. (4.10)

6. Why don't intelligent persons worship the demigods? (4.12)

7. List the corresponding modes predominantly influencing the four divisions of human society. (4.13)

8. If the Lord is impartial, how is it that different grades of living beings suffer? How can living beings become free from the results of *karma*? (4.14)

9. Who are the twelve *mahājanas*? Why were they considered great in relation to transcendental knowledge?

10. Why is a Kṛṣṇa conscious person compared to a machine part that requires maintenance? (4.21)

11. What does matter regain when dovetailed for the cause of the Absolute Truth? (4.24)

12. Describe a devotee's attitude to longevity. (4.29)

LEARNING HARMONIES

Multiple-choice questions
to quiz your memory

(Choose the most complete answer.)

1. What is the main theme of this chapter?
   a. The importance of devotion to God.
   b. The knowledge of the self.
   c. Transcendental knowledge and the process of sacrifice.
   d. The nature of material existence.

2. Who is eligible to receive transcendental knowledge?
   a. Only those born in noble families.
   b. Only those who engage in deep meditation.
   c. A devotee who is free from envy and attachment.
   d. Anyone who practices austerities.

3. How does Kṛṣṇa describe the process of passing down transcendental knowledge?
   a. Through ritualistic sacrifices.
   b. Through the *paramparā* (disciplic succession).
   c. Through self-study and reflection.
   d. Through meditation.

4. What is the significance of *yajña* (sacrifice)?
   a. *Yajña* is a ritual done by priests and *brāhmaṇas* as a holy fire sacrifice.
   b. It is an offering made to Lord Viṣṇu to earn heavenly rewards.
   c. It is the process of purifying one's consciousness and offering everything to the Supreme.
   d. It is primarily a material transaction for wealth and prosperity.

5. What is the relationship between action and knowledge?
   a. Knowledge alone is sufficient to attain liberation; action is unnecessary.
   b. One must perform actions without attachment while maintaining knowledge of the self.
   c. Only knowledge can lead to the removal of material desires; actions have no effect.
   d. All actions should be performed with some motivation to gain success.

6. What does Kṛṣṇa say about the concept of "old knowledge" in the beginning of this chapter?
   a. The knowledge is always new and never repeated.
   b. It is timeless knowledge that was once lost but now is being imparted to Arjuna.
   c. The knowledge is ancient but is not always relevant.
   d. Old knowledge is irrelevant and must be replaced with new techniques of self-realization.

7. What are the reasons for Kṛṣṇa's divine appearance in the world?
   a. To teach the secret of eternal life and immortality.
   b. To demonstrate the power of the material world and its illusions.
   c. To protect the righteous, destroy the wicked, and reestablish the principles of *dharma*.
   d. To fulfill the desires of His devotees and grant them material success.

8. What does Kṛṣṇa reveal about the "sacrifice of knowledge" (*jñāna-yajña*)?
   a. It is the highest form of sacrifice and requires no physical offerings.
   b. It involves offering material possessions to the priests for spiritual benefit.
   c. It is a ritual that is more beneficial than physical *yajñas*.
   d. It is a process of gaining wealth and material prosperity by learning sacred *mantras*.

9. How can one attain the perfection of action?
   a. By abandoning all actions and living in complete renunciation.
   b. By acting without selfish desires and dedicating all actions to Kṛṣṇa.
   c. By performing actions only in a state of absolute mental focus.
   d. By avoiding any interaction with the world and staying in solitude.

10. How should one receive transcendental knowledge from a bona fide spiritual master?
    a. By inquiring submissively and rendering selfless service.
    b. By offering material gifts in exchange for the teachings.
    c. By showing you are learned and capable of absorbing the knowledge.
    d. By following the instructions and applying them without questioning.

MEDLEY ACTS

A variety of fun activities
to learn from

THEME TRACK 1 ACTIVITIES

ARTISTIC ACTIVITY

Foldable Frame: Guru Paramparā

In this chapter we learn about the importance of receiving knowledge in *paramparā* and hearing from and serving a bona fide spiritual master in disciplic succession.

Let's make a foldable frame of our *ācāryas* that you can gift to a friend or use on your home altar. It is ideal to fold up and travel with.

Let us design it with the prominent *ācāryas* in our *paramparā*: 1) Śrīla A. C. Bhaktivedānta Swami; 2) Śrīla Bhaktisiddhānta Sarasvatī; 3) Śrīla Gaura-kiśora dāsa Bābājī; 4) Śrīla Bhaktivinoda Ṭhākura; 5) Śrīla Jagannātha dāsa Bābājī; 6) The Six Gosvāmīs. You may also do two or four frames, starting from Śrīla Prabhupāda.

Materials needed: Cardboard box, transparent sheets (or cut plain Ziploc bags), printed pictures of the *ācāryas* (of the same size) or taken from old magazines, gold paint/foil, decorative stickers, a plain cloth, glue, tape, scissors.

Steps:

1. Cut a rectangular piece from the cardboard box. The piece should be large enough to leave at least a one-inch border on all sides of the *ācārya* picture (see Image 1).
2. Paste the picture exactly at the center of the rectangle.
3. Paint all the sides with gold paint or any color of your choice. You can also glue gold foil (see Image 1).
4. Wrap the frame with the transparent sheet and secure it at the back with tape.
5. Repeat steps 1 to 4 for the remaining frames. The frames and pictures should all be of the same size.
6. Place all the frames in the sequence mentioned above starting from left to right.
7. Turn them all over. Join them using glue tape at the back and glue the entire back portion with a plain cloth for sturdiness and a neat finish (see Image 2).
8. Decorate the borders of the frames with stickers (see Image 3).

Your foldable frame is ready.

Image 1

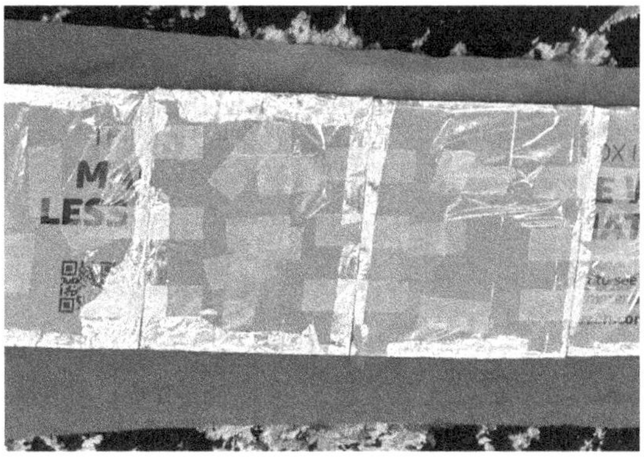

Image 2

Image 3

In class discuss a few highlights of each of these *ācāryas*' contributions and lives, from which we can draw many valuable lessons. It is our responsibility to keep their message intact, so it's not lost again as it was before.

WRITING AND LANGUAGE ACTIVITIES

Exploring Kṛṣṇa's Timeless Teachings

Instructions:

1. **Read the purports to 4.1–3** and reflect on Kṛṣṇa's explanation of how the *Bhagavad-gītā's* divine knowledge has been passed down through the disciplic succession, from Vivasvān to Arjuna. Pay attention to the role of *rājarṣis* (saintly kings) in preserving and sharing this wisdom.

2. **Write a paragraph** (5–6 sentences) based on the following:

- Summarize how Kṛṣṇa describes the history of imparting the *Bhagavad-gītā*.
- Discuss how Kṛṣṇa intervened when the chain of knowledge was broken over time.
- Explain the importance of this system in ensuring that the teachings remain pure and accessible to all.

3. **Reflect on Kṛṣṇa's love and compassion:** In 2 to 3 sentences, describe how Kṛṣṇa's love for all beings is evident in His actions. How does He continue to remind us of our spiritual identity? How can we accept His love and overcome illusion in our lives?

The Royal Legacy of the Bhagavad-Gītā

Instructions:

1. **Read 4.1–2 and Śrīla Prabhupāda's Purports:**
   Focus on the verses where Kṛṣṇa explains the transmission of the *Bhagavad-gītā* to the royal order, starting with Vivasvān (the sun-god) and then to Manu and the kings. Notice how the *rājarṣis* (saintly kings) are central to passing on this wisdom.

2. Reflect on the meaning of the statement in 4.2, *sa kālena mahatā yogaḥ naṣṭaḥ* (over time, this knowledge was lost) and its significance for ISKCON's mission, both in the present and future.

3. **Reflect and answer the following in your notebooks:**
   a. How do the royal kings and leaders in the *Bhagavad-gītā* set an example for modern leaders, including leaders of spiritual movements like ISKCON?
   b. Why do you think Śrīla Prabhupāda emphasizes spreading the *Bhagavad-gītā's* teachings to all people, starting with the leaders? How does this help spread spiritual wisdom to the masses?
   c. What does Kṛṣṇa's statement *sa kālena mahatā yogaḥ naṣṭaḥ* imply about the challenges of maintaining spiritual knowledge in the world?
   d. How does ISKCON work to keep the teachings of the *Bhagavad-gītā* alive and relevant today, despite the passage of time?
   e. In what ways can you, as a young member of ISKCON, help ensure that this knowledge continues to be passed on to future generations?

Optional:

Draw or create a short presentation (a poster, video, or digital art) that illustrates how the *Bhagavad-gītā's* knowledge has been passed down through time and how it can be kept vibrant in the future, especially by the younger generation.

INTROSPECTIVE ACTIVITY

From Familiarity to Understanding

Kṛṣṇa chose Arjuna to be the recipient of the science of the *Bhagavad-gītā* because Arjuna was a devotee and a friend, which made him capable of understanding Kṛṣṇa's transcendental appearance, activities, and relationship with him. Understanding Kṛṣṇa's birth and activities purifies one of all contamination, including material attachment, fear, and anger, and makes one eligible to enter Kṛṣṇa's abode.

In this activity you will try to experience the effects of absorbing your mind and intelligence in one of Kṛṣṇa's pastimes.

- Choose a pastime of Kṛṣṇa you feel drawn to. You may choose any other incarnation of Kṛṣṇa as well.
- For one month, immerse yourself in learning this pastime, either from *Śrīmad- Bhāgavatam* or the Kṛṣṇa book. You may also listen to lectures and study commentaries by Vaiṣṇava *ācāryas* on the pastime.
- Make notes of Kṛṣṇa's qualities, protection, love, opulence, and sweetness related to the pastime.
- Try memorizing a key verse from the chosen pastime.
- Discuss your findings with friends and family to deepen your understanding.
- After a month, review your notes and answer these questions:
    1. What is the difference between being familiar with and understanding a pastime (*vetti tattvataḥ*)?
    2. Which qualities of Kṛṣṇa charmed you?
    3. Did you feel any reciprocation from Kṛṣṇa while studying His pastimes?
    4. Did any misconceptions dissolve?
    5. Are you convinced that understanding Kṛṣṇa's transcendental position can free one from material attachment?
    6. What can we learn from Arjuna's mood in his approach to Kṛṣṇa's teachings? (Consider Arjuna's humility, openness, and willingness to surrender to Kṛṣṇa's wisdom.)

CRITICAL-THINKING ACTIVITY

The Divine Detective Agency: Mystery of Kṛṣṇa's Divine Mission

In this activity you will present arguments to establish that Kṛṣṇa's appearance is transcendental. And you will also understand the reasons for the Lord's appearance in this world. To do this, play the part of a detective in The Divine Detective Agency.

Materials needed: "Case files" prepared in advance (either printed or written on pieces of paper). Each case file contains a brief "mystery" or puzzle to solve, based on key ideas from Chapter 4; pens and paper; a board or wall space to post clues and conclusions.

Instructions:

1. **Introduction**: Divide your class into groups. The teacher will begin by explaining that Kṛṣṇa's appearance and divine mission are like a great cosmic mystery. Students are given the position of "Divine Detectives," hired by a special organization (perhaps a mystical agency dedicated to unraveling divine truths!). Your job is to uncover the mystery behind Kṛṣṇa's transcendental nature and His purpose for coming to Earth.

2. Your teacher will hand out some case files to each group. Each case file will contain:

- A brief mystery (describing a particular scenario related to Kṛṣṇa's transcendence or His mission, based on verses 4.5–9 and 4.7–8).
- A list of "clues" (quotes from the *Bhagavad-gītā*, paraphrased or direct) that will help solve the mystery.

See examples of case files in Resource 1 at the end of the chapter. You may help your teacher create more case files. (Also refer to Analogy 1 at the end of this chapter.)

3. **Group Work and Presentation**: Divide the class into groups of 3 or 4 students. Each group will work on their own "case file," using the clues provided to come to a conclusion about Kṛṣṇa's transcendental nature and the reason for His appearance on Earth. You must:

- Analyze the clues and work together to solve the mystery.
- Write down your findings and arguments, connecting them to specific verses in the *Bhagavad-gītā*.

- Give a brief presentation to the class in which you explain:
  - → How Kṛṣṇa's appearance is transcendental (based on the clues).
  - → Why Kṛṣṇa incarnates in this world, focusing on the mission He has outlined in the *Gītā*.
- After each presentation, other groups can ask one question to check understanding and dig deeper into the analysis.

Reflection:
Reflect on how understanding Kṛṣṇa's transcendental nature and His reasons for appearing in the world can influence your actions. How can your actions bring balance and righteousness (*dharma*) into your own lives by following Kṛṣṇa's teachings?

THEME TRACK 2 ACTIVITIES

THEATRICAL ACTIVITY

Role-Play: Who Follows Kṛṣṇa's Path?

In verse 11, Kṛṣṇa says that everyone follows His path in all respects. This means that devotees lovingly follow the Lord to please Him, and nondevotees also follow Him indirectly through various Vedic processes or systems. Even atheists and materialists follow His path, having no choice but to surrender to material nature and take birth after birth in ignorance in the material world. Let us try to understand this through role-play.

Divide your class into pairs. Each pair is provided one set of cards printed in Resource 2 at the end of this chapter. Separate the Kṛṣṇa cards from the character cards. One person takes on the role of Kṛṣṇa, and the other plays the character on their card.

Then fill in the table below:

TYPE OF PERSONALITY	DIRECT/INDIRECT FOLLOWER?	HOW DOES HE/SHE FOLLOW THE LORD'S PATH?
Gopī		
Impersonalist		
Mystic *yogī*		
Kṛṣṇa's parent		
Demigod worshiper		
Atheist/ Materialist		

1. Did you conclude that everyone follows Kṛṣṇa's path directly or indirectly?
2. State briefly how you can use this understanding to preach the Lord's glories to different types of people.
3. Do you think that all paths lead to Kṛṣṇa? Substantiate your answer with reference to verse 42 purport. What is the criterion to reach Kṛṣṇa in different paths?
4. Related to the different paths, what does Kṛṣṇa mean by "as all surrender unto Me, I reward them accordingly"?

CRITICAL-THINKING ACTIVITY

The Varṇa Portfolio

In verse 13, Kṛṣṇa discusses the *varṇāśrama* system, which is a Vedic social system that organizes society into four *varṇas* (social orders) and four *āśramas* (stages of life) to ensure spiritual and material well-being. The *varṇas* facilitates a society's material progress and harmony, and the *āśramas* facilitate an individual's spiritual progress.

The Varṇas

	VARṆA	DOMINANT MATERIAL MODES OF NATURE	CHARACTERISTICS
brāhmaṇas	Priests	*sattva* (goodness)	Sense and mind control, austerity, purity, religiosity
kṣatriyas	Administrators/ warriors	*sattva-rajas* (goodness-passion)	Heroism, leadership, power, resourcefulness
vaiśyas	Merchants/Farmers	*rajas-tamas* (passion-ignorance)	Businessmen, cow protectors, farmers
śūdras	Workers	*tamas* (ignorance)	Helpers to other classes

The Āśramas

	ĀŚRAMA	SPIRITUAL RESPONSIBILITY
brahmacārī	Celibate Student	Studies the scriptures and practices sense control
gṛhastha	Householder	Works and maintains a family and continues to progress with them
vānaprastha	Retired life	Studies the scriptures, shares spiritual knowledge, and goes on pilgrimage
sannyāsa	Renunciant	Travels and preaches spiritual knowledge and exclusively worships the Lord

In this verse, Kṛṣṇa mentions that we should consider a person belonging to a certain *varṇa* and *āśrama* based on *guṇa* (nature) and *karma* (work), not *janma* (birth) as commonly misunderstood.

Look at the following Varṇa Bulletin Board that appeared in your *Bhakti-śāstrī* classroom and prepared by someone with this misconception:

brāhmaṇas

Paraśurāma

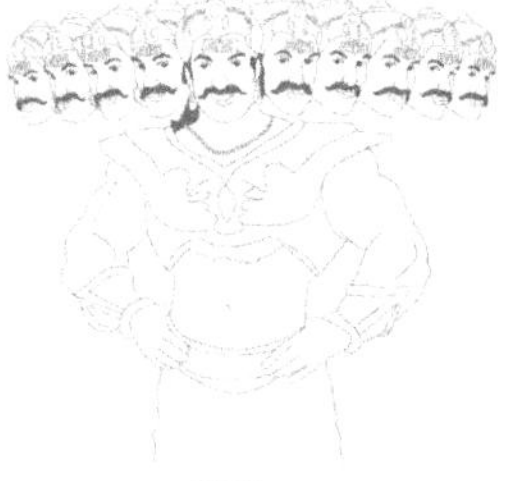

Rāvaṇa

kṣatriyas	 Viśvāmitra  Nanda Mahāraja
vaiśyas	 Raghunātha dāsa Gosvāmī  Śrīla Prabhupāda
śūdras	 Vālmīki  Karṇa  Haridāsa Ṭhākura  Vidura
Transcendental *varṇa*	

Your *Bhakti-śāstrī* teacher has asked you to reorganize the personalities in their proper *varṇas*, based on their qualities, not birth. Remember that pure devotees do not fall under any *varṇa* irrespective of their birth *varṇa*, so classify them under Transcendental Varṇa and also place them under the *varṇa* they functioned.

1. How do you think your final Varṇa Bulletin Board will look?
2. From the examples above, give reasons why birth is not a good criterion to classify people into *varṇas*, but *guṇa* and *karma* are.
3. Why did Kṛṣṇa create the four *varṇas*? Explain who is responsible for the suffering of the living entities with reference to *BG* 4.14.

THEME TRACK 3 ACTIVITIES

LANGUAGE ACTIVITIES

Comic Strip: Action or Not

Verses 19 to 24 describe how a *niṣkāma-karma-yogī* who acts in full knowledge burns up the reactions of work. Although engaged in work, he doesn't work. Let's understand more clearly what this means. Read this comic strip featuring Madhu and Priya from our *Bhagavad-gita* study group and answer the questions that follow.

Questions:

1. Why does Priya say, "I don't think that's what Kṛṣṇa meant"? Explain her statement in terms of Arjuna not wanting to act in the battle. (Refer to verse 18.)
2. How has Madhu misunderstood inaction? What does he "get" in the end?
3. How would you classify Priya's actions in the last panel in terms of *karma*, *akarma*, or *vikarma*. Explain why.
4. How would a *niṣkāma-karma-yogī* act without incurring a reaction in the same situation as Priya? Refer to Sanskrit verses and analogies from *BG* 4.19–24 to explain your answer. (Also refer to the Analogy Anthology section at the end of this chapter.)
5. How does *karma-yoga* done for Kṛṣṇa liberate us?
6. How can Priya perform *akarma*?
7. Does Priya striving for an A+ in her test mean she is attached to the result? In other words, should devotees strive to excel, or should they simply work without any ambition?

How Matter Regains its Spiritual Quality

Śrīla Prabhupāda explains in his purport to verse 24: "Matter dovetailed for the cause of the Absolute Truth regains its spiritual quality." Let's understand this better and see how this is related to Śrīla Prabhupāda's mood and mission.

Śrīla Prabhupāda explains that everything in existence is situated within the *brahmajyoti* of the Lord, but because it is covered by *māyā* or sense gratification, it is called matter. This matter can be uncovered by Kṛṣṇa consciousness, so when matter is dovetailed for Kṛṣṇa's service it regains its spiritual quality. Kṛṣṇa consciousness is the process of converting the illusory consciousness into Brahman, or the Supreme. Dovetailing material things in Kṛṣṇa's service so that they become spiritualized is called *yukta-vairāgya*.

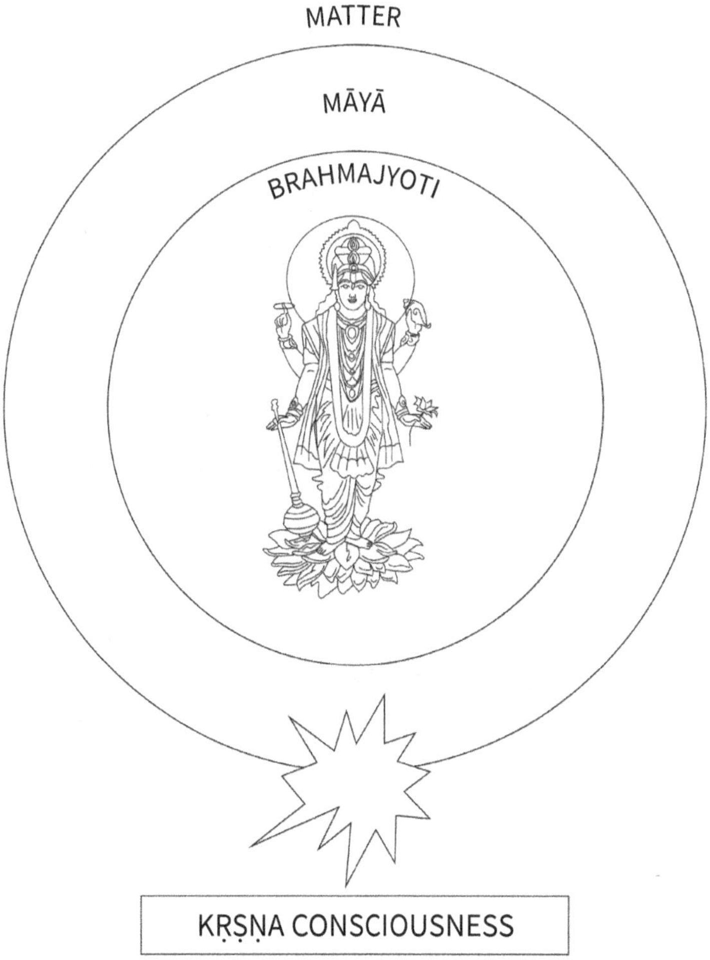

In the table below, let's see how we can use these objects/things, which are usually used for sense gratification, in Kṛṣṇa consciousness. Fill in how these things are used for sense pleasure and how they can be spiritualized by using them for Kṛṣṇa's pleasure:

	OBJECTS/THINGS	SENSE GRATIFICATION	KṚṢṆA CONSCIOUSNESS
1.	Sound system		
2.	Food		
3.	Books		
4.	Musical instruments		
5.	Airplane		
6.	House		
7.	Eyes		
8.	Ears		
9.	Legs		
10.	Cellphone		

After reading the purport to understand the following terms, choose one of the examples from the table and state what each term refers to:

For example: Food

1. Offering: Food
2. Consuming agent: Person eating
3. Process of consumption: Food being converted to *prasādam*
4. Contributor: Person offering the *bhoga*
5. Result: Spiritual upliftment

Then discuss in groups more examples of material things that Śrīla Prabhupāda used for spreading Kṛṣṇa consciousness.

THEME TRACK 4 ACTIVITIES

LANGUAGE ACTIVITIES

The Purpose of Sacrifices

Verses 30 to 33 describe the purpose of various sacrifices. Study the diagram below to analyze the purpose of all sacrifices; then discuss with your class:

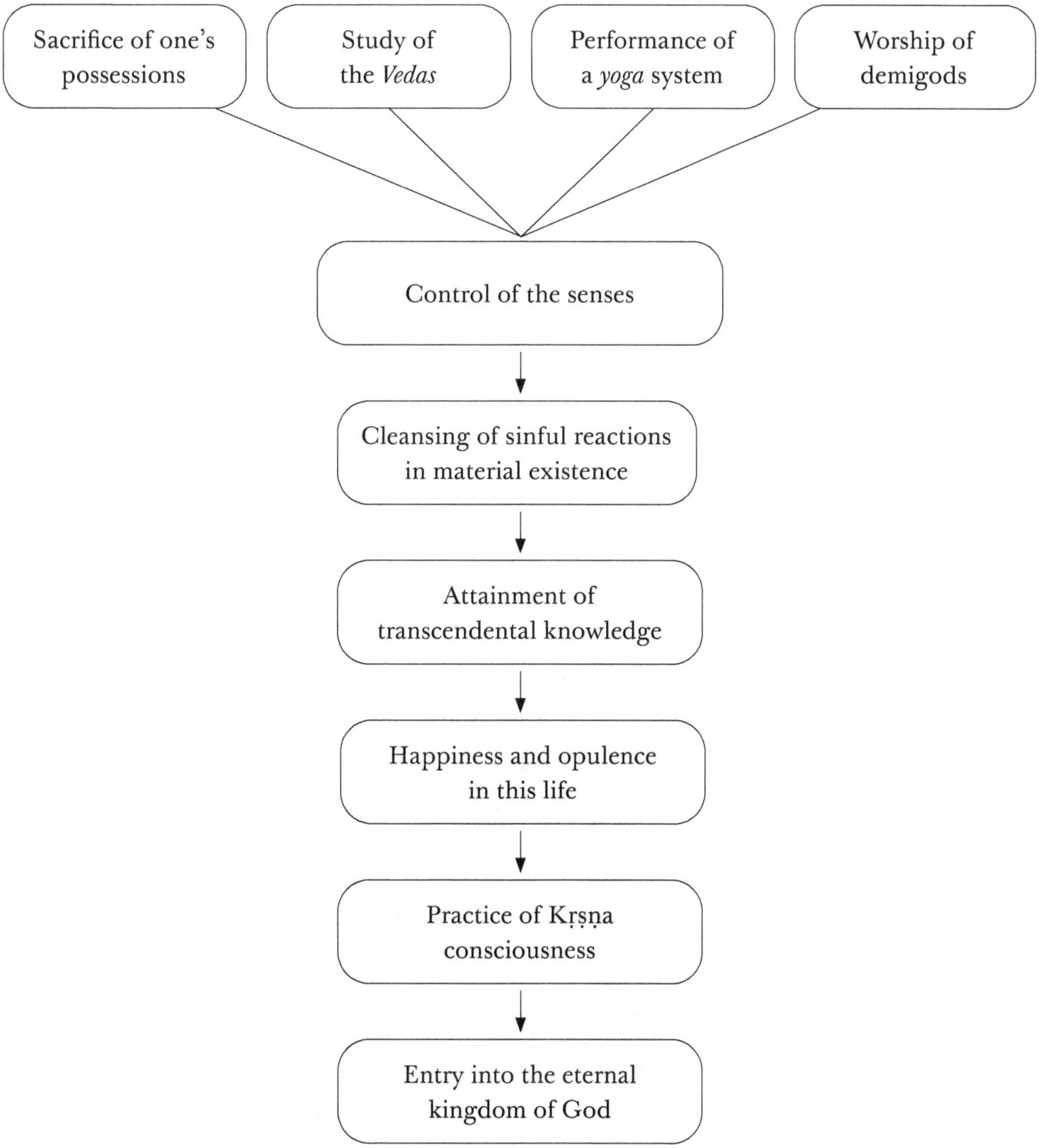

In the table below, categorize the sacrifices given in the first column into four categories. Put a tick in the right box. Then in pairs discuss more examples.

SACRIFICE	SACRIFICE OF ONE'S POSSESSIONS	STUDY OF THE VEDAS	PERFORMANCE OF A YOGA SYSTEM	SACRIFICE IN KṚṢṆA CONSCIOUSNESS
1. A student sacrifices TV time to study for an upcoming test.				
2. A *brahmacārī* controls his senses to study the scriptures.				
3. A *yogī* controls his breath to attain mystic powers.				
4. A devotee sacrifices sleep on Ekādaśī night and does *kīrtana*.				
5. A little girl sacrifices her pocket money to buy a chain for her pet dog.				
6. A student studies hard to attain top results so she can use her career in Kṛṣṇa's service.				

What is the greatest sacrifice according to Kṛṣṇa in verse 33? Explain.

Article: Transcendental Knowledge

Write an article for your local ISKCON magazine describing the glories of transcendental knowledge and the role of faith in obtaining transcendental knowledge.

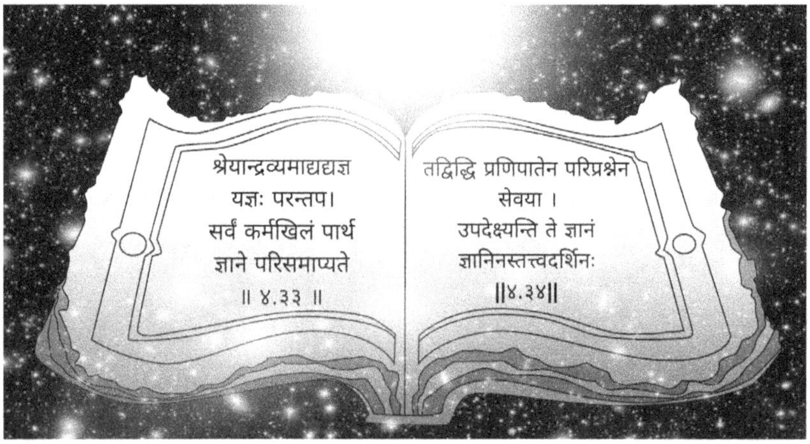

Article Structure and Key Points

1. **Introduction: What is Transcendental Knowledge?**

- Define transcendental knowledge.
- Key Verse: *BG* 4.33: "The knowledge of the Supreme is the best form of knowledge, for it removes all doubts and leads to liberation."

2. **The Glories of Transcendental Knowledge (*BG* 4.35-38)**

- **Benefits of Knowledge**:
    - → Liberation from Ignorance: Transcendental knowledge removes the darkness of ignorance (*BG* 4.37).
    - → Seeing the Divine Everywhere: It allows one to see the divine presence in all living beings and the material world (*BG* 4.38).
    - → Freedom from Material Bondage: It frees one from the cycle of birth and death, leading to liberation.

3. **The Role of Faith in Attaining Transcendental Knowledge (*BG* 4.39–40)**

- Faith and Knowledge: Faith in the teachings of the *Gītā* and the guidance of a spiritual master is essential for obtaining transcendental knowledge.
- Key Verses:
    - → *BG* 4.39: "A person who has faith and is free from doubts attains the transcendental knowledge."
    - → *BG* 4.40: "But a person without faith cannot attain knowledge and remains entangled in material life."
- Application: Faith is crucial in following instructions, practicing spiritual discipline, and sharing knowledge with others.

4. **Personal Realization**

- Reflect on how transcendental knowledge and faith have impacted your personal spiritual journey. How has your practice of these teachings helped you grow spiritually or overcome challenges?

Guidelines for Writing the Article:

1. Clarity: Organize your article with an introduction, main sections, and conclusion.
2. Use of Verses: Support your points with direct quotes from *Bhagavad-gītā As It Is* (particularly from *BG* 4.35–40).
3. Personal Insight: Share your own reflections on how the teachings of *Bhagavad-gītā* have influenced your life and how your faith has helped you to share it with others.

ACTION ACTIVITY

Game: "Broken Telephone"

As we've learned from this chapter, it is very important that spiritual knowledge be handed down from the Supreme Lord intact. This is done by a bona fide spiritual master. On the other hand, cheaters who pose as *gurus* speculate and propagate their own ideas as real knowledge, thereby creating confusion in religious circles.

Let's explore the principle of obtaining knowledge in the correct way from our *Bhagavad-gītā* study group, who are playing a fun game of "Broken Telephone." The first person whispers a message into the ear of the second person, and each of the participants whispers the message into the ear of the next person to see if the message remains the same at the end.

Tamal: (in a commanding tone) Alright, let's play. Remember, no loud talking! I'll start the phrase. Ready? Here we go . . . (he whispers in Balu's ear) "The penguin wore a fluffy hat and danced on a table."

Balu: (grinning, trying not to laugh) Got it.

Balu turns to Priya, looking super serious.

Balu: (whispers to Priya) "The penguin wore a fluffy cap and danced with a table."

Priya: (frowning slightly) Uh, okay… (whispers to Tara) "The penguin had a happy nap before a dance-off with a table."

Tara nods thoughtfully, her face scrunching up as she tries to figure out what she just heard.

Tara: (whispers to Madhu) "The penguin had a happy nap and got in a dance-off with a taco."

Madhu: (laughing to himself) This is gonna be good. (leans in to whisper to Tamal) "The penguin ate a taco and danced on a table after a happy nap."

Tamal: (wide-eyed, about to burst out laughing) What? That's totally different from what I said!

Everyone bursts out laughing. They all turn to Tamal for the final reveal.

Tamal tells them the original message: "The penguin wore a fluffy hat and danced on a table."

Balu: (laughing) How did we go from a stylish penguin to a taco dance-off?

Priya: (giggling) I don't even know how we got to a happy nap.

Tara: (innocently) I just thought tacos sounded fun.

Madhu: (shrugs, still laughing) Honestly, I think we improved it. Who doesn't want a taco dancing penguin?

Balu: (smirking) This is why none of you can be trusted with important information.

(They all laugh at little Balu trying to be the wise man.)

Tamal: On a serious note, Balu has a point here. Śrīla Prabhupāda has always taught us that no one can be spiritually realized by manufacturing his own process.

Balu: What does that mean?

Now answer the following questions:

1. What do you think is Tamal's answer?
2. We sometimes hear about deceptive *gurus* in the market of spirituality. What do these *gurus* do to actual spiritual knowledge?
3. What is the difference between Śrīla Prabhupāda and unauthorized *gurus*?
4. Why can't one progress in spiritual life by independent study of books of knowledge?
5. Discuss points of personal significance regarding verse 34. How can you benefit from serving and hearing submissively from a spiritual master?

Now that you have more clarity in understanding how knowledge needs to be passed on as it is, you can play the "Broken Telephone" game with your friends. Be aware and conscious about how easily knowledge can get distorted if we don't pay proper attention.

ANALOGY ANTHOLOGY

A collection of analogies
for easier understanding

Analogy 1: Appearance and Disappearance of Kṛṣṇa

His appearance and disappearance are like the sun's rising, moving before us, and then disappearing from our eyesight. When the sun is out of sight, we think that the sun is set, and when the sun is before our eyes, we think that the sun is on the horizon. Actually, the sun is always in its fixed position. – *BG* 4.6, purport

One may think the Lord is born and leaves at the end, but the Lord neither takes birth nor dies. He just appears and disappears in different places in the universe, just like the sun appears and disappears in different places on the planet.

Analogy 2: Rain Clouds

Cloud: "Those fruits are yours to enjoy if they are sweet. I didn't pour so I could enjoy them."

The proprietor never desires the low-grade happiness such as the workers may desire. He is aloof from the material actions and reactions. For example, the rains are not responsible for different types of vegetation that appear on the earth, although without such rains there is no possibility of vegetative growth. – *BG* 4.14, purport

Material enjoyment is inferior, and the Lord never desires it. He is *ānanda mayo 'bhyāsāt*, one who is situated in spiritual enjoyment.

Analogy 3: A Machine in Service

As a machine part requires oiling and cleaning for maintenance, so a Kṛṣṇa conscious man maintains himself by his work just to remain fit for action in the transcendental loving service of the Lord. He is therefore immune to all the reactions of his endeavors.
– *BG* 4.21, purport

A Kṛṣṇa conscious person acts for the pleasure of the Lord, and not for sense gratification. He therefore does not enjoy or suffer reactions to his actions.

Analogy 4: Milk and Yogurt

For example, a patient who is suffering from a disorder of the bowels due to overindulgence in milk products is cured by another milk product, namely curds. The materially absorbed conditioned soul can be cured by Kṛṣṇa consciousness as set forth here in the *Gītā*.
– *BG* 4.24, purport

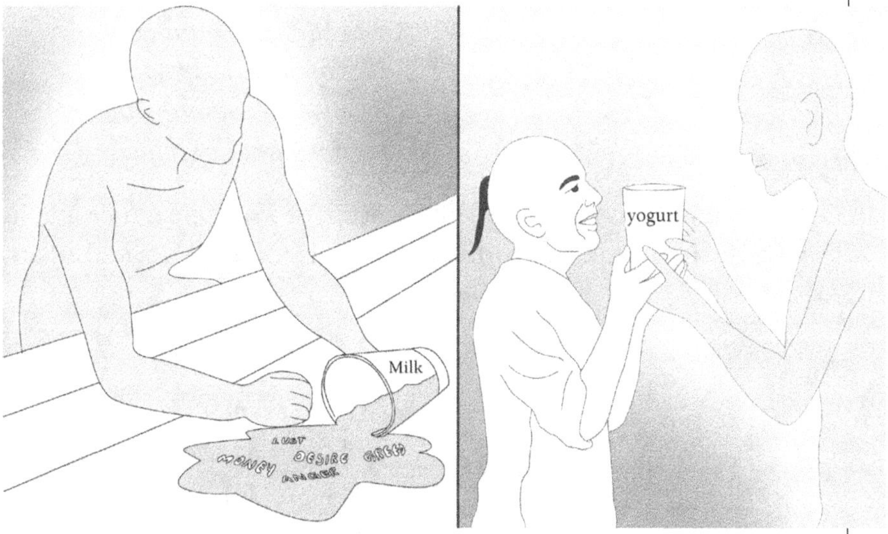

From hurt to healed, when spiritual knowledge is revealed.

A diseased soul acts in a way that he becomes entangled, but the way to end his entanglement is also to act, but in Kṛṣṇa consciousness.

SACRED RHYTHMS

Important verses
to memorize

***BG* 4.2**

evaṁ paramparā-prāptam
imaṁ rājarṣayo viduḥ
sa kāleneha mahatā
yogo naṣṭaḥ paran-tapa

This supreme science was thus received through the chain of disciplic succession, and the saintly kings understood it in that way. But in course of time the succession was broken, and therefore the science as it is appears to be lost.

***BG* 4.8**

paritrāṇāya sādhūnāṁ
vināśāya ca duṣkṛtām
dharma-saṁsthāpanārthāya
sambhavāmi yuge yuge

To deliver the pious and to annihilate the miscreants, as well as to reestablish the principles of religion, I Myself appear, millennium after millennium.

***BG* 4.9**

janma karma ca me divyam
evaṁ yo vetti tattvataḥ
tyaktvā dehaṁ punar janma
naiti mām eti so 'rjuna

One who knows the transcendental nature of My appearance and activities does not, upon leaving the body, take his birth again in this material world, but attains My eternal abode, O Arjuna.

***BG* 4.34**

tad viddhi praṇipātena
paripraśnena sevayā
upadekṣyanti te jñānaṁ
jñāninas tattva-darśinaḥ

Just try to learn the truth by approaching a spiritual master. Inquire from him submissively and render service unto him. The self-realized souls can impart knowledge unto you because they have seen the truth.

ANSWERS

Learning Harmonies
1. c; 2. c; 3. b. 4. c; 5. b; 6. b; 7. c; 8. a; 9. b; 10. a

The Divine Detective Agency *(Solutions)*:

Case 1: The detectives must argue that Kṛṣṇa's appearance is not ordinary but transcendental, supported by the clues from the *Bhagavad-gītā*.

Case 2: The detectives must deduce that Kṛṣṇa's appearance is for the protection of *dharma* (righteousness) and to destroy *adharma* (evil).

Case 3: The detectives must conclude that Kṛṣṇa's appearance is not only to restore *dharma* but to reciprocate the love of His pure devotees. As He states in *BG* 10.10, He personally guides those devoted to Him, offering them the understanding to return to Him. He appears because He wants to interact in intimate relationships with His devotees, to personally protect them, and through His pastimes, attract everyone to Him.

The Varṇa Portfolio

1. Transcendental *varṇa* devotees: Nanda Mahārāja, Śrīla Prabhupāda, Raghunātha dāsa Gosvāmī, Vālmīki, Vidura, Haridāsa Ṭhākura
   Brāhmaṇas: Vidura (functioned so, as he counseled Dhṛtarāṣṭra), Vālmīki (penned the Rāmāyaṇa), Viśvāmitra, Haridāsa Ṭhākura
   Kṣatriyas: Karṇa, Rāvaṇa, Paraśurāma
   Vaiśyas: Nanda Mahārāja; *Śūdras*: none
2. Reasons: Birth provides an opportunity to train in a certain *varṇa*, but one may not take that opportunity and develop the qualities (e.g., Aśvatthāmā); a person's natural inclination for work may be different from the *varṇa* he was born in; a person's *guṇas*, or modes that control him, can change – uplift or degrade him – within a lifetime (e.g., Ajāmila); classifying *varṇas* based on birth can cause confusion in society; it can lead to pride (e.g., *brāhmaṇa* boy Śṛṅgi who cursed Parīkṣit Mahārāja) or exploitation of a lower *varṇa* by a higher *varṇa* (modern-day caste system).
3. The *varṇas* ensure the structural roles of individuals in society, resulting in a harmonious and well-developed society. They also ensure a person's spiritual growth according to one's individual position. The living entities are responsible for the reactions of their work and actions – not the Lord. He simply sanctions activities but is aloof from work and its reactions.

Comic Strip

1. There will be no karmic reaction when one does the right action for Kṛṣṇa. Arjuna will not incur negative reactions if he does his duty of fighting in a mood of detachment and devotion. But there are reactions when one stops doing one's duty in service to Kṛṣṇa. Arjuna's not wanting to engage in the battle will incur a karmic reaction because he is a *kṣatriya*. He has to do his *kṣatriya* duty and fight for the pleasure of Kṛṣṇa. Similarly, Madhu is a student and has to do his duty and study for his test.
2. Madhu misunderstood, thinking that by not doing anything he remains unattached. He only understood partially, seeing that he shouldn't focus on the outcome. However, he still needed to act. In the end he understands that he needs to work to get results, but also not to be attached to the results like Priya.
3. *Karma*. Although she understood what *akarma* was and tried to imbibe it by studying hard and doing her duty, her disappointment in her results shows that she has some element of *karma* with attachment to the results.
4. Detached workers (*niṣkāma-karma-yogīs*) act but do not accrue reactions to their work. Therefore, their work is *akarma*, or inaction, although performing *karma* (action). The fire of knowledge burns up reactions of work. They know that because they are part and parcels of the Supreme, it is not their own activity but is being done through them by the Lord. They therefore move like a part of a machine. Just as a machine part requires oiling and cleaning for maintenance, so do Kṛṣṇa conscious persons maintain themselves by their work – to remain fit for action in the transcendental loving service of

the Lord. In relation to Priya's situation, a *niṣkāma-karma-yogī* will see studies in relation to Kṛṣṇa, do their best, and not be attached or affected by the results.

5. Any work done with attachment causes bondage. When doing *karma-yoga*, we perform our worldly duties in a mood of detachment (not focusing on the results), thus realizing our spiritual identity as souls and progressing towards disentanglement.
6. By doing her duty of studying and trying her best, as she did, but not being attached to the results. If she is satisfied by the results, whatever they are, knowing that she is an instrument of Kṛṣṇa's and the fruits of her studies will be offered to Kṛṣṇa, she can perform *akarma* and not be distressed or more entangled in fruitive work.
7. No, it doesn't necessarily mean she is attached to the result. She could simply desire to do the best for the pleasure of Krsna and leave the results to Him. Similarly, devotees can strive to excel in their service or work, as Srila Prabhupada had encouraged his disciples, but for Krsna's pleasure, not for personal enjoyment.

The Purpose of Sacrifices

1. Sacrifice of one's possessions; 2. Study of the *Vedas;* 3. Performance of a *yoga* system; 4. Sacrifice in Kṛṣṇa consciousness; 5. Sacrifice of one's possessions; 6. Sacrifice in Kṛṣṇa consciousness.

The greatest sacrifice is of transcendental knowledge. Real knowledge is knowledge of Kṛṣṇa consciousness, which elevates one to the spiritual platform. Other sacrifices are simply material activities if they are not meant for serving and pleasing Kṛṣṇa.

"Broken Telephone"

1. Tamal means that spiritual knowledge should be learned only from a bona fide spiritual master. One learns from a *guru* and then after realizing the knowledge, one may pass it on to disciples without changing anything, not by manufacturing one's own knowledge process.
2. They distort the knowledge and teach their disciples their own manufactured lessons. The original knowledge thus gets lost as it is passed on to the next generation.
3. Śrīla Prabhupāda comes in a line of *paramparā* or disciplic succession in which knowledge is handed over to the next generation as it is. This means he did not distort the knowledge but passed it to his disciples intact. Unauthorized *gurus* try to speculate and interpret knowledge, giving their own meanings, which may not be aligned to original knowledge.
4. Just as we need a teacher for transmitting material knowledge, we need a spiritual teacher from whom we can hear and learn spiritual knowledge. The spiritual master also teaches by example and can destroy all our doubts.

RESOURCE 1

Examples of Case Files (Mysteries) for The Detective Agency Activity:

Case 1: The Mysterious Identity of Kṛṣṇa

Mystery: A divine figure has appeared on Earth, and some say He is just a prince born in a royal family. But is He more than just a regular human?

Clues:

- "Although I appear to be born in this world, I am beyond birth." (4.6)
- "My transcendental body does not undergo birth and death." (4.5)
- "I am the source of all creation." (4.9)

Case 2: The Universal Mission of Kṛṣṇa

Mystery: Why did this extraordinary figure, Kṛṣṇa, take birth in this world? What was His purpose?

Clues:

- "Whenever there is a decline in righteousness and a rise in unrighteousness, I appear." (4.7)
- "To protect the righteous, to destroy the wicked, and to reestablish the principles of *dharma,* I appear age after age." (4.8)
- "I incarnate to restore balance and guide the world back to the path of virtue." (4.8)

Case 3: The Internal Reason for Kṛṣṇa's Descent

Mystery: Kṛṣṇa could have easily destroyed the demons and established religion through the forces of nature or His pure devotee agents. So, why did He come Himself? Was there something more to His appearance beyond the need to eliminate evil and reestablish *dharma*?

Clues:

- "I am never manifest to the foolish and unintelligent. For them I am covered by My internal potency, and therefore they do not know that I am unborn and infallible." (7.25)
- "To those who are constantly devoted and who always remember Me with love, I give the understanding by which they can come to Me." (10.10)
- "I am the swift deliverer of My devotees from the ocean of birth and death." (12.7)
- "I am the source of all spiritual and material worlds. Everything emanates from Me. The wise who perfectly know this engage in My devotional service and worship Me with all their hearts." (10.8)

RESOURCE 2

Role-Play Cards: Who Follows Kṛṣṇa's Path?

A *gopī* from Vṛndāvana (Character Card)

A *gopī*, a pure cowherd damsel of Vṛndāvana, is automatically attracted to Kṛṣṇa and always follows His path.

Role Play: Recite this verse from the *gopī-gīta* to Kṛṣṇa (*SB* 10.31.18):

"O beloved, Your all-auspicious appearance vanquishes the distress of those living in Vraja's forests. Our minds long for Your association. Please give to us just a bit of that medicine, which counteracts the disease in Your devotees' hearts."

Kṛṣṇa's Response to the *gopī*

Respond to the *gopī*, while conveying how she follows Your path in all respects.

Refer to the following verse to help you formulate your response:

"I am not able to repay My debt for your spotless service, even within a lifetime of Brahmā. Your connection with Me is beyond reproach. You have worshiped Me, cutting off all domestic ties, which are difficult to break. Therefore please let your own glorious deeds be your compensation." (*SB* 10.32.22)

Impersonalist (Character Card)

An impersonalist wants to merge into Brahman.

Role play the impersonalist seeking liberation. Use the following prompt to help you:

"Being a *jñānī,* I scrutinizingly study the *Vedas.* I understand that the Supreme Brahman is ultimate, and I aspire to become one with Him. By thus negating my material identity and gaining liberation, I will become situated in *brahmānanda.*"

Kṛṣṇa's Response to Impersonalist

Explain how he follows You indirectly, although wishing to avoid You.

Use the following quote from *BG* 12.3–4 to help you formulate your answer:

"But those who fully worship the unmanifested, that which lies beyond the perception of the senses, the all-pervading, inconceivable, unchanging, fixed and immovable – the impersonal conception of the Absolute Truth – by controlling the various senses and being equally disposed to everyone, such persons, engaged in the welfare of all, at last achieve Me."

Mystic Yogi (Character Card)

As a *yogi*, you look inward, trying to find spiritual bliss within.

Use the following prompt to help you formulate your answer:

"As a *yogi*, I prefer going within and meditating. I seek the Supersoul within, finding whom I will be freed from material illusion."

Kṛṣṇa's Response to Mystic Yogi

You explain to the *yogi* that you are the Supersoul he is seeking:

"I am the Supersoul, seated in the hearts of all living entities. I direct the wanderings of all beings." (*BG* 15.15)

Demigod worshiper (Character Card)

A demigod worshiper does not directly worship Kṛṣṇa but worships the demigods to quickly fulfill material desires. He does not know this is indirect worship of Kṛṣṇa.

Role play a demigod worshiper using this quote based on *BG* 4.12:

"I desire to be happy. I therefore worship all the *devatās* because they give us happiness. Worship of the sun-god gives good health, worship of Sarasvatī gives knowledge, worship of Gaṇeśa removes all obstacles, and so on. I always make sure they are all satisfied."

Kṛṣṇa's Response to Demigod Worshiper

Explain how he actually follows You indirectly, although not worshiping You.

Use the following quote from *BG* 9.23 to help you formulate your answer:

"Whatever a man may sacrifice to other gods, O son of Kuntī, is really meant for Me alone, but it is offered without true understanding."

Parent (Character Card)

As a parent, Mother Yaśoda cares for and protects the Lord. Her path is thus one with Kṛṣṇa's.

Role play using this prompt where Mother Yaśoda is ready to chastise Kṛṣṇa after discovering that He has eaten dirt:

"Upon hearing this from Kṛṣṇa's playmates, mother Yaśodā, who was always full of anxiety over Kṛṣṇa's welfare, picked Kṛṣṇa up with her hands to look into His mouth and chastise Him." (*SB* 10.8.33)

Kṛṣṇa's Response to Parent

You allowed Yourself to be bound by Mother Yaśodā as a tribute to her love. Show how the Dāmodara pastime reveals Your recognition of her love:

"O Mahārāja Parīkṣit, this entire universe, with its great, exalted demigods like Lord Śiva, Lord Brahmā and Lord Indra, is under the control of the Supreme Personality of Godhead. Yet the Supreme Lord has one transcendental attribute: He comes under the control of His devotees. This was now exhibited by Kṛṣṇa in this pastime." (*SB* 10.9.19)

Atheist/Materialist (Character Card)

An atheist does not believe in Kṛṣṇa and does not want to follow Him. Yet, he indirectly follows the Lord because the Lord keeps the atheist in the material world in ignorance, and the atheist can neither detect this nor do anything about it.

Use this quote from *BG* 16.13–15 to role play the atheist:

"So much wealth do I have today, and I will gain more according to my schemes. So much is mine now, and it will increase in the future, more and more. He is my enemy, and I have killed him, and my other enemies will also be killed. I am the lord of everything."

Kṛṣṇa's Response to Atheist/Materialist

You recognize atheistic mentality but also know that the atheist cannot follow a path independent of You. Respond to him by using the following quote from *BG* 16.19:

"Those who are envious and mischievous, who are the lowest among men, I perpetually cast into the ocean of material existence, into various demoniac species of life."

CHAPTER 5

Karma-yoga – Action in Kṛṣṇa Consciousness

CHAPTER BEATS

An overview

Arjuna was still confused. He asked, "O Kṛṣṇa, first you told me to renounce work, and then you recommended that I work in devotion. Kindly tell me which is more beneficial?"

Kṛṣṇa smiled and replied, "Both are good for liberation, dear Arjuna, but devotional service is better than renunciation of work."

Kṛṣṇa explained that *jñāna*, knowledge that one is not the material body but a spirit soul, is not sufficient for liberation. One has to *act* as the spirit soul. This action in Kṛṣṇa consciousness does not involve acting for material gain but acting in full knowledge as a servant of Kṛṣṇa. Such action does not incur reactions. However, mere renunciation without Kṛṣṇa consciousness doesn't purify the heart or give one happiness. Yet a Kṛṣṇa conscious person engaged in devotional service can achieve the Supreme without delay. This is how action in Kṛṣṇa consciousness is superior to renunciation.

Arjuna tried to absorb Kṛṣṇa's words. He desired to know how such a Kṛṣṇa conscious *karma-yogī* acts.

Kṛṣṇa explained that a

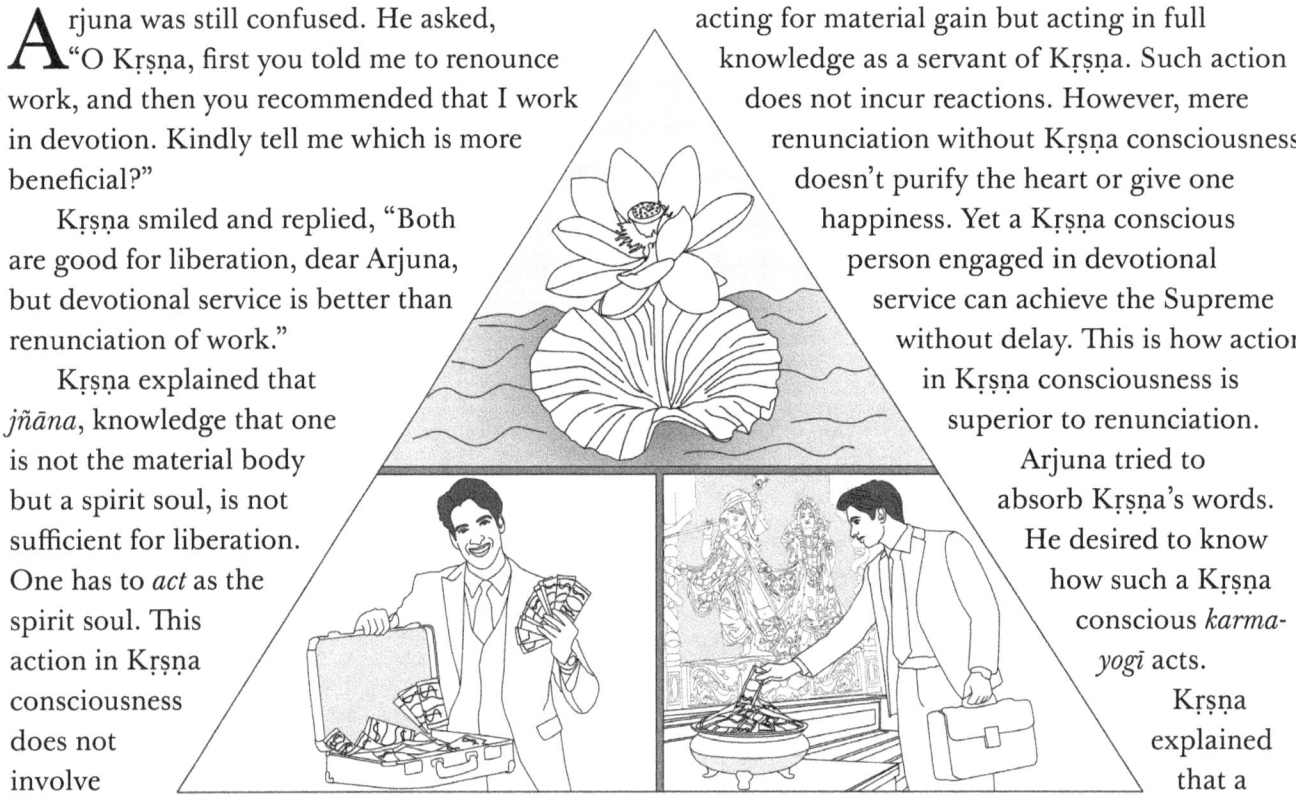

pure soul who controls the mind and senses cannot think of anything separate from Kṛṣṇa, just as the leaves and branches of a tree are not separate from the tree. Therefore, such people are never entangled in material life.

They are dear to everyone, and everyone is dear to them. While acting they know they don't do anything at all. They understand that while speaking, eating, moving, sleeping, or breathing that only the material senses are engaged with their objects and that they are aloof from them. They offer the results of their work to the Supreme Lord while performing their duties without attachment. They are unaffected by sins just as a lotus leaf is untouched by water. Therefore *karma-yogīs* attain peace, because they offer the results of their activities to Kṛṣṇa, whereas *karmīs* are greedy for the fruits of labor and become entangled.

Kṛṣṇa then said firmly, "So it is not action that causes bondage or liberation but the consciousness in which we act."

Kṛṣṇa explained that *niṣkāma-karma-yogīs* understand the relationship between the living entity, material nature, and the Supersoul. They don't blame the Lord or material nature for their suffering but understand that when we desire to enjoy material nature, the modes of nature carry out our actions with the permission of the Supersoul.

"Conditioned souls, however, are bewildered," added Kṛṣṇa. "When they are enlightened with knowledge, darkness is destroyed and their knowledge reveals everything, as the sun lights up everything. By such knowledge, the humble sages see with equal vision a learned and gentle *brāhmaṇa*, a cow, an elephant, a dog, and a dog-eater. Such persons with equanimity conquer the conditions of birth and death and are always situated in Brahman. They are constantly in trance, enjoying sublime pleasure within because of concentrating on the Supreme.

"O son of Kunti, an intelligent person does not participate in the sources of misery. Such pleasures have a beginning and an end, and so the wise man does not delight in them. If one can tolerate the urges of the material senses and give up material desire and anger, one is happy in this world. Those who are beyond the dualities of this world, whose minds are turned within, who are always busy working for the welfare of others, who are free from all sins, and who are self-realized and self-disciplined achieve liberation in the Supreme.

"One who shuts out all external objects, who keeps the eyes and vision concentrated between the two eyebrows, controlling one's breathing, mind, senses, and intelligence is certainly liberated."

Kṛṣṇa's eyes scanned the battlefield as He contemplated the death that lay before everyone. Real peace could only come about in one way. He looked at Arjuna and said in a soft voice, "A person who is fully conscious of Me, knowing Me to the supreme controller, enjoyer, and proprietor, and the benefactor and well-wisher of all living entities, attains peace from the pangs of material miseries."

THEME TRACKS

Themes and key messages
to contemplate and discuss

THEME TRACKS	REFERENCES	KEY MESSAGES
Theme Track 1 *Karma-yoga* is better and easier than renouncing work.	5.1–6	As in Chapter 3, Arjuna again asked Kṛṣṇa which is better: renouncing work (*karma-sannyāsa*) or working without attachment to the results (*karma-yoga*). Kṛṣṇa explained that both ultimately give liberation from material existence, since the aim of both *yogas*, *jñāna-* and *karma-yogas*, is Viṣṇu. However, renunciation is difficult and distressful to perform whereas *karma-yoga* is easier. Kṛṣṇa consciousness, or *karma-yoga*, is also superior because it frees one from good and bad reactions so that one doesn't come down to the material platform, whereas a *jñāna-yogī* has the risk of fall down. *Jñāna* is not sufficient for liberation. However, a *jñānī* who performs *niṣkāma-karma-yoga* becomes fixed in knowledge, while a *karma-yogī* can automatically be a *sannyāsī* because of not being attached to the fruits of action. Renunciation without Kṛṣṇa consciousness cannot make one happy, but devotional service can allow one to achieve the Lord quickly. Therefore, Kṛṣṇa advised Arjuna to perform *karma-yoga*, which is more relevant to him.

THEME TRACKS	REFERENCES	KEY MESSAGES
Theme Track 2 Performing *niṣkāma-karma-yoga* frees one from bondage.	5.7–12	A *yoga-yukta*, a *karma-yogī* who works in devotion, is never entangled because he cannot think of anything separate from Kṛṣṇa, just as the leaves and branches of a tree are not separate from the tree. He is dear to everyone and everyone is dear to him. He controls his mind and senses; he's the doer yet the non-doer, because he knows that the material senses are only interacting with the sense objects, and so he is aloof from them. He offers the results of his work to the Supreme Lord while performing his duties without attachment. He is unaffected by sins just as a lotus leaf is untouched by water. Therefore a *karma-yogī* attains peace, because he offers the results of his activities to Kṛṣṇa, whereas a *karmī*, who is greedy for the fruits of his labor, becomes entangled. So it is not action that causes bondage or liberation but the consciousness in which action is performed.
Theme Track 3 Knowledge of the three doers allows one to become detached, understand the Supreme, and attain liberation.	5.13–16	There are three doers – the soul, material nature, and the Supersoul. Although the modes of nature or the Supersoul may appear to be the cause of action and reaction, they are not responsible. When the soul (*jīva*) works but renounces the results of actions, the *jīva* is happy in the material body, but if the *jīva* desires to enjoy material nature, the modes of material nature influence or impel the *jīva*'s particular nature, his *sva-bhāva*. Then the Supreme Lord simply witnesses and sanctions these actions; He is not responsible for anyone's sinful or pious activities and the consequent reactions. When one is enlightened with knowledge about the soul, material nature, and the Supreme Lord, one will take shelter of the Lord and attain liberation.
Theme Track 4 One can attain liberation and peace by focusing on the Supreme Lord and seeing Him as the supreme enjoyer, proprietor, and true well-wisher.	5.17–29	A *yogī* attains liberation by fixing his mind on the Supreme Lord. He sees every living being with equal vision. He tolerates the temptations of the senses and redirects his pleasure-seeking propensity from matter to spirit. He detaches from external pleasures and focuses inwards because he understands that material enjoyment is not substantial and is foolish. One who delights inwards is on the *brahma-bhūta* stage and attains the Supreme. He works for the welfare of all living beings. When one understands Kṛṣṇa to be the supreme enjoyer, proprietor, and well-wisher, one becomes free from material miseries and attains real peace.

SOLO QUESTIONS

To enhance your self-study

(Find the answers in the verse and purport references provided in brackets.)

1. How is work in full knowledge (*karma-yoga*) the same as inaction, or not doing work? (5.1)
2. Briefly describe what is action in Kṛṣṇa consciousness. (5.2)
3. How is a Kṛṣṇa conscious person automatically a renouncer? (5.3–4)
4. How is Sāṅkhya and *karma-yoga* the same? (5.4)
5. How is Sāṅkhya study for the Māyāvādī *sannyāsī* more difficult than devotional service performed by the Vaiṣṇava *sannyāsī*? What are the results of each? (5.6)
6. Killing usually involves sinful reactions. How then would Arjuna not be entangled in the reactions of work if he chose to fight? (5.7, 10)
7. How is a Kṛṣṇa conscious person already liberated while still in the material world? (5.11)
8. What is the cause of anxiety expressed by Śrīla Prabhupāda? (5.12)
9. The devotee is free from both the inner and outer activities of the material body. Relate this to the nine gates of the body and the Lord living within the body. (5.13)
10. How is the Lord (*vibhu*) not responsible for the conditional life of the living entity (*aṇu*)? (5.15)
11. Give the English meaning of the phrase *paṇḍitāḥ sama-darśinaḥ*, the amazing quality of a Kṛṣṇa conscious person. What is this due to? (5.18)
12. List the eight limbs of *aṣṭāṅga-yoga*, the results of which are automatically achieved in Kṛṣṇa consciousness. (5.27)

LEARNING HARMONIES

Multiple-choice questions
to quiz your memory

(Choose the most complete answer.)

1. What is the main theme of Chapter 5?
   a. The path of devotion (*bhakti-yoga*).
   b. Renunciation and selfless action (*karma-yoga*).
   c. The nature of the material world.
   d. The superiority of knowledge (*jñāna-yoga*).

2. Which of the following is superior to renunciation (*sannyāsa*)?
   a. Mystical practices.
   b. *Karma-yoga* (the path of selfless action).
   c. Pure meditation (*dhyāna-yoga*).
   d. Physical austerities and penance.

3. What does Lord Kṛṣṇa say about those who perform their duties with detachment?
   a. They will experience continuous difficulties in the material world.
   b. They will attain the highest spiritual perfection.
   c. They will be liberated from the cycle of birth and death.
   d. They will gain fame and power in society.

4. Who is a genuinely renounced person?
   a. A person who gives up all duties and lives in isolation.
   b. A person who performs actions with no attachment to results.
   c. A person who constantly focuses on meditation and knowledge.
   d. A person who performs actions for personal spiritual gain.

5. What is the difference between a renunciant (*sannyāsī*) and a *karma-yogī*?
   a. A *karma-yogī* works for personal benefit, while a *sannyāsī* renounces all material desires.
   b. A *sannyāsī* renounces all worldly work, while a *karma-yogī* works with detachment.
   c. A *karma-yogī* performs actions to gain material rewards, while a *sannyāsī* seeks liberation.
   d. Both are essentially the same, with no significant difference.

6. How does a true *yogī* view all living beings?
   a. As separate and distinct from themselves.
   b. As obstacles to be avoided for spiritual progress.
   c. With equal vision, as spirit souls with the Lord manifested in the heart.
   d. As beings who are ignorant and covered by material nature.

7. What is the result for people who practice *karma-yoga*?
   a. They gain material wealth and fame.
   b. They attain liberation and eternal peace.
   c. They experience continued suffering in the material world.
   d. They are blessed with various powers.

8. Why don't the wise delight in material pleasures?
   a. They realize that such sense pleasure is available to even the hogs.
   b. They enjoy the pleasure within in connection with the Supreme.
   c. They realize that material pleasures are temporary and are sources of eventual misery.
   d. All of the above.

9. What is the position of people whose minds are engaged within and work for the welfare of others?
   a. They are spiritually inferior to those who meditate in solitude.
   b. They have realized their oneness with the Supreme and are true *yogīs*.
   c. They continue to experience difficulty in life but remain detached.
   d. They are free from all sins and achieve liberation in the Supreme.

10. What is the key to attaining peace?
   a. To meditate in solitude.
   b. To become renounced.
   c. To know Kṛṣṇa as the supreme enjoyer, proprietor, and well-wisher.
   d. To endeavor for material prosperity.

MEDLEY ACTS

A variety of fun activities to learn from

THEME TRACK 1 ACTIVITIES

LANGUAGE ACTIVITY

The Highest Philosophy

In the third chapter Kṛṣṇa explains that a person who is on the platform of knowledge no longer has duties to perform. In the fourth chapter the Lord tells Arjuna that all kinds of sacrificial work culminate in knowledge. However, at the end of the fourth chapter, the Lord advises Arjuna to wake up and fight and be situated in perfect knowledge in this way. Therefore, by simultaneously stressing the importance of both work in devotion (*karma-yoga*) and inaction in knowledge (*jñāna -yoga*), Kṛṣṇa has perplexed Arjuna. He inquires, therefore, whether he should cease work altogether or work with full knowledge. (*BG* 5.1 purport)

Kṛṣṇa then explains that both ultimately give liberation from material existence, since the aim of both *yogas*, *jñāna-* and *karma-yogas*, is Viṣṇu. However, renunciation is difficult and distressful to perform whereas *karma-yoga* is easier. The Lord further clarifies as follows (*BG* 5.2–6 verses and purports):

1. *Jñāna* (or knowledge that one is not this material body but spirit soul) is not sufficient for liberation. One has to act as the spirit soul. Performing devotional service is acting as a spirit soul.
2. Work in Kṛṣṇa consciousness is working in full knowledge and doesn't incur reactions. It is, therefore, the same as inaction.
3. Activities performed in full knowledge give practical realization and thereby support one's advancement.
4. Without Kṛṣṇa consciousness, mere renunciation does not actually purify the heart of a conditioned soul.
5. Action in Kṛṣṇa consciousness is always superior to renunciation, which always has a risk of falldown due to lack of complete connection with Kṛṣṇa.
6. Work done to satisfy Kṛṣṇa automatically pleases the Lord and the servant.
7. When one acts in Kṛṣṇa consciousness, one acts in one's constitutional position. One is detached from matter and attached to Kṛṣṇa, who is all attractive.
8. The Vaiṣṇava *sannyāsīs* are happy in their transcendental duties, and they have the guarantee of ultimate entrance into the infinite kingdom of God.

Study and discuss the above points and complete the following acronym to show the superiority of Kṛṣṇa consciousness (*bhakti-yoga*):

Philosophy (Kṛṣṇa consciousness is the highest philosophy)

P
H
I
L
O
S
O
P
H
Y

Examples:

P: Practical and pleasing to all the senses (Kṛṣṇa consciousness is practical, and anyone from any sphere of life can practice and achieve real happiness.)

H: High-minded (Kṛṣṇa consciousness makes one conquer the mind and washes traces of all sinful desires and thoughts.)

INTROSPECTIVE ACTIVITY

Yukta-Vairāgya

The following are statements by Śrīla Prabhupāda regarding *phalgu-* and *yukta-vairāgya*:

A. *Vairāgya* means renunciation, and *phalgu* means without any value, or little, very little. Why should we give up this world? But the process is that give up the idea of sense enjoyment. That is required. That is real renunciation. "I shall not use it for my sense gratification. I shall utilize it for Kṛṣṇa's service." That is Kṛṣṇa consciousness. (SP lecture, *BG* 5.17–24, 1969, Los Angeles)

B. There is a river, Phalgu, in the Gaya. Those who have gone to Gaya . . . There is a river. The Gaya city is situated on the river Phalgu. This river is got name Phalgu because on the bed you'll find only sand, but if you push your hand within the sand, you'll find water. Similarly, *phalgu-vairāgya* means the so-called *sannyāsīs*, they have taken the dress of renounced order, but within the heart they have got all desires to fulfill (want to become God). Within the heart. If you push your hand within his heart, you'll find he has got all desires for material enjoyment. That is called *phalgu-vairāgya*. On the surface there is no water; sand. But within, oh, there is flow of water going on. (SP lecture, *Nectar of Devotion*, 1973, Calcutta)

C. So everything created or given by God, we should not say it is false, but we should know that "This is God gifted, it is God's possession, so I must utilize it for God's purpose." That is Kṛṣṇa consciousness. That is the knowledge of science of Kṛṣṇa. Everything . . . *nirbandhaḥ kṛṣṇa-sambandhe yuktam vairāgyam ucyate.* And,

prāpañcikatayā buddhyā
hari-sambandhi-vastunaḥ
mumukṣubhiḥ parityāgo
vairāgyaṁ phalgu kathyate
[*Bhakti-rasāmṛta-sindhu* 1.2.258]

[When one is not attached to anything but at the same time accepts anything in relation to Kṛṣṇa, one is rightly situated above possessiveness. On the other hand, one who rejects everything without knowledge of its relationship to Kṛṣṇa is not as complete in his renunciation.] (SP lecture, *BG* 5.17-24, 1969, Los Angeles)

D. You know the story, jackal? He wanted to take the grapes, jumping, jumping, jumping. When he could not get it, he says, "Oh, grapes are sour. I have no necessity. I have no necessity." Similarly, these rascals, they renounce the world. What renouncement? What you had, you are renouncing? This is also wrong. The real happiness is *sevā*. "This is Kṛṣṇa's, and it must be used for Kṛṣṇa's purpose." That is real happiness. (SP Lecture, *Nectar of Devotion*, 1973, Calcutta)

1. Read the above excerpts and note the differences between *phalgu-vairāgya* and *yukta-vairāgya*.
2. For a few days observe how everything you see is Kṛṣṇa's property. Try to label things – people, creations, materials, animals, nature, energies, etc. – as Kṛṣṇa's in your mind's eye.
3. Then think of how these things can be used to please Kṛṣṇa.
4. Now contemplate on your possessions, strengths, and activities. Note the good and bad use of them. Then see how you can connect them to Kṛṣṇa.
5. Share with a friend: A. the most creative use of anything in Kṛṣṇa's service; B. a quality or object most difficult to use in Kṛṣṇa's service.

THEME TRACK 2 ACTIVITIES

LANGUAGE ACTIVITY

Anagram Fun: Work Without Attachment

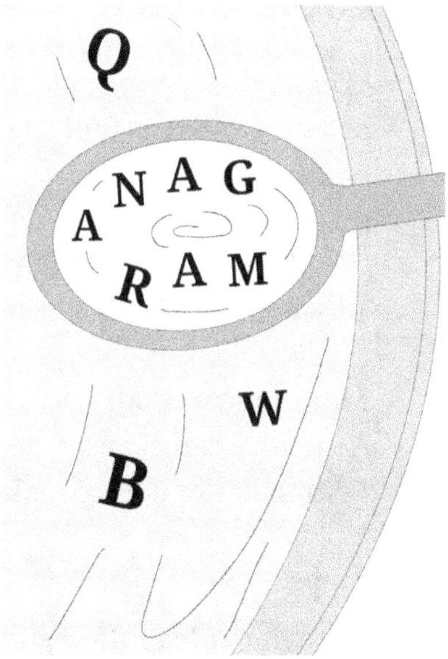

On the path of Kṛṣṇa consciousness, or *niṣkāma-karma-yoga*, the practitioner performs work without incurring reactions. Such a devotee is dear to everyone and attains complete peace.

The extract below will help you understand this better. Fill in the missing words, using anagrams.

An anagram is a word or phrase that when rearranged makes up another word. For example, the word "secure" is an anagram of the word "rescue." In an anagram all the letters of the original word are used. However, for this activity we will modify this rule and not use all letters. For example, an eight-letter word "retrieve" may have a seven-letter anagram of "retiree."

Read the extract on the next page. For the highlighted words, find the corresponding anagram and fill in the blanks. The number of letters in the anagram is specified in brackets.*

* At the end of the exercise, you may also think of some of your own fun anagrams in relation to the topic. (For example, "Attachment" is an anagram of "Match at ten.")

A person in Kṛṣṇa consciousness is always conscious of his actual position as a servitor of the Lord, and thus he is ______ (5) to always serving. Just as leaves and branches of a tree are not separate from the tree, a Kṛṣṇa conscious person cannot think of living a life separate from Kṛṣṇa. He knows that an ______ (6) of water to the root is enough to nourish the leaves and branches too. Thus, by serving the Lord, he also ________ (5) for the Lord's parts and parcels, the living entities. And because he is a servitor to all, he is dear to everyone.

As a devotee is always engaging in service, he is pure in consciousness, his mind and senses are controlled, and he never thinks of ________ (7) anything. There is no chance for such a person to deviate from Kṛṣṇa. He knows that everything in the material world belongs to Kṛṣṇa and that its ________ (8) to think otherwise. He knows that the results of his work also belong to Kṛṣṇa, and so he offers the results to Kṛṣṇa. He remains unattached to the results of his work, like a lotus leaf that remains untouched by the water surrounding it. Like this he performs work, unattached to the results, thereby incurring no reaction; he thus remains aloof from the ________ (8).

By performing work in such consciousness, a devotee gets further purified of material contamination. He has no anxiety over the results of an activity; he can ________ (4, 3) troublesome situation smoothly, and therefore he is never in duality. His activities are on a transcendental plane and have no material effect. Thus he is filled with peace in any ______ (5) of work. To rationalize that there is no existence besides Kṛṣṇa is true __________(11) of peace and fearlessness.

ARTISTIC ACTIVITY

Lotus Incense Holder

Śrīla Prabhupāda explains in his purport to verse 10 that one who knows that everything belongs to Kṛṣṇa and engages everything in His service becomes detached from the results of one's activities just like a lotus leaf remains untouched in water. See Analogy 1 at the end of this chapter.

Make this beautiful lotus incense holder to remind you how the lotus blossoms, floating above the muddy waters of attachment and desire.

Materials needed:
A circular cardboard cutout: diameter around 7 cm; 50 to 60 pistachio shells or plastic spoons (with handles cut) to make lotus petals; hot glue gun; red and green paints; 2 paint brushes.

Steps:

1. Paint at least 45 shells with red paint and around 15 shells with green paint on both sides and let them dry.

2. Use any strong glue and stick two red petals at the center of the circular cardboard. Glue the red shells one by one in a circular pattern as shown in Image 2.

3. As you keep sticking the petal shells, increase the inclination of the petals slightly outward (Image 3).
4. Once the red petals are glued, stick the green petals as the last concentric circle.
5. Light incense sticks and insert them into the small opening at the center of the lotus to offer them to the Deities or Deity images on your altar (Image 4).

Image 1

Image 2

Image 3

Image 4

Explore further why different limbs of the Lord are described as lotus feet, lotus eyes, lotus face, etc. Discuss how you can engage your body, possessions, intelligence, expertise, and all such attributes in the Lord's service so that you can be detached from the results of those activities.

SCIENCE ACTIVITY

The Lotus Effect

Verse 10 states that one who performs his duty without attachment and surrenders the results to the Supreme Lord is unaffected by sinful action, as the lotus leaf is untouched by water.

Did you know that the phenomenon Kṛṣṇa mentions in this verse is called the "Lotus Effect" in science? The Lotus Effect is a natural phenomenon where surfaces, like the leaves of a lotus plant, repel water and dirt from their surfaces. Engineers even use this concept to design water-repellent materials, like raincoats, exterior paints, and antibacterial surfaces. Amazing how nature inspires technology, isn't it?

Learning about the Lotus Effect stimulated Balu's scientific instinct. He is trying to investigate the Lotus Effect with help from Tamal. Here is what Balu is trying to ascertain:

1. How does the lotus leaf repel water, despite water being its habitat?
2. Is the lotus the only plant species that adapts like this?
3. What characteristics do plants without this adaptation display?
4. How different are the two categories of water plants?

Write down what you think Balu came up with.

After he completed his investigation, Balu drew the following picture and shared it with Tamal:

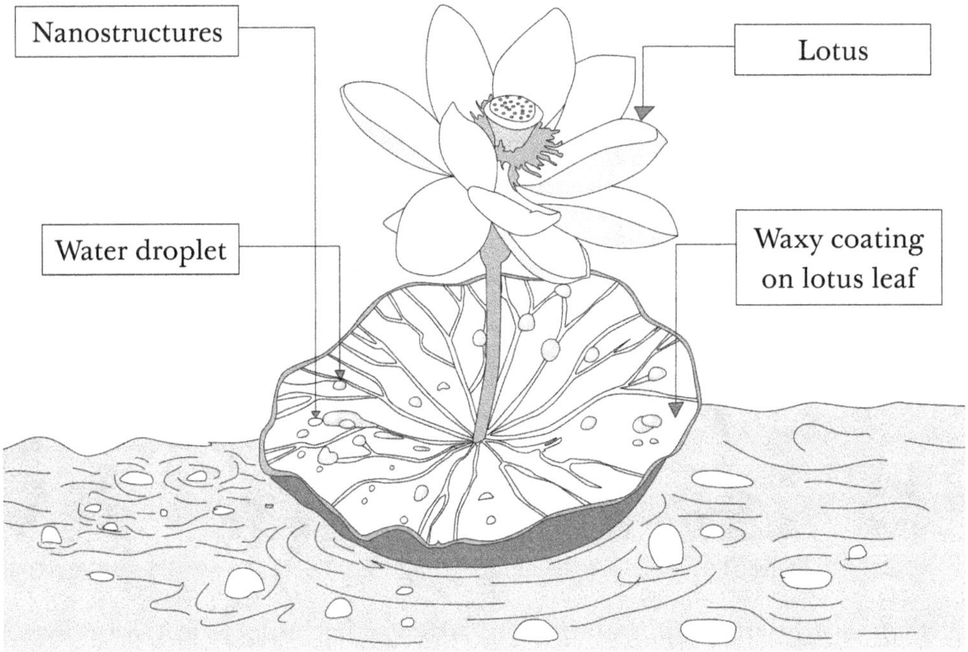

Now Tamal asks Balu to extend his investigation and find the *Bhagavad-gītā* connection to it. Here are three clues Tamal gives Balu:

1. Look at verses 5.7–12 to find the answer. First find the verse that specifically mentions the Lotus Effect.

2. Now read the other verses. Find the key message of these verses. Connect it to the lotus leaf.

3. Illustrate what you understood.

Here is what Balu drew.

Can you explain what Balu understood?

THEME TRACK 3 ACTIVITIES

THEATRICAL ACTIVITY

Whose Fault?

Enact the following skit with a partner and then discuss in class what you learned about who is responsible for our suffering with reference to *BG* 4.14 and *BG* 5.14–15.

Brahmacārī Vidura is reading *Bhagavad-gītā* when Bhakta Neil bursts in. Neil sinks to the ground in an exaggerated manner and covers his face. Neil is wearing lace-up sneakers and western attire.

Bhakta Neil: I'm suffering.

Vidura looks up from his book.

Brahmacārī Vidura: Everyone is.

Neil: No, my suffering is worse. It's suffering squared. No. I lie. It's suffering cubed.

Vidura: People are dying, Neil. Earthquakes, wars, and famines are still happening.

Neil: Vidura, you know what the worst part is?

Vidura: I wait with bated breath.

Neil: Kṛṣṇa did this. It's all Kṛṣṇa's fault.

Vidura: Okay, that was a waste of my bated breath. How did you reach that conclusion?

Neil: I was asleep, dreaming about pizza and cheesecake. You don't happen to have any cheesecake here, do you?

Vidura: No, I don't.

Neil: Too bad. I really need some cheesecake right now. Well, anyway, my phone alarm didn't go off.

Vidura: Okay. So?

Neil: So I didn't wake up in time.

Vidura: In time for what?

Neil: In time for the most important meal of the day: breakfast. So I had to skip breakfast and rush to catch the bus.

Vidura: And did you catch the bus?

Neil: My laces opened, and I tripped and fell. Look at these scratches on my arm.

Vidura examines the scratches.

Vidura: Maybe I need a magnifying glass. Does it still even hurt?

Neil: No, but that's not the point. The point is I missed the bus and was late for my interview for my part-time job.

Vidura: Did you get the job?

Neil: Of course not. All this wouldn't have happened if my alarm had gone off. Why did Kṛṣṇa let this happen? He should have woken me up.

Vidura: Why didn't your alarm go off? Did your phone break?

Neil: No, the battery died.

Vidura: The battery died because you didn't charge it, right?

Neil: Yes, but –

Vidura: Did Kṛṣṇa tell you not to charge your phone?

Neil: No, but –

Vidura: Did Kṛṣṇa tell you not to tie your laces properly?

Neil: No, but –

Vidura: Who didn't charge the phone and tie the laces?

Neil: Me.

Vidura: You like to play board games, right? Let's say you are playing a game. You choose to play the game, but you start losing. Can you blame the owner of the board game for losing?

Neil: No . . . because I rolled the dice and decided to play.

Vidura: Kṛṣṇa owns this board of life. You are the player who chose to play. So why are you blaming Kṛṣṇa for actions that you took or didn't take?

Neil crosses his arms.

Neil: I don't know.

Vidura: Yes, you do. We always know. We just don't want to accept it.

Neil (reluctantly): Because it's easy.

Vidura: Yes. It's easier to blame Kṛṣṇa than to accept responsibility for our own actions.

Neil: I guess . . . This is soooo hard.

Vidura: Neil, you are on a journey. You have to expect bumps, potholes, and road detours along the way. But there's always cheesecake to make you feel better.

Neil (perks up): Cheesecake? I thought you said you didn't have any.

Vidura: I don't. But Govinda's does. Let's go.

Neil smiles.

They walk off stage together with Vidura carrying his *Bhagavad-gītā.*

THEME TRACK 4 ACTIVITIES

LANGUAGE ACTIVITY

Equal Vision

Let's learn the true meaning of "equal vision" as given in verse 18:

"The humble sages, by virtue of true knowledge, see with equal vision a learned and gentle *brāhmaṇa*, a cow, an elephant, a dog and a dog-eater [outcaste]."

Choose one or all of the following short activities:

Activity 1: (Class discussion)
Look at an earth globe or a world map. Students can be called to the front of the classroom and asked to point out a particular country or continent. Discuss a few points that make the people from this place different from others. Note them down on a chart. Then note down what makes them similar. What is the one common spiritual factor in all of them?

Activity 2: (Class art discussion)
Each student dips their hands in various color paints and then prints it on a big chart paper. Then they write their names below it. Learning: All the hands are of a different color, yet they are very similar.

Activity 3: (Current-topics discussion)
Discuss how various discriminations and prejudices – racial, social, economic, gender, and others – can be overcome on the spiritual platform.

Activity 4: (Poem)
In a poem, compare human beings to a rainbow of colors or a forest of various trees, etc. Show that there is beauty in diversity, but on the spiritual platform we are all Kṛṣṇa's children.

Activity 5: (Examples of eyes with equal vision)
In the following table briefly state how each of the characters demonstrated their vision of equality. Include some of your own:

	CHARACTER	PASTIME
1.	King Śibi	
2.	Caitanya Mahāprabhu	
3.	Nityānanda Prabhu	
4.	Śrīla Prabhupāda	
5.		
6.		

CRITICAL-THINKING ACTIVITY

The Happiness Within

Verses 19 to 26 describe the qualities a spiritual seeker should cultivate. Lord Kṛṣṇa says that such a person's mind "is engaged within" (25) and his "happiness is within" (24). Let us understand what this means and how to cultivate these qualities.

Looking within means to understand that our true self is the soul and not the body or senses with which we try to enjoy. Such sense gratification makes us forget our identity as a soul.

In verse 22, Lord Kṛṣṇa describes the limitation of sense enjoyment and encourages us to stop focusing on it. Let us first understand why sense enjoyment isn't worth it.

In verse 22, Kṛṣṇa ironically calls sense enjoyment a "source of misery" and "having a beginning and an end." In other parts of the *Gītā*, He further explains the dangers of sense enjoyment. It is not hard to see why material sense enjoyment cannot bring us full satisfaction or happiness.

The table below lists some characteristics of material happiness. Against each characteristic, write down one or two instances when you may have experienced the listed characteristic of material happiness to be true.

NATURE OF MATERIAL HAPPINESS	EXPERIENCES
Material happiness does not last forever – it has a beginning and an end.	
With time, the intensity of happiness reduces.	
When someone is enjoying more than us, we become dissatisfied with our own happiness.	
When we fail to find material happiness, we end up frustrated.	
We realize that we are not as happy as we expected to be after getting what we wanted.	
We are stopped from fully enjoying our happiness due to sudden tragic events that occur at the same time.	
Material happiness is never completely satisfying – after some time, we feel we have not got enough and want to experience a higher level of happiness.	

Do you now agree with Kṛṣṇa's assessment that sense enjoyment is a source of misery?

As an alternative to sense enjoyment, Kṛṣṇa describes the "happiness within" and that one who seeks this kind of enjoyment becomes liberated. These verses also describe some of the qualities we can cultivate to seek that happiness within.

Given below are the qualities Kṛṣṇa lists in these verses that make a person truly happy and liberated. Again, draw from your personal experience and discuss how each of these qualities can bring you closer to real happiness and help you focus on reviving a spiritual relationship with the Lord.

QUALITY	HOW DOES IT HELP ME TO BECOME HAPPY AND KṚṢṆA CONSCIOUS? HOW DO I CULTIVATE IT?
Is equal to everyone	
Knows that the body is not the true self	
Not attracted to material sense pleasure	
Controls anger	
Experiences happiness in spiritual activities	
Works for the spiritual welfare of all	
Is self-disciplined	
Is constantly trying for perfection (to please the Lord)	

INTROSPECTIVE ACTIVITY

Steps to Liberation

As mentioned in the last activity, Kṛṣṇa describes the qualities of a person that lead to liberation in verses 19 to 26:

a. Has equal vision, which conquers birth and death.

b. Does not rejoice or lament.

c. Realizes that sensual pleasures is an illusion and have a beginning and an end.

d. Fixed in intelligence; not bewildered.

e. Tolerates urges of the senses and checks the forces of desire and anger.

f. Works for everyone's welfare.

g. Directs happiness inwards.

h. Situated in transcendence and knows the science of God.

i. Free from sins, duality, and doubt.

L I B E R A T I O N

In our practice of Kṛṣṇa consciousness, we may see some of these qualities manifest in small ways, which encourage us to continue. In the table below are examples of real-life situations, in which some of these qualities may manifest. Categorize them in the qualities above (write the corresponding letter in the category column). Then think of other situations in your life in which these qualities manifested, and write them in your notebook.

SITUATION	CATEGORY
1. You buy a new shirt, but the pleasure of having it fades away after a few days.	
2. A new pizza corner tempts you every day, but you know that it is not *prasādam*, so you resist it. You are invited to a party where delicious pizza is served.	
3. You have difficulty in controlling bursts of anger. You have had many breakups with friends because of this and you begin to realize this and try to change.	
4. A friend buys the latest model iPhone, and you are also tempted to buy one. You then realize that most of the apps are the same and it is not worth buying.	
5. You enjoy the chips and dip from the nearby takeaway. Next day you are down with stomach pain.	
6. Some of your school friends invite you to the latest nightclub in town, but you bluntly refuse.	
7. You feel sorry for the stray dogs in Vṛndāvana and start collecting funds for their care.	

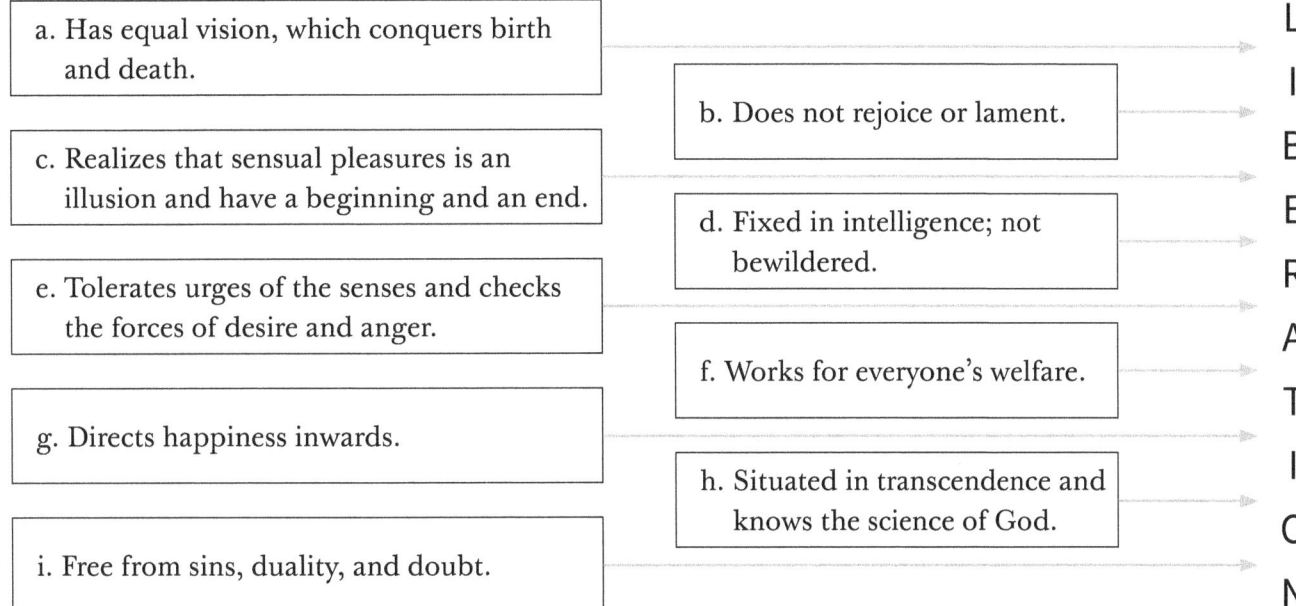

ACTION ACTIVITIES

The Highest Welfare

In his purport to verse 25, Śrīla Prabhupāda states, "Only a person who is fully in Kṛṣṇa consciousness can be said to be engaged in welfare work for all living entities." Why do you think that reviving Kṛṣṇa consciousness is higher than, for example, giving charity or helping others materially? Refer to the purport to find the answer.

Choose either A or B activities:

A. Śrīla Prabhupāda gave us several different ways to perform this welfare work through his temples and communities.

With your study group, a partner, or class, design a series of service-based challenges in which your group and other community members can participate. Roll out these challenges and encourage as many devotees as possible to participate in them. Here are some ideas:

1. Distribute ten books in ten days.
2. Start a book club to read the Kṛṣṇa book.
3. Post at least three devotional stories on your social media accounts in a month.
4. Memorize ten *Bhagavad-gītā* verses (with translations) in five weeks.
5. Visit the temple five times in a month.

When you design a challenge, clearly state how it reflects Śrīla Prabhupāda's mood and mission of benefiting everyone spiritually. After you have completed the challenge, share your experience of the positive impact it had on you and on others.

B. We see Śrīla Prabhupāda's mood of spiritual compassion reflected in the motivated leaders of ISKCON, his disciples, and grand disciples. They carry out Śrīla Prabhupāda's mission of sharing Kṛṣṇa consciousness with others – the highest welfare activity. They run temples, maintain farm communities, write and distribute books, spread the holy name, among many other activities, to revive people's remembrance of Kṛṣṇa.

Make a reel, video, or slide presentation of your favorite leader and their Kṛṣṇa conscious welfare projects that inspire you. Illustrate how they are following Śrīla Prabhupāda's mood of compassion and mercy.

Role-play: The Real Peace Formula

The last verse of this chapter, verse 29, is very important. After clearing Arjuna's doubt about whether renunciation is better than work in devotion, Kṛṣṇa now tells Arjuna that by working with the understanding that Kṛṣṇa is the real master, enjoyer, and friend, Arjuna will attain peace.

Let us understand each aspect properly and why working with this understanding will bring us peace.

Lord Kṛṣṇa says He is the supreme creator and master because:

- He created everything in the material and spiritual worlds.
- He created all living entities.
- He knows every detail of how His creation works.
- He is fully capable of controlling everything in creation.

Lord Kṛṣṇa says He is the supreme enjoyer because:

- As the creator of everything, He has a natural right to enjoy everything within His creation.
- In the spiritual world everything and every action is meant for His enjoyment.

Lord Kṛṣṇa says He is the supreme friend because:

- He is always present with us as a friend as the Supersoul in our hearts.
- He supplies us with all our needs to sustain ourselves and fulfill our desires.
- He speaks the *Bhagavad-gītā* to make us aware of our relationship with Him.
- He sends His intimate associates to teach us how to love and serve Him.

Your *Bhakti-Sastri* mentor has formed a Kṛṣṇa Bhakti World Assembly (similar to the United Nations) with students in your class. If there are more than five students, form groups.

Each student or group is given a statement (from one of the members of our *Bhagavad-gītā* study group) based on verse 29 to work with. Each statement represents the atheistic (or opposite) understanding of what Lord Kṛṣṇa is stating in this verse. Each student is expected to present how a person with this understanding can never attain peace. Then they should each present how adopting a Kṛṣṇa-centric understanding can bring peace. The class is given no more than ten minutes to prepare, and no more than three minutes each to present.

Role-play the character given to you and then prepare a short talk to present to your group or class. The prompts below should help you prepare. Try to make your talk interesting and relevant by adding *śāstric* as well as everyday examples, anecdotes, news stories, or facts that may be intriguing or proving the point. And don't forget, you are role playing, so you can make up some personal experiences based on your character and present that too!

Balu:

Kṛṣṇa as the supreme creator: An atheist thinks that the universe came into existence on its own, and since we are the most intelligent species on Earth, we can exploit it for our own purposes.

Effect (clue): A person may start cultivating greed, covetousness, and an excessive desire to possess things and attain power, etc.

Suggestion to attain peace: ______________________________

Madhu:

Kṛṣṇa as the supreme creator/master: Atheists believe that human life is a rat race in which only the fittest survive, so it is acceptable to exploit others to get ahead.

Effect (clue): Failure to get what we want leads to depression, frustration, and anger. It may make us resort to unfair practices.

Suggestion to attain peace: ______________________________

Tamal:

Kṛṣṇa is the supreme enjoyer: Atheists believe that the world has been created for their own enjoyment, and they have a right to do as they please.

Effect (clue): We become concerned with only our sense pleasure, sometimes disregarding the rights of others and thus exploiting them. We also forget that self-purification is the aim of life.

Suggestion to attain peace: ____

Tara:

Kṛṣṇa as the supreme friend: Atheists believe that everything in the world is a matter of luck and not predestined or determined by God.

Effect (clue): A person may believe only in his own abilities and neither credit God for success nor take shelter of Him in failure.

Suggestion to attain peace: ____

Priya:

Kṛṣṇa as the supreme friend: Atheists believe that God is just an imaginative person created by humans; He neither exists nor helps in times of need.

Effect (clue): We may never have the opportunity to understand the Lord as a loving, caring person who is always with us.

Suggestion to attain peace: ____

ANALOGY ANTHOLOGY

A collection of analogies
for easier understanding

When love for the Divine flows,
attachment to the "likes" goes.

Analogy 1: The Lotus Leaf

One who performs his duty without attachment, surrendering the results unto the Supreme Lord, is unaffected by sinful action, as the lotus leaf is untouched by water.
– *BG* 5.10

Karma only affects those who work for sense gratification; one who works for Kṛṣṇa's pleasure is not bound by *karma*.

Analogy 2: The Soul's Proof

The Lord is the constant companion of the living entity as Paramātmā, or the Supersoul, and therefore He can understand the desires of the individual soul, as one can smell the flavor of a flower by being near it.
– *BG* 5.15, purport

The Paramātmā, who is always with the living being, understands the soul's desires.

If even an app's algorithm can understand what we may like, imagine how much more the Paramātmā understands us!

SACRED RHYTHMS

Important verses
to memorize

***BG* 5.22**

ye hi saṁsparśa-jā bhogā
duḥkha-yonaya eva te
ādy-antavantaḥ kaunteya
na teṣu ramate budhaḥ

An intelligent person does not take part in the sources of misery, which are due to contact with the material senses. O son of Kunti, such pleasures have a beginning and an end, and so the wise man does not delight in them.

***BG* 5.29**

bhoktāraṁ yajña-tapasāṁ
sarva-loka-maheśvaram
suhṛdaṁ sarva-bhūtānāṁ
jñātvā māṁ śāntim ṛcchati

A person in full consciousness of Me, knowing Me to be the ultimate beneficiary of all sacrifices and austerities, the Supreme Lord of all planets and demigods, and the benefactor and well-wisher of all living entities, attains peace from the pangs of material miseries.

ANSWERS

Learning Harmonies

1. b; 2. b; 3. c; 4. b; 5. b; 6. c; 7. b; 8. d; 9. d; 10.c

The Highest Philosophy *(Potential Answers)*

Practical and pleasing to all the senses.
High-minded.
Incomparable: No other process is comparable to it in terms of knowledge, application, and the goal.
Logical: There is no artificial imposition; loving and serving the Lord is natural to the soul.
Optimistic: A small endeavor on this path saves one from the greatest danger.
Service: Loving service to the Lord and His parts and parcels is the greatest welfare activity.
Omnipotent: Bhakti is so powerful that it conquers the unconquerable Lord.
Purifies: Acquired conditioning and inclinations.
Harmonious: With our eternal identity.
Youthful: Kṛṣṇa consciousness is ever fresh and joyful.

Anagram Fun

prone; onrush; cares; gaining; thievery; creation; exit any; field; realization

The Lotus Effect

What Balu discovered about the Lotus Effect: 1. The leaf has a waxy coating that repels water, and micro- and nanostructures, or tiny bumps, collate the water into droplets, which roll off the surface; 2–3. Some other plants like the water lily and Indian mustard have similar adaptations, but hydrilla and duckweed do not – they get wet; 4. "Wet" plants have different kinds of adaptations to protect themselves, which are different from the lotus.

Verse 5.10 mentions the Lotus Effect. The verses related to it describe how a *niṣkāma-karma-yogī* (lotus leaf), while living in the material world (lake), performs all kinds of activities and offers the results to the Lord. Since he acts for the Lord, he does not incur reactions to the actions (waxy coating), although always acting. In the example Balu drew, the boy is distributing books and collecting donations; although he appears to be a salesman, he does not incur reactions like an ordinary salesman because he is engaged in the service of the Lord.

Equal Vision

Activity 5: King Śibi: He saved a pigeon's life from a vulture by offering his own flesh; Caitanya Mahāprabhu: He gave His remnants to a dog, who had accompanied Śivānanda Sena to Jagannātha Purī, and liberated it. He inspired all the animals in Jhārikhaṇḍa forest to dance and chant in ecstasy; Nityānanda Prabhu: He showed mercy to Jagāi and Mādhāi, one of the most sinful people of the time; Śrīla Prabhupāda: He made Kṛṣṇa consciousness available to everyone, irrespective of any external designation.

Steps to Liberation

1. c; 2. e; 3. e; 4. d & e; 5. c; 6. d; 7. f

CHAPTER 6

Dhyāna-yoga

CHAPTER BEATS

An overview

"A *karma-yogī*, one who is not attached to the results of one's work, is a true *sannyāsī* and *yogī*," Kṛṣṇa continued to explain, "not one who is inactive and doesn't perform any duty. One cannot be a *yogī* unless they are free from the desire to enjoy the senses."

Kṛṣṇa was trying to make Arjuna understand that real *sannyāsa* and *yoga* means that one should understand one's spiritual position as a loving servant of the Lord and act accordingly. Such a person renounces sense enjoyment and engages the senses only for pleasing Kṛṣṇa – not for self-satisfaction. In this way, a devotee is the perfect *sannyāsī* and *yogī*.

Kṛṣṇa then explained that *aṣṭāṅga-yoga*, the eightfold *yoga* system, is another way to control the mind and senses and reach the liberated stage. It consists of *yama*, regulations or prohibitions (don'ts); *niyama*, rules or prescriptions (do's); *āsana*, physical exercises; *prāṇāyāma*, breathing exercises; *pratyāhāra*, withdrawing the senses from sense objects; *dhāraṇā*, focusing the mind on the Lord's form; *dhyāna*, deep meditation on the Lord; and *samādhi*, complete absorption or trance. The process can be compared to a ladder, the lower rung called the *yogāruruksu* stage and the highest rung the *yogārūḍha* stage. The *yogāruruksu* stage involves early efforts in meditation by following rules and regulations and practicing different sitting postures to control the mind and senses. It is meant to bring one to the *yogārūḍha* stage, one of perfect self-realization and absorption in the Lord, called *samādhi*. But first one needs to control the mind and become detached from material things.

Arjuna listened attentively. He wondered how he could reach this level of pure spiritual consciousness.

Kṛṣṇa said, "You must deliver yourself with the help of your mind, O Arjuna, not degrade yourself. The mind can be your best friend, if you control it, or your greatest enemy, if you don't.

"Those who have conquered the mind are on the *yogārūḍha* stage. Because they control the mind, they can follow the guidance of the Supersoul in the heart. As a result, they are equipoised in happiness and distress, heat and cold, and honor and dishonor. Such a *yogī* is fully satisfied through transcendental knowledge. He sees everything – whether pebbles or gold – the same. He also sees friends and enemies and the pious and the sinners with an equal mind.

"In this *yogārūḍha* stage, one engages one's body, mind, and self in *samādhi*; one lives alone in a secluded place, controls the mind, and doesn't think he owns anything.

"An *aṣṭāṅga-yogī* sits upright, fixes the mind, and meditates on My form. Withdrawing the mind from sense objects, he makes Me the goal of life. And what is the result?"

Arjuna smiled, beginning to see his friend and relative in a different light.

"He attains the kingdom of God!" Kṛṣṇa exclaimed. "And while living in this world, he who is regulated in eating, sleeping, recreation, and work can become free from material miseries. He stays steady in meditation on the self, like a lamp that doesn't waver in a windless place. In perfect *samādhi* (trance), a *yogī* gets boundless spiritual bliss; having obtained this he thinks there's no greater gain; in full determination he is never shaken even in the greatest difficulty. A *yogī* withdraws the mind through his intelligence and brings it under the control of the self. He is peaceful by being fixed on the Supreme. He sees every living being in the Lord and the Lord everywhere. Such a devotee is never lost to the Lord, nor the Lord is lost to him."

Arjuna's face became grave. He said, "O Madhusūdana, this system of *yoga* that you've summarized appears impractical and too difficult to follow, for the mind is restless, unsteady, and obstinate. It is very strong, O Kṛṣṇa, and I think controlling it is harder than controlling the wind."

Kṛṣṇa smiled and nodded reassuringly. "O mighty-armed son of Kunti," He said, "it is undoubtedly very difficult to subdue the restless mind, but it is possible by practice and detachment. If you don't control the mind, self-realization is difficult, but if you strive to control it, you will be successful."

Arjuna thought for a while and then asked, "What happens to someone who falls away from both material and spiritual paths, with no position, like a riven cloud in the sky?"

Kṛṣṇa, the Supreme Personality of Godhead, answered, "Son of Pṛthā, a transcendentalist can never be destroyed in this world or in the spiritual world, because one who does good, My friend, is never defeated by evil.

"After many years of enjoyment in the higher planets, the unsuccessful *yogī* is born into a righteous or aristocratic family. And if he is more fortunate, he is born into a family of devotees who have great wisdom. Such a birth is rare. He then gets the chance to revive his spiritual consciousness from his past life and achieve complete success.

"My dear Arjuna, a *yogī* is greater than an ascetic (*tapasvī*), a great thinker (*jñānī*), or someone who works for rewards (*karmī*). So be a *yogī*, O Arjuna.

"And of all *yogīs*, do you know who is the best?"

Arjuna shook his head.

"Of all *yogīs*, the one who has great faith in Me, who always thinks of Me and serves Me with love, is most closely connected with me in *yoga* and is the highest of all. This is my opinion, O Arjuna."

For Arjuna, Kṛṣṇa's opinion mattered the most. He understood and accepted that all other forms of *yoga* lead toward *bhakti-yoga*. When *karma-yoga* increases in knowledge and renunciation, the stage is called *jñāna-yoga*; when *jñāna-yoga* increases in meditation on the Supersoul, it is called *aṣṭāṅga-yoga*; and when one surpasses this stage and comes to Kṛṣṇa, it culminates in *bhakti-yoga*.

Arjuna gazed at Kṛṣṇa, whose beautiful complexion resembled a monsoon cloud, whose lotuslike face shone like the sun, whose dress sparkled like jewels, and who radiated a resplendent luster.

His heart leapt with joy as he began to see Kṛṣṇa for who He truly was and appreciated that Kṛṣṇa was teaching him the highest truths.

THEME TRACKS

Themes and key messages
to contemplate and discuss

THEME TRACKS	REFERENCES	KEY MESSAGES
Theme Track 1 *Aṣṭāṅga-yoga*, the eightfold *yoga* system, is a means to control the mind and senses.	6.1–9	Chapter 5 describes *niṣkāma-karma-yoga* and touches on *aṣṭāṅga-yoga* to obtain liberation. In this chapter, Kṛṣṇa explains *aṣṭāṅga-yoga* in more detail. The beginning stage, called *yogārurukṣu*, which involves cultivating detachment and performing *āsanas*, etc., gradually purifies the heart of material desires. The advanced stage, *yogārūḍha*, is when one is completely purified of material desires. One neither acts for sense gratification nor engages in fruitive activities. This is the stage of steady meditation (*dhyāna*). One needs to control the mind, as the mind can be one's best friend if one conquers it or the worst enemy if one does not.
Theme Track 2 The different stages of the *aṣṭāṅga-yoga* system are meant to bring one to the stage of *samādhi*, exclusive meditation on the Supreme.	6.10–32	The practices in the *yogārūḍha* stage are meant to bring one to the platform of meditating on the Lord's form. The goal is the cessation of material existence and attainment of the Lord's kingdom. In perfect *samādhi* (trance), a *yogī* gets boundless spiritual bliss; having obtained this he thinks there's no greater gain; in full determination he is never shaken even in the greatest difficulty. On this *brahma-bhūta* platform, realizing the *ātmā*, a *yogī* can withdraw the mind and bring it under the control of the self. He is peaceful by being fixed on the Supreme. He sees every living being in the Lord and the Lord everywhere. Such a devotee is never lost to the Lord, nor is the Lord lost to him.
Theme Track 3 *Aṣṭāṅga-yoga* is difficult due to the fickle mind.	6.33–36	Arjuna tells Kṛṣṇa that for an ordinary person the process of *aṣṭāṅga-yoga* is impractical and difficult, for the mind is restless and unsteady. To subdue the mind is more difficult than controlling the wind. Kṛṣṇa advises Arjuna that the mind can only be controlled by practice and detachment. One has to control the mind to practice *yoga* and seek self-realization. *Yoga* practice without mind control is a waste of time, like pouring water onto a fire while trying to ignite it.

THEME TRACKS	REFERENCES	KEY MESSAGES
Theme Track 4 *Bhakti-yoga* is the best path because it is the most direct method of God realization; all other paths culminate in *bhakti-yoga*.	6.37–47	To attain self-realization, one can follow the path of *karma-yoga*, *jñāna-yoga*, *aṣṭāṅga-yoga*, or *bhakti-yoga*. *Bhakti-yoga* is the most direct path to the Lord, and all other paths are supposed to lead to *bhakti-yoga*. With even a little endeavor on this path of *bhakti*, one can be delivered. An unsuccessful *yogī* goes to the higher planets, after which he is born on earth into a righteous or rich family. He revives the divine consciousness of his previous life and strives again for complete perfection. Since *bhakti-yoga* is the topmost of all *yoga* practices, a *bhakti-yogī* is the best *yogī*, according to Kṛṣṇa, greater than a *karmī*, *jñānī*, or *tapasvī*. One who always thinks of Kṛṣṇa and worships and serves Him with great faith is intimately united with Him in *yoga*.

SOLO QUESTIONS

To enhance your self-study

(Find the answers in the verse and purport references provided in brackets.)

1. How is a Kṛṣṇa conscious person a true *yogī* and *sannyāsī*? (6.1)
2. Why is a Kṛṣṇa conscious person considered to be situated on the upper rung of the *aṣṭāṅga-yoga* process? (6.3)
3. When is the mind the best friend and when is it the greatest enemy? (6.6)
4. When one is absorbed in the Supreme, what state of mind does one achieve? (6.7)
5. How is a Kṛṣṇa conscious person the perfect *yogī*? (6.10)
6. What is the result of extravagance in eating, sleeping, defending, and mating? (6.17)
7. Give the English meaning of the term *yukta*. How is a *yogī* well situated and distinguished from an ordinary person? (6.18)
8. *Yogīs* who are attracted to sense enjoyment cannot attain the stage of perfection. How is Kṛṣṇa consciousness – *karma-yoga* and *bhakti-yoga* – the best practice of *yoga*? (6.23)
9. What is *pratyāhāra* and how can one achieve this? (6.25)
10. Describe how the devotee becomes "one with Kṛṣṇa." (6.30–31)
11. Why does Arjuna describe the *aṣṭāṅga-yoga* system as impractical and difficult? (6.33–34)
12. Describe what happens to an unsuccessful or fallen *yogī*. (6.41–42)

LEARNING HARMONIES

Multiple-choice questions
to quiz your memory

(Choose the most complete answer.)

1. What is the true definition of a *sannyāsī* and a *yogī*?
   a. One who renounces all actions and possessions.
   b. One who performs prescribed duties without attachment to the results.
   c. One who sits in meditation all day.
   d. One who lives in solitude and avoids all material activities.

2. What is said to be the purpose of *yoga*?
   a. To detach oneself from family and society.
   b. To elevate the self and not degrade it.
   c. To achieve material success through discipline.
   d. To focus solely on renunciation.

3. What does Kṛṣṇa explain about the mind?
   a. The mind is always one's best friend.
   b. For one who has conquered the mind, the mind is the best friend.
   c. The mind cannot be controlled by anyone.
   d. The mind is always an enemy, whether conquered or not.

4. Where does Kṛṣṇa recommend an *aṣṭāṅga-yogī* to meditate?
   a. In a crowded place to test their concentration.
   b. On a sacred mountain surrounded by disciples.
   c. In a secluded, sanctified, clean, and quiet place.
   d. In a temple.

5. What type of lifestyle is considered unsuitable for a *yogī*?
   a. A life of excessive eating or fasting.
   b. A life of devotion to spiritual practices.
   c. A life of renunciation of all work.
   d. A life of arduous penances and austerities.

6. What is the state of the mind of a successful *yogī*?
   a. Disturbed by material desires but focused on renunciation.
   b. Completely pacified, focused on the self, and free from material desires.
   c. Restless but disciplined through austerities.
   d. Detached but focused on acquiring mystic powers.

7. What does Kṛṣṇa say about the vision of a *yogī*?
   a. A *yogī* sees only spiritual things and ignores the material world.
   b. A *yogī* sees all living beings as equal and sees the Lord in all beings.
   c. A *yogī* focuses on personal needs and disregards others.
   d. A *yogī* is blind to differences and avoids worldly interactions.

8. What does Kṛṣṇa declare about the highest *yogī*?
   a. He sits in the forest and meditates.
   b. He renounces all worldly duties.
   c. He worships Kṛṣṇa with love and faith.
   d. He has mastered physical postures.

9. What does Kṛṣṇa say about the fate of unsuccessful *yogīs*?
    a. They are doomed to be born into lower species of life.
    b. They are granted a chance to continue their practice in the next life.
    c. They lose all spiritual progress and start over.
    d. They remain in eternal suffering until liberation.

10. What is the ultimate goal of *yoga*?
    a. Achieving physical perfection and mental clarity.
    b. Realizing oneself as Brahman and attaining liberation.
    c. Becoming detached from society and material possessions.
    d. Developing unalloyed love for Kṛṣṇa.

MEDLEY ACTS

A variety of fun activities to learn from

THEME TRACK 1 ACTIVITIES

LANGUAGE ACTIVITY

Aṣṭāṅga-Yoga and Bhakti-Yoga

Aṣṭāṅga-yoga consists of two stages: the practicing stage of meditation (*yogārurukṣu*) and the perfected stage of meditation (*yogārūḍha*). In a short paragraph explain these stages, referring to verses 3 and 4 and their purports, and then describe how the practice of Kṛṣṇa consciousness (*bhakti-yoga*) can easily help one to reach the perfected stage without the tedious practices of *aṣṭāṅga-yoga*. Also compare the intentions and the results of *bhakti-yoga* to *aṣṭāṅga-yoga*.

INTROSPECTIVE ACTIVITY

Mind: Friend or Enemy?

The purpose of *yoga* practice is to control the mind and use it to uplift, not degrade, oneself. One who cannot control the mind lives with the greatest enemy. However, if one can subdue the mind with intelligence and Kṛṣṇa conscious practices, the mind becomes the greatest friend.

With the help of a partner, analyze the following scenario to see how the mind can act as an enemy, and as a friend.

Mind as an enemy:

"Go, talk to her! She is the only one who can help you with your project," whispered my friend, Rohit, into my ears. Rohit was right. I needed Anushka's help badly. I started walking towards her when my mind cried out, "Wait! She's a girl! Girls like to talk only to smart boys." My heart sank. I looked at Rohit, who was now talking to another girl, Amisha, about his project. My mind barged in again, "But Rohit has always been popular with girls, remember? He is smart! You are not! You stammer when you talk to girls!"

Well, maybe my mind was right. My head hung in shame and my body grew heavy; I knew I could not get myself to speak with Anushka at all now. As I turned back, my mind again reeled with negative thoughts, "You've never been able to make others laugh by saying something witty. Half the time you are unable to even understand what others have to say . . . you are hopeless, and you always will be hopeless."

I returned to my hostel room, threw myself onto my bed, and spent the rest of the day mindlessly watching reels on Instagram. My project remained untouched, and without Anushka's help or any work on my part, I got an E grade on my assignment.

Mind as a friend:

"Girls like to talk to smart boys, true," said my mind when I was reluctant to speak to Anushka about my project. "But they also like to talk to gentle and kind-hearted boys. You are one of them."

Then when I began to doubt my ability to speak, my mind reminded me: "Sometimes you do stammer when you talk to friends, boys or girls, but that's okay. The more you talk with new friends, the more you will overcome your nervousness, and stammering will stop."

The mind added, "You may not be witty, but you are a storyteller. You always have brilliant anecdotes to share with your friends. And you will learn more with time."

When we can train our mind to act as a friend, we will observe how our mind will act as our friend and also encourage us on the path of devotion.

Now think of a scenario in your life in which your mind acted as an enemy. Write down the incident as done in the example above. Then reframe your thoughts so your mind learns to act as your friend.

Finally, summarize the role of the mind in *yoga* practice with reference to verses 5 and 6.

THEME TRACK 2 ACTIVITIES

ARTISTIC ACTIVITY

Aṣṭāṅga-Yoga Ferris Wheel

Description: In this chapter Kṛṣṇa emphasizes the importance of controlling the mind through a disciplined practice, a key aspect of *aṣṭāṅga-yoga*. *Aṣṭāṅga-yoga* is the eight-limbed (*aṣṭa-aṅga*) path with the goal of achieving self-realization. It includes the following stages:

1. *Yama*: Don'ts: Regulations or prohibitions
2. *Niyama*: Do's: Rules or prescriptions
3. *Āsana*: Bodily exercises
4. *Prāṇāyāma*: Breathing exercises
5. *Pratyāhāra*: Withdrawal of the senses from sense objects
6. *Dhāraṇā*: Absorption of the mind on the Lord's form
7. *Dhyāna*: Intensified meditation on the Lord (limb by limb starting from His lotus feet).
8. *Samādhi*: Complete absorption/trance

In the highest stage of perfection, *samādhi*, the *aṣṭāṅga-yogī* sees Paramātmā (the Supersoul) in all living beings and every living being in the Lord. In other words, he sees Kṛṣṇa everywhere.

Have you ever taken a ride in a Ferris wheel at an amusement park? If so, what was it like at the highest point? Wasn't it breathtaking or thrilling? Let's bring out your creativity in making an *aṣṭāṅga-yoga* Ferris wheel.

Materials needed: Popsicle sticks (around 60), glue gun, scissors, 2 circular cutouts (8 cm in diameter), thin cardboard for making frames, skewers (around 10), one-hole hand punch.

Steps:

1. Glue eight popsicle sticks around the center of the circular cutout and complete the triangles with eight more sticks to make an octagonal wheel. Make another similar wheel (Image 1).
2. Attach four 11cm popsicle sticks to the center of one wheel as shown in Image 1.
3. Now attach the four sticks to the second wheel, connecting them in such a way that all the triangles coincide with each other (Image 2).
4. Make rectangular frames with thin cardboard for the eight stages of *aṣṭāṅga-yoga* and add brief details as in the description section above (Image 3).
5. Then take eight skewers of 14 cm each and 16 small circular cutouts with holes punched at the center of each. Insert two circles at the end of each of the skewers. Attach and glue the frames between the circles as shown in Image 3.

6. Now let's make the stand. Make two triangles with their longer sides crossing each other slightly at their ends to form a small "V" shape at their intersection.
7. Go for a broader rectangular base and attach the triangles on both the ends, slightly bent towards each other. Hold the triangles until the glue dries up and they become firm, as in Image 4.
8. Insert a skewer to pass through both the centers of the wheels and place the whole structure in between the triangles of the stand, with the ends of the skewers on the "V" shapes. Leave at least an inch between the center of the wheel and the stands to ensure the free movement of the wheel (Image 5).
9. Hang the frames at the corners of the octagon, along the wheel, following the right sequence as in the description.
10. Our amazing *aṣṭāṅga-yoga* Ferris wheel is now ready to rotate (Image 6). Add any further decorations as desired.

Image 1

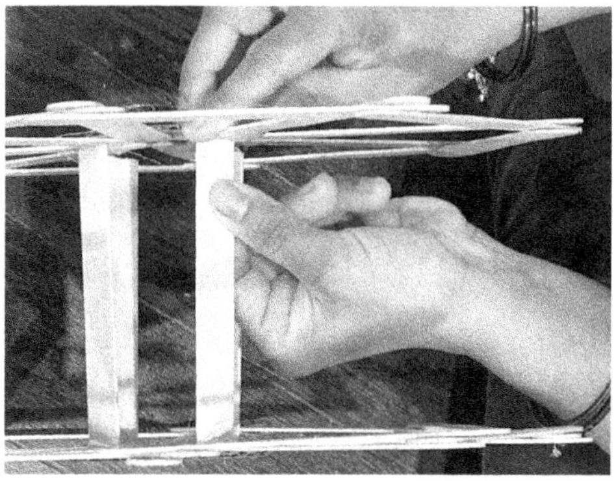
Image 2

Image 3

Image 4

Image 5

Image 6

Meditate on when *samādhi* is reached at the top, how one's "view" is the best.

LANGUAGE ACTIVITY

Results of Various Yoga Practices

In the table below fill in the respective description and results of *karma-kāṇḍa*, *karma-yoga*, *jñāna-yoga*, and *dhyāna-yoga*, with reference to the appropriate verses from *Bhagavad-gītā*.

YOGA	BG REFERENCES	DESCRIPTION AND RESULTS
1. *Karma-kāṇḍa*	2.42–43	
2. *Karma-yoga*	3.9 (rest of Chapter 3)	
3. *Jñāna-yoga*	4.41	
4. *Dhyāna-yoga*	6.10–32	
5. *Bhakti-yoga*	6.47	

THEME TRACK 3 ACTIVITIES

LANGUAGE ACTIVITIES

Yoga for the Modern Age

In this chapter Lord Kṛṣṇa describes *aṣṭāṅga-yoga* as a means of achieving liberation. But Arjuna doubts its practicality in this age due to many factors. One is the difficulty to control the mind, which is an essential element in the practice of *yoga*. However, the mind can be easily controlled by engaging it in the service of Lord Kṛṣṇa.

The table below presents other challenges in the practice of *aṣṭāṅga-yoga*. First read verse 33 and purport and then match each challenge in the table with the corresponding advantage of practicing *bhakti-yoga* instead:

	AṢṬĀṄGA-YOGA CHALLENGES		BHAKTI-YOGA PRACTICALITIES
1	Renouncing material desires mechanically.	a	Meant for all ages, genders, and health conditions.
2	Meditating on objects.	b	Purifies material desires by associating with Kṛṣṇa and His devotees.
3	Giving up home and family.	c	Engaging home, family, resources, and everything in Kṛṣṇa's service.
4	Denying sense gratification.	d	Meditating on the supremely pure and purifying Kṛṣṇa.
5	Practicing difficult postures and breathing techniques is not practical in Kali-yuga due to our short lifespan, laziness, and disturbed minds.	e	Satisfying the senses of Kṛṣṇa satisfies our senses.

AṢṬĀṄGA-YOGA CHALLENGES		BHAKTI-YOGA PRACTICALITIES	
6	Practicing in solitude in the *yogārūḍha* stage can lead to falldown.	f	Chanting of the holy names is the easiest and most powerful and the panacea for diseased minds in Kali-yuga.
7	Not practical for all age groups, health conditions, etc.	g	Associating with likeminded devotees helps in all stages of practice.

Essay: Aṣṭāṅga-Yoga in Kṛṣṇa Consciousness

Śrīla Prabhupāda explains in verse 32 purport: "Kṛṣṇa consciousness is the highest stage of trance in *yoga* practice."

In an essay discuss how the principles of *aṣṭāṅga-yoga* are automatically included in Kṛṣṇa consciousness.

First discuss the eightfold steps as described in the story summary. Then draw a correlation between them and Kṛṣṇa consciousness. For example, just as *aṣṭāṅga-yoga* begins with following regulations and prohibitions, *bhakti-yoga* also begins by following certain rules and regulations, hearing about Kṛṣṇa (*śravaṇaṁ*), glorifying Kṛṣṇa (*kīrtanaṁ*), and then remembering Him (*smaraṇaṁ*). Just as *aṣṭāṅga-yoga* has different stages of remembrance, *bhakti-yoga* has five progressive stages of remembrance and meditation, as explained by Śrīla Prabhupāda in the purport to verse 8 of *Śrī Upadeśāmṛta* (*Nectar of Instruction*). These are recollection, absorption, meditation, constant remembrance, and trance. Refer to the descriptions of each of these stages in *NOI*. Then choose an example of a devotee who was immersed in thoughts of the Lord and describe their progressive stages of remembrance and absorption, e.g., Bhīṣmadeva, Ambarīṣa Mahārāja, Dhruva Mahārāja, Prahlāda Mahārāja, the *gopīs*, etc.

ACTION AND INTROSPECTIVE ACTIVITY

Practice and Detachment

In verse 35, Kṛṣṇa indicates that it's not impossible to control the mind: "O mighty-armed son of Kunti, it is undoubtedly very difficult to curb the restless mind, but it is possible by suitable practice and detachment." Practice means regularly and sincerely doing activities that help

us grow in Kṛṣṇa consciousness. Detachment means avoiding activities that weaken our relationship with Kṛṣṇa. Both practice and detachment support each other. Of all favorable activities, hearing about Kṛṣṇa and chanting His holy names are the most important and powerful ways to develop attraction for Him. This attraction brings spiritual satisfaction, and thus the mind becomes peaceful.

Activity: Select an activity of hearing about Kṛṣṇa. It could be the holy name in *japa* or *kīrtana* or hearing and reading about Kṛṣṇa's pastimes. Choose a peaceful space, a fixed time and duration (more or less half an hour), and practice this routine every day. This helps in increasing our absorption. Every day, before you begin, state your intention to hear the sound vibration with concentration. Hearing attentively engages three senses: tongue, ears, and mind. Try your best to hear every syllable. The mind may drift but be alert and bring it back to the sound.

To the examples given below, add important factors to improve your practice and to develop more detachment. You may add more to the list later from your experience:

Practice (do's): Sit in a comfortable position; choose a solitary or disturbance-free place; bring the mind back when distracted; ______________________________

____

____

Detachment (don'ts): Don't have a phone near you; don't let the mind wander; don't make a to-do-list in the mind while hearing; ______________________________

____

____

At the end of five days review your observations with a friend. Were you aware that the mind can wander so frequently? Did you observe common distractions? Did you remember to bring the mind back to hearing? Did you feel peaceful after attentive hearing? What changes would you like to make in your daily routine to improve your focus? Please continue for another five days.

THEME TRACK 4 ACTIVITIES

LANGUAGE ACTIVITY

The Destination of a Fallen Yogī

In verses 37–39, Arjuna asks Kṛṣṇa about the fate of a *yogī* who somehow falls from the path of spiritual practice. In verses 40–45, Kṛṣṇa explains that fallen *yogis*, after spending some time in the heavenly planets, are born either in rich or pious families or in a family of devotees. They are given another chance to attain spiritual perfection, and their endeavors are never wasted. Śrīla Prabhupāda also says that some great families raise transcendentalists generation after generation and that great souls are still born in such families.

The *Bhāgavatam* gives several examples of such personalities. Some, including exalted souls who were born in devotee families, are shown in the pictures below.

Identify each personality and choose three to write a short paragraph about (50–75 words each). Remember to include:

a. The name of the personality
b. Whether they were a fallen practitioner or a great transcendentalist
c. How they either got a second chance to continue their spiritual journey and perfect their lives, or how they used their special birth to help with the Lord's mission

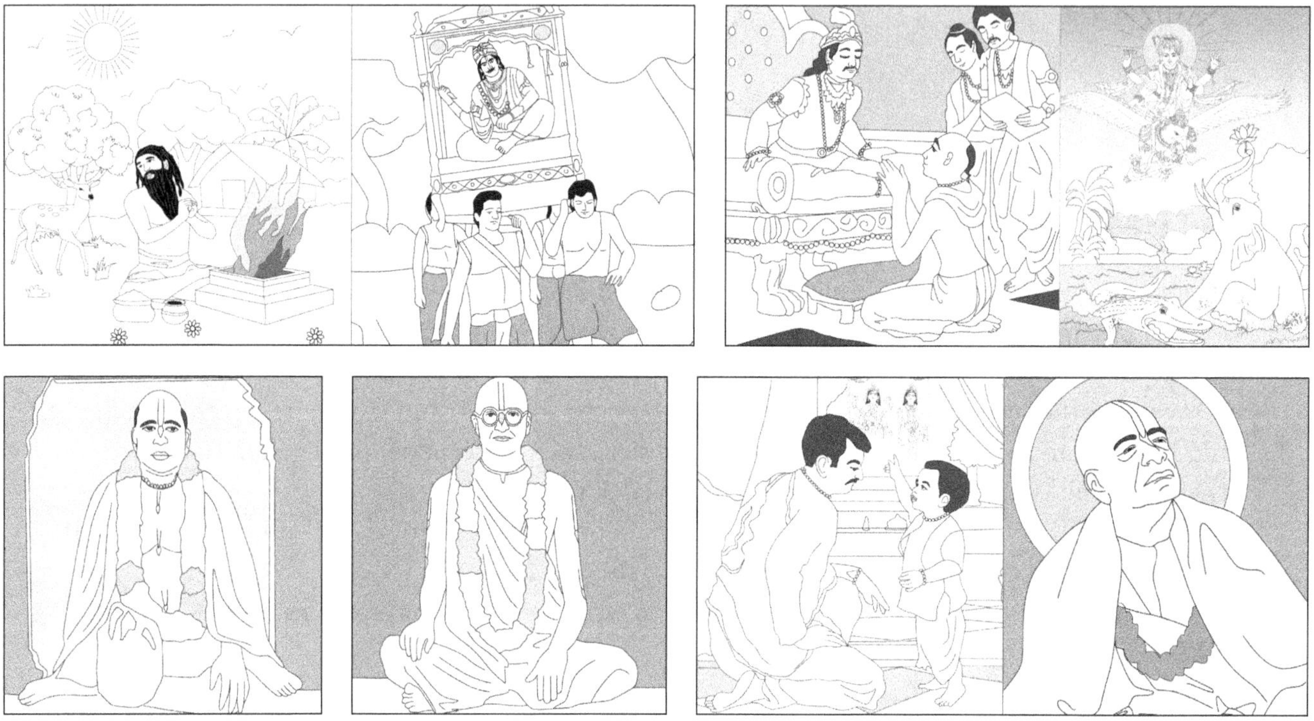

Śrīla Prabhupāda also states that children born or raised in ISKCON are Vaikuṇṭha children. What do you understand about this in the context of these verses?

SCIENCE ACTIVITY

The Yoga Ladder

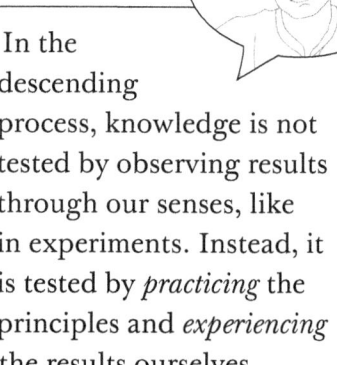

> In the descending process, knowledge is not tested by observing results through our senses, like in experiments. Instead, it is tested by *practicing* the principles and *experiencing* the results ourselves.

A body of knowledge can be called scientific if it meets three main principles: universality (it holds true across cultures, societies, and contexts), generality (it applies in different places and circumstances), and repeatability (it gives the same accurate results when tested again and again). The *yoga* process Kṛṣṇa describes in the *Bhagavad-gītā* meets these criteria and is therefore scientific. It follows the descending (*śabda*) process.

The word *yoga* means "linking" or "connecting" with the Supreme.

Yoga helps us connect to Kṛṣṇa, or God. So far, Kṛṣṇa has described the process of *sakāma-karma yoga*, *niṣkāma-karma yoga*, *jñāna-yoga*, *aṣṭāṅga-yoga*, and by the end of this chapter He will introduce *bhakti-yoga*. All these types of *yoga* help us connect with the Lord, either directly or indirectly.

They are arranged in a sequence called the "Yoga Ladder," based on how strongly each one connects the *yogī* with the Lord. Let's explore the rungs of this ladder and understand the following:

a. What a *yogī* needs to do to be situated on each of the rungs.
b. To what extent a *yogī* situated on each rung can realize the Lord.

Look at the Yoga Ladder here. It rests against a "Yoga Wall," which gives helpful information about each *yoga* process and shows how much the Lord can be realized at each stage.

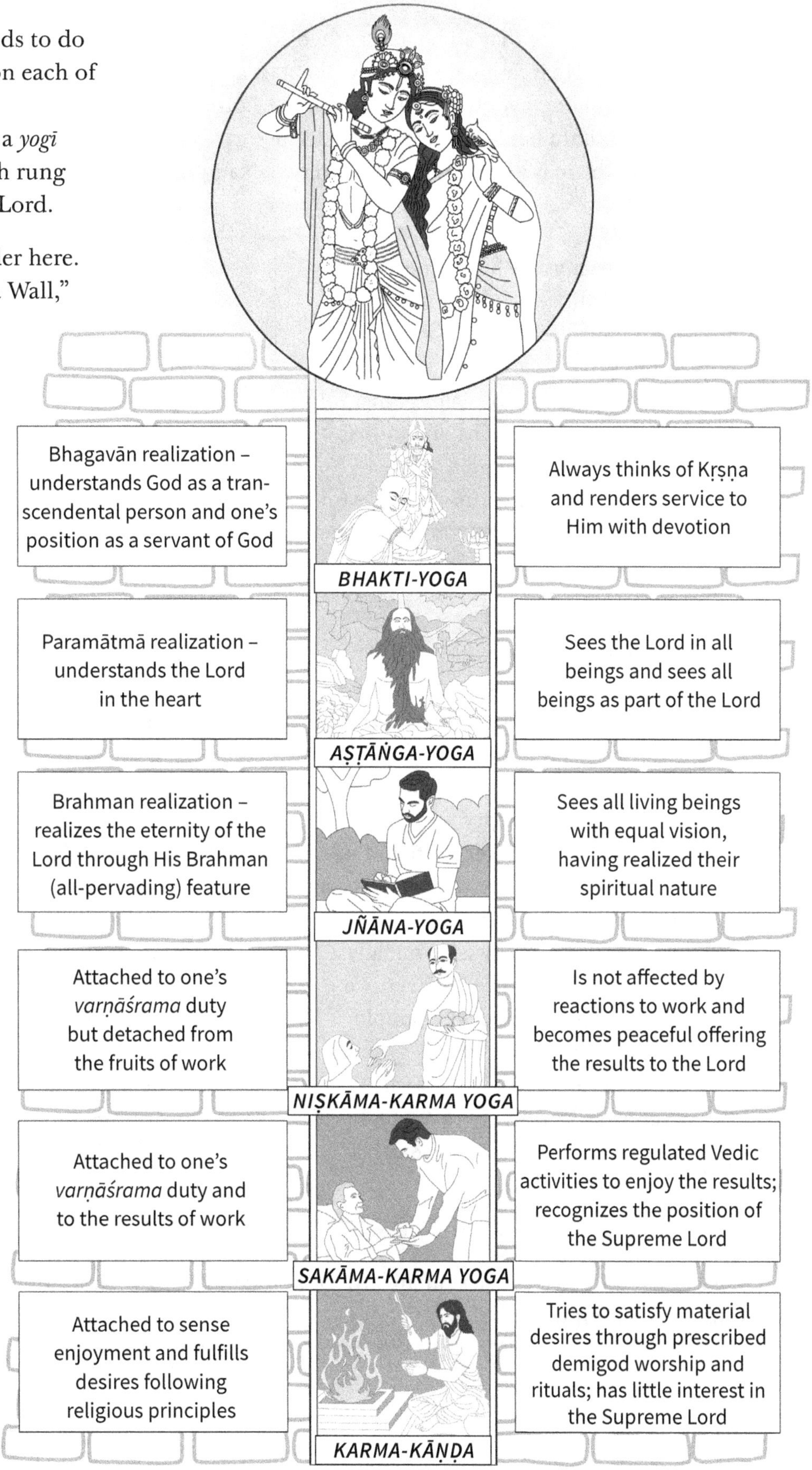

Bhagavān realization – understands God as a transcendental person and one's position as a servant of God
Always thinks of Kṛṣṇa and renders service to Him with devotion
BHAKTI-YOGA
Paramātmā realization – understands the Lord in the heart
Sees the Lord in all beings and sees all beings as part of the Lord
AṢṬĀṄGA-YOGA
Brahman realization – realizes the eternity of the Lord through His Brahman (all-pervading) feature
Sees all living beings with equal vision, having realized their spiritual nature
JÑĀNA-YOGA
Attached to one's *varṇāśrama* duty but detached from the fruits of work
Is not affected by reactions to work and becomes peaceful offering the results to the Lord
NIṢKĀMA-KARMA YOGA
Attached to one's *varṇāśrama* duty and to the results of work
Performs regulated Vedic activities to enjoy the results; recognizes the position of the Supreme Lord
SAKĀMA-KARMA YOGA
Attached to sense enjoyment and fulfills desires following religious principles
Tries to satisfy material desires through prescribed demigod worship and rituals; has little interest in the Supreme Lord
KARMA-KĀṆḌA

Balu is thrilled to see that all he has learned so far in the *Bhagavad-gītā* has been placed into a Yoga Ladder. He is fascinated by how the *yoga* systems connect as rungs, with each system progressively giving a higher realization of the Lord. He is looking to understand deeper.

In school, Balu has learned to create science cards to study how different phenomena work scientifically. Here is a definition card and two example cards he has created:

Scientific analysis – 3 parameters

1. Universality – the knowledge/principle works everywhere, no matter the place or culture.
2. Generality – the principle can apply to different situations or contexts.
3. Repeatability: If you test the principle multiple times in the same way, you get the same results.

Card 1: Gravity

Gravity is the force that pulls objects toward each other. For example, Earth attracts all objects toward itself, which is why things fall when dropped.

1. Universality: Gravity works everywhere, both on earth and in space. All objects with mass pull on other objects with mass.
2. Generality: Gravity acts in many different situations wherever two masses are present; for example, when an apple falls to the ground or the moon orbits the Earth.
3. Repeatability: Every time an object is dropped, it falls to the earth at the same predictable rate.

Card 2: Photosynthesis

Photosynthesis is the process by which plants make their own food. They use sunlight, carbon dioxide, and water to produce sugar (their food) and oxygen.

1. Universality: Photosynthesis takes place in all green plants and some bacteria, no matter where they are in the world.
2. Generality: Even though plants live in different ecosystems, green plants make food using the same basic process.
3. Repeatability: When a plant receives sunlight, water, and carbon dioxide, it will always carry out photosynthesis in a predictable way.

Balu now wants to create a similar card for at least one of the rungs on the Yoga Ladder. Can you help him?

CRITICAL-THINKING ACTIVITY

The Highest Yogī

In many of the *Bhagavad-gītā* verses leading up to verse 47 in this chapter, Lord Kṛṣṇa explains the different *yoga* processes. We have studied these processes in some detail, and we understand how they relate to each other through the Yoga Ladder. Now let's try to understand these processes in relation to modern religious practices and philosophies.

Look at the processes on the Yoga Ladder again. This time let's find modern-day examples of each type of *yogī* and place them on the appropriate rungs of the ladder (use the space next to the Yoga Ladder of the previous activity).

The list below gives some types of practitioners of different *yoga* systems. While many may not strictly follow the proper Vedic process of performing their respective *yoga*, they still show traces of yogic practice through their mood or intention. Can you put these practitioners or practices on the appropriate rung of the Yoga Ladder? (Only write the letter next to the appropriate rung of the ladder.)

a. Charity given to the poor at temples or other places of worship
b. ISKCON devotee going out on *saṅkīrtana* on the order of the *guru*
c. *Yajña* done to appease Goddess Kālī to prevent an outbreak of a disease
d. Religions teaching about the Lord's impersonal feature
e. "Green" initiatives taken up to preserve the environment
f. Interfaith dialogues arranged among different faiths
g. *Pujārī* performing Deity worship
h. Food for Life programs offering disaster relief
i. *Nāga bābās* covered with ash performing arduous austerities

You can think of more activities to add to each rung of the ladder. Remember, though, that the activities should somehow connect the doer to the Lord, since the process of *yoga* relates to linking with the Lord.

Now, in verse 46 Lord Kṛṣṇa says that a *yogī* is the best among those who practice austerity, those who seek knowledge, and those who work for material gains. In verse 47 He further clarifies that of all *yogīs*, the *bhakti-yogī* is the best. Let us look more closely at these two verses and understand them deeper.

Staying with the Yoga Ladder, find examples of different types of *yogīs*. Against each type of *yoga*, fill out the name of one *yogī* who practiced it. Then, discuss verse 46: why does Kṛṣṇa say a *yogī* is better than a *karmī* (person who works for fruitive results), a *tapasvī* (austere person), or a *jñānī* (empiricist)? Use the examples to analyze.

Finally, try to understand verse 47 using all the information you have filled out on the Yoga Ladder in this activity. Also refer to the activity "Results of Various Yoga Practices" to compare the results of each *yoga* type. Now discuss: Why does Kṛṣṇa consider the *bhakti-yogī* to be the highest of all and most intimately connected with Him in *yoga*?

LANGUAGE ACTIVITY

Comic Strip: Yoga Matters

Read the following comic strip in which Vidura Brahmacari and Bhakta Neil contemplate which *yoga* path is best for this age. Then answer the questions that follow.

Questions:

1. Neil says *it's all so difficult*. Explain why he is correct by discussing the challenges of *karma-yoga*, *jñāna-yoga*, and *dhyāna-yoga*.
2. How can *bhakti-yoga* be easily practiced by Neil? Why doesn't he have to practice the previous *yogas* on the Yoga Ladder?
3. How can Vidura explain to Neil that *bhakti-yoga* contains all the elements of the other *yoga* systems, with reference to appropriate verses from this chapter?
4. Discuss the superiority of *bhakti* over the other *yoga* systems with reference to suitable verses from this chapter.

ANALOGY ANTHOLOGY

A collection of analogies
for easier understanding

Analogy 1: The Chariot of the Body

The individual is the passenger in the car of the material body, and intelligence is the driver. Mind is the driving instrument, and the senses are the horses. –*BG* 6.34, purport

The passenger will have a smooth ride if the horses are controlled by the chariot driver, else the ride is bound to be bumpy.

Similarly, if our senses and mind are controlled by steady intelligence, we can become peaceful.

Analogy 2: Mental Infection

The mind is so strong and obstinate that it often overcomes even one's own intelligence, as an acute infection may surpass the efficacy of medicine.
– *BG* 6.34, purport

We may not be able to do the right thing even when we know what it is, because the desire of the mind can be stronger than the reasoning ability of the intelligence.

Analogy 3: The Riven Cloud

If the aspiring transcendentalist fails, then he apparently loses both ways; in other words, he can enjoy neither material happiness nor spiritual success. He has no position; he is like a riven cloud. A cloud in the sky sometimes deviates from a small cloud and joins a big one. But if it cannot join a big one, then it is blown away by the wind and becomes a nonentity in the vast sky.
– *BG* 6.38, purport

If a person who is trying to practice spirituality loses his interest in it, he may also not be well situated materially. He may not fully adjust to either path.

Body at the party, mind in the temple, heart stuck in between.

SACRED RHYTHMS

Important verses
to memorize

***BG* 6.47**

yogināṁ api sarveṣāṁ
mad-gatenāntar-ātmanā
śraddhāvān bhajate yo māṁ
sa me yukta-tamo mataḥ

And of all *yogīs*, the one with great faith who always abides in Me, thinks of Me within himself, and renders transcendental loving service to Me – he is the most intimately united with Me in *yoga* and is the highest of all. That is My opinion.

ANSWERS

Learning Harmonies

1. b; 2. b; 3. b; 4. c; 5. a; 6. b; 7. b; 8. c; 9. b; 10. d

Results of Various Yoga Practices

1. *Karma-kāṇḍa*: Practitioners are attached to the flowery words of the *Vedas* and perform activities to attain material results, like the attainment of the heavenly planets, good birth, power, fame, etc.
2. *Karma-yoga*: *Karma-yogīs* perform work as a sacrifice to Lord Viṣṇu, and *niṣkāma-karma-yogīs* perform prescribed duties for His satisfaction without expecting anything in return. As a result, the *yogī* achieves freedom from material bondage and inner satisfaction and happiness in service.
3. *Jñāna-yoga*: *Jñānī-yogīs* study the *Vedas*, are situated in transcendental knowledge, and are renounced from worldly affairs. They are situated in Brahman and achieve impersonal liberation.
4. *Dhyāna-yoga*: A mechanical meditative practice to control the mind and the senses so that one can focus on the Supreme Lord in one's heart. Results: attaining control of the mind and senses, becoming detached from material enjoyment, attaining equal vision and eventually residence in the Lord's kingdom.
5. *Bhakti-yoga*: *Bhakti-yogīs* perform devotional service to Lord Kṛṣṇa, which is the highest and most expedient means for attaining pure love for God. They develop divine qualities, become free from material entanglement and reactions to work, burn up past sinful reactions, and become very dear to the Lord. They attain the personal association of the Lord in the spiritual world.

Yoga for the Modern Age

1. b; 2. d; 3. c; 4. e; 5. f; 6. g; 7. a

The Yoga Ladder

Every type of *yoga* on the Yoga Ladder follows the three mentioned principles – they are all universal, in the sense that each type of *yoga* can be practiced anywhere, they are all general in the sense that people from different walks of life/*varṇas*/different life situations/controlled by different modes can take to *yoga* practice according to their current capacity (the process will work for all of them), and it is repeatable in the sense that the respective *yoga* processes yield similar results for all genuine practitioners when they accurately follow the process. For example, ISKCON practitioners, who follow the *bhakti-yoga* process, can practice it anywhere in the world (universality), can practice it throughout their lives – even as they face different situations (generality), and can all potentially obtain the results of *bhakti* – *prema* – simply by regularly and consistently following the process (repeatability).

The Highest Yogī

a. *sakāma-karma yoga*; b. *bhakti-yoga*; c. *karma-kāṇḍa/ sakāma-karma yoga*; d. *jñāna-yoga*; e. *niṣkāma-karma yoga*; f. *jñāna/bhakti-yoga*; g. *bhakti-yoga*; h. *niṣkāma-karma yoga*; i. *aṣṭāṅga-yoga*

Examples for each *yoga*: *sakāma-karma yoga*: Indra – anyone wanting to become Indra needs to do a hundred *aśvamedha-yajñas*; King Daśaratha doing a *yajña* to have sons; *niṣkāma-karma yoga*: King Janaka and King Pṛthu – ruled the kingdom being detached from the results of their activities, just to set an example; *jñāna-yoga*: Śaṅkarācārya; Śukadeva Gosvāmī and the four Kumāras before they became devotees – were detached, had full sense control, and cultivated knowledge from Vedic scriptures; *aṣṭāṅga-yoga*: Dhruva Mahārāja; Nārada Muni in his previous life, who followed intense discipline and austerity to see the Lord in the heart; *bhakti-yoga*: Hanumān; Prahlāda Mahārāja – performed nine processes of devotional service to the Lord.

Why a *yogī* is better than others: *Yoga* means to link with the Supreme, so performing any kind of *yoga* connects one with the Lord, whereas a *karmī* who works only for sense gratification without any connection with the Supreme doesn't have the chance of connecting with the Lord and progressing spiritually.

Why a *bhakti-yogī* is considered the highest: The perfection of *yoga* is to link most intimately with the Supreme Lord. A *bhakti-yogī* has the best understanding of the Lord as Bhagavān, the original person, and therefore acts as a servant of the Lord to please Him.

From 6.46 purport: *Bhakti-yoga* is full spiritual knowledge, and therefore nothing can excel it. Asceticism without self-knowledge is imperfect. Empiric knowledge without surrender to the Supreme Lord is also imperfect. And fruitive work without Kṛṣṇa consciousness is a waste of time. Therefore, the most highly praised form of *yoga* performance is *bhakti-yoga*.

Other *yoga* practitioners are incomplete in their understanding, and they rarely directly and selflessly serve the Lord. Therefore, a *bhakti-yogī* is the highest *yogī*.

Yoga Matters

1. In *karma-yoga* one may have understanding about the Supreme Lord but not that the Supreme Lord is Lord Kṛṣṇa. Advancing from *sakāma-karma yoga* to *niṣkāma-karma yoga* is difficult and may take many lifetimes because one has to completely be detached from the results of one's work.

   For *jñāna-yogīs*, renunciation means negation, suppressing one's desires and emotions and remaining inactive. But because souls cannot remain inactive and need constant engagement in connection with Kṛṣṇa, *jñāna-yoga* is dry and not pleasing to the heart.

   To practice *dhyāna-yoga* in this age of Kali is difficult because people are short lived and their minds are restless and agitated. Finding a secluded place is also challenging as one has to leave one's home.

2. There is no prerequisite to perform *bhakti-yoga*; everyone is eligible. The emphasis is not much on separately trying to control the mind and senses, as in the other *yoga* systems, but on using the mind and senses in serving Kṛṣṇa, which automatically curbs the mind and pleases the senses, thus making devotional service easier and more attractive to perform.

3. Śrīla Prabhupāda explains, "The culmination of all kinds of *yoga* practices lies in *bhakti- yoga*. All other *yogas* are but means to come to the point of *bhakti* in *bhakti-yoga*. *Yoga* actually means *bhakti-yoga*; all other *yogas* are progressions toward the destination of *bhakti-yoga*." (6.47, purport)

   In *karma-* and *jñāna-yogas* one may come to the stage of Brahman realization. So the destination will be the Brahman effulgence. In *dhyāna-yoga* one may come to the stage of Paramātmā realization. But only in *bhakti-yoga* can one achieve Bhagavān realization, which is the topmost and allows the devotee to attain Kṛṣṇa and return to His spiritual abode.

4.a Anyone can perform *bhakti-yoga* irrespective of age, gender, or any material designation.

4.b It is easier to control the mind and senses in *bhakti-yoga* than the other processes because one uses the senses and mind in serving Kṛṣṇa. By being absorbed in serving Kṛṣṇa, through the process of hearing and chanting His names and glories, the senses, mind, and heart automatically get purified.

4.c *Bhakti-yoga* revives one's relationship with Kṛṣṇa while other processes strive to renounce the world and any relationship. However, the soul hankers for personal connection and can only be fully satisfied in one's everlasting relationship with Kṛṣṇa.

4.d In *bhakti* one works with devotion for Kṛṣṇa's pleasure whereas even in *niṣkāma-karma yoga*, one works out of duty.

4.e Kṛṣṇa automatically reveals knowledge in *bhakti-yoga*, and the devotee understands and acts in his constitutional position as the servant of Kṛṣṇa.

4.f Purification is easier and much quicker in *bhakti-yoga*, especially in the association of pure devotees, whereas in other processes it may take a long time.

These benefits establish *bhakti-yoga* as the topmost *yoga*, confirmed by Lord Kṛṣṇa: "And of all *yogīs*, the one with great faith who always abides in Me, thinks of Me within himself and renders transcendental loving service to Me – he is the most intimately united with Me in *yoga* and is the highest of all. That is My opinion." (6.47)

www.ingramcontent.com/pod-product-compliance
Lightning Source LLC
Chambersburg PA
CBHW081159070526
44583CB00021B/2915
* 9 7 8 1 7 3 6 9 6 1 0 6 3 *